The Tragic Imagination in
Shakespeare and Emerson

Also Available from Bloomsbury

The Ethical Imagination in Shakespeare and Heidegger, Andy Amato
Classical American Philosophy, Rebecca L. Farinas
Encounters in the Arts, Literature, and Philosophy, ed. Jerome Brillaud and Virginie Greene
Philosophy, Literature and Understanding, Jukka Mikkonen

The Tragic Imagination in Shakespeare and Emerson

Andy Amato

BLOOMSBURY ACADEMIC
LONDON • NEW YORK • OXFORD • NEW DELHI • SYDNEY

BLOOMSBURY ACADEMIC
Bloomsbury Publishing Plc, 50 Bedford Square, London, WC1B 3DP, UK
Bloomsbury Publishing Inc, 1359 Broadway, 12th Floor, New York, NY 10018, USA
Bloomsbury Publishing Ireland, 29 Earlsfort Terrace, Dublin 2, D02 AY28, Ireland

BLOOMSBURY, BLOOMSBURY ACADEMIC and the Diana logo are trademarks of Bloomsbury Publishing Plc

First published in Great Britain 2024
This paperback edition published 2025

Copyright © Andy Amato, 2024

Andy Amato has asserted his right under the Copyright, Designs and Patents Act, 1988, to be identified as Author of this work.

For legal purposes the Acknowledgments on pp. xx–xxii constitute an extension of this copyright page.

Series design by Charlotte Daniels
Cover image: "And there upon a heath did King Lear wander out". Arthur Rackham (1867–1939) (© The History Emporium / Alamy Stock Photo)

All rights reserved. No part of this publication may be: i) reproduced or transmitted in any form, electronic or mechanical, including photocopying, recording or by means of any information storage or retrieval system without prior permission in writing from the publishers; or ii) used or reproduced in any way for the training, development or operation of artificial intelligence (AI) technologies, including generative AI technologies. The rights holders expressly reserve this publication from the text and data mining exception as per Article 4(3) of the Digital Single Market Directive (EU) 2019/790.

Bloomsbury Publishing Inc does not have any control over, or responsibility for, any third-party websites referred to or in this book. All internet addresses given in this book were correct at the time of going to press. The author and publisher regret any inconvenience caused if addresses have changed or sites have ceased to exist, but can accept no responsibility for any such changes.

A catalogue record for this book is available from the British Library.

A catalogue record for this book is available from the Library of Congress.

ISBN: HB: 978-1-3503-7357-0
PB: 978-1-3503-7361-7
ePDF: 978-1-3503-7358-7
eBook: 978-1-3503-7359-4

Typeset by Newgen KnowledgeWorks Pvt. Ltd., Chennai, India

For product safety related questions contact productsafety@bloomsbury.com.

To find out more about our authors and books visit www.bloomsbury.com and sign up for our newsletters.

Contents

Preface	vi
Acknowledgments	xx
1 A Silent Fool	1
2 The Riddle Is an Elegy	19
3 The Perpetual Messiah	47
4 Wiles of Innocence	93
5 A Fool Speaks	123
Notes	145
Bibliography	177
Index	189

Preface

The Tragic Engine. Tragedy is the dark engine of being. It names the cruel industry of nature, the original curse, and the first swindle.[1] We find ourselves, to varying degrees and intensities, ever entangled in treacherous plots and betrayed by our passions.[2] And despite all lamentations to the contrary, human life seems strangely receptive to these deceptions. From the earth's most disquieting, astonishing, and necessary qualities, a tragic ontology emerges to reveal—for those honest enough to bear it—an endless cycle of power always destructively becoming, beyond absolute identification and our influence. Even the old word itself, "tragedy" (*tragōidía*), only insufficiently captures what it indicates.[3] Tragedy, after all, unyieldingly turns (*strophḗs*) and counterturns (*àntistrophḗs*). Prior to our customs and collective acts of law-giving, and even ever after we erect such shields against terror, nature itself resists all attempts at perfect representation, especially epistemic ones.[4] Nevertheless, our earliest rituals testify to our concurrent needs to set the world in order and to honor those forces that refuse to be ordered. In this tension art arises.[5] It is a choreographed recognition and attempted appeasement of it. Accordingly, from our vantage, upon the smaller stage of human life, tragedy becomes something subsequently acted out: the veneration of a god—*Dionysus*—and a theatrical performance celebrating his terrible truths. Truths narrativizing our recurrent drive to madness, violence, excess. Truths reminding us that, in spite of what we like to believe about ourselves, we live irrationally. Remarkably, tragedy is a sacred celebration of our shared miseries and psychic entrapments. It is an orchestrated festival for what can never be fixed or fully apprehended. Tragedy underscores the fate of all dying dreamers, however ordinary or kind. It remembers and commemorates the inescapable personal and political burdens we cyclically create for ourselves. And these two senses of tragedy—the ontological and the performed—tell us that nothing escapes the ordinances of time and that the play of being is forever sorrow. Tragedy, subsequently, signals no mere temporary condition or mere genre of drama or mere existential theory. We cannot evolve, or think, or legislate ourselves out of it. We live life insecurely and in absolute danger, always. And it is not merely a pessimistic perspective of human affairs but the way things are and have always been. Stars dying, mountains collapsing into dust, species vanishing. Worlds and creatures and phenomena we never even had the opportunity to marvel at, fear, use, or love. Gone. Entire languages and cultures never known or now faded from memory. You and I, our children, our friends, this place we have made. Our beliefs and techniques and cures do not spare us. Politics cannot save us. *Nothing* can. This is life as it truly is.

That the tenebrous sobriety of this truth took shape as a festival among the ancient Greeks and as the meridian of modern drama with Shakespearean tragedy should continue to assail and perplex us today. It is itself a riddle.

———

Greek Tragedy. Ancient Greek tragedy sets in stark contrast—as *relief*—the most horrifying and most humane aspects of social life within a state. It lingers upon unspeakable events that highlight the tensions born between honor and shame, piety and politics, *zōé* and *bíos*, grief and rage. Tragedy venerates those terrible events as divinely fated. As a sacred civic spectacle, in a way that seems difficult to understand today, ancient tragedy occurs at the intersection of religion, art, and politics. And it is this original theatrical sense of the tragic, rather than the purely ontological or the contemporary (often reductive) genric sense, that agonistically educates through affirmation without offering explicit "lessons" about life or the nature of the gods. It arrives poetically as a celebratory design—as *art*—of the ceaseless rifts running through our world.[6] Perhaps aptly comported, we can, in our own way, as the ancients did in their own way, apprentice ourselves to tragic works, taken performatively or artifactually, in such a way as to open up their pedagogical prospects, however equivocal and alien. We should recall that beyond being merely "writers of plays," the Greek playwrights—as *poiētḗs* and *didáskaloi*—served as "teachers of plays."[7] They educated their audience. They served the city by helping to create a literate citizenry capable of participating in a functioning democracy.[8] The Athenians considered dramatic festival attendance so vital to civic life that they went as far as to subsidize admission for the poor and to compel the wealthiest citizens to become impresarios, financing and organizing these elaborate performances. They released prisoners and welcomed foreigners. Military generals and war orphans and the public festival fund (*theōriká*) were paraded on stage before the play began as propagandistic embodiments of Athenian ideology.[9] The whole affair displayed the city's idealized image of itself, and the works of art that followed offered a humbling correction to that image. The Great Dionysia, which commenced annually with a grand procession marking the advent of the fertile wine god of mad ecstasy and regeneration from *outside* the city *into* the city, clearly held as much sociopolitical importance as it did artistic and religious. We would do well to remember that as the image of the god entered the theater, it transformed the space, making it sacred. The audience that followed in the festival procession thus entered as religious celebrants. Playgoers became worshippers of Dionysus.

And yet, why? Why endow such happenings with sacrality? Was it the underlying ontological significance of tragic drama? That the performances spoke to mortality and aspects of sociality otherwise obfuscated by the everyday array of habits and aspirations? Perhaps the plays' cultic inheritance—Dionysian dithyrambs, fertility and mystery rites, animal sacrifice—suggests a perennial concern for divine appeasement? A way of dealing with, by piously honoring, festively ritualizing, and performatively translating, irrational drives, natural forces, and historic events seemingly beyond anyone's control? An acknowledgment of the uncertainty always accompanying a culture? Accentuated in times of crisis and transition? An indication of a subconscious awareness of the true state of affairs belying all hollow confidence in economic and political conditions whatsoever? On some level, they knew—as we, on some ancient subterranean level, also suspect—a fall is forthcoming? That they deserve it? That all things become fit for their end?[10]

Of the victims of tragedy—those theatrically highlighted and heroized in powerful relief as scene-stealing actors (*hypokritēs*) brought into line by time's equilibrium, which indulges exaggeration only momentarily—Emerson tells us, "They must perish, and there is no overgod to stop or to mollify this hideous enginery that grinds or thunders, and snatches them up into its terrific system."[11] This fate is not reserved only for tragic heroes and heroines, only conspicuously them. Nature's pronouncements to our species through the very voice of our species that it will forever refuse adaptation to human law or apprehension.

Our interest in the forgoing work turns upon a historically informed phenomenological interpretation of tragic drama and its cultural implications today, always keeping in mind its Greek origin and its Shakespearean summit. Theatrical form and audience appetites change. Particular contexts differ. Political and economic conditions differ. Distinct material environments constitute distinct biases and assumptions. Consequently, though both have become synecdochic with tragedy, the tragedies of Shakespeare are not the tragedies of Sophocles. They both educate us about the age in which they lived. And yet, as masterful tragedians whose works have become transhistorical, they also have much to tell us about ourselves, about society, about the tragic engine. About an unfamiliar, unforgiving, ever evasive and occult universe that cannot be placated, tamed, befriended. And though our understanding, if not our appreciation, of tragic art has strayed in more modern times, it continues to carry—emblematically—our mortal signature in the key of time and the timing of necessity. This signature illustrates the compulsive pull of *pathos*, of what befalls us.

Or, tragedy as *the beautiful curse*.

Our tragic accounts dilate a localized instance of the curse of being. A "hero." They give it names and features and detailed contours. A "plot." They show how very powerfully and passionately and ironically and irresistibly life occurs *as life*: it wields its own instruments of destruction, deceptively and wondrously clothed in the artifice of its own vitality. This occurs seasonally, cyclically, and theatrically, as a masked Dionysus whose tragic dance brings healing (*kátharsis*) only in the wake of destruction.[12] Despair's epiphany leads us back to the granularity and grandiosity of all preceding facts and we find the texture of life transformed. We learn that a surfeit of gifts is necessary but insufficient to mark out the hero. Greatness lights upon him because the tragic engine made humanity's fate explicit with him. We witness her family fall around her. Gloom covers the whole city.[13] Elsewhere and earlier, gods foretell the doom of other gods as prophetic speech, fate, and necessity reveal their roles within the tragic cosmos.[14] Whether ancient as *Antigone* or modern as *Macbeth* or contemporary as postindustrialism and late capitalism, the end—displayed with all of the terrible marvelousness and exquisitely grotesqueness that dramatic tensions allow—appears as the only genuinely democratic principle of an uncaring universe unaroused by our prayers, our progress, or our appreciation for its indifference.

―――――

The Beautiful Curse. The curse of being at all and the public cursing of being mark no mere isolated acts of revenge.[15] We might very well engage in technologically mediated behaviors that correlate to the ancient practice of inscribing our private desires for retribution upon tablets of clay or silver and seal them up for the gods to find and act upon.[16] But tragedy is for everyone and it is about everyone. We are all cursed to pay the high price of existence. What stance do we take in response? The curse of being is no rare affair. Though we consider ourselves as individuals, the same enginery drives all of us. When properly considered, this is, in part, what tragedy—as the child of the Homeric epic and the progenitor of the Gospels[17]—attempts to do: to reveal the hidden relation between life and death. And that all beings find themselves compelled to become "things" by an irresistible *force* (*Bía*) that draws them into itself.[18] We have no choice. *Nothing* does. The old curse: knowing engenders suffering and no aspect or degree of knowing can totally relieve that suffering. It provides us, however, with the requisite humility to experience shame with thanksgiving.[19] Nietzsche, therefore, thinks we—"we" in an aristocratic sense—ought to take joy in this curse-song. This drama suggests no catharsis in the usual sense, no sympathetic magic, or ardent litany. Rather, it descends from rapturous hymns and sumptuous dances celebrating Dionysus' death and resurrection. Instead, tragedy resists reduction to any purely psychological mechanism or mere civic function. It puts knowledge and politics whatsoever in their place. The tragic curse-song and drama strangely affirms reality *as reality*; not for what we wish it would be at the expense of the actual or genuinely possible. Our affirmative response to the tragic curse speaks to a life aesthetic: an elective imperative and accompanying existential invitation. "It is Dionysus' task," Deleuze writes, "to make us graceful, to teach us to dance, to give us the instinct to play."[20] We learn not to long for light by which to dispel the darkness, for the darkness hides half of the god's treasures. Treasures banished by the light of a ratiocinative apprehension of irrational and appetitive forces for practical applications and, ultimately—seemingly consensually—ideological hegemony.

A mystical poet might respond: "*Men do mightily wrong themselves* when they refuse to be present in all ages: and neglect to see the beauty of all kingdoms."[21]

The beauty of *all kingdoms*. We lust for life, full and overflowing. Misery. We work against life's foe, death. Ruin. We do not normally celebrate all the powers and events that seem to work against life. "Disorders" and "accidents" and "disasters." Inauthentically, usually—ostensibly—we categorize what weakens and kills as non-life-affirming. Banished from our rational considerations and all healthy imaginations. And yet they belong together. Dying gods *are* fertility gods. All life dies. Death and life are in truth one idea. Death is the totalized identity of life, life the unending multiplicity of death. Philosophers ancient and modern wonder how *nothing* and *everything* belong to one another. We find a key to this relation, or a suggestion of one, in those moments when beauty arrests the senses or deeply wounds the heart. Like when our star dies in a thousand colors at twilight or our daughter dances in her mother's dress. "The greatest delight which the fields and woods minister," Emerson tells us of wild beauty, "is the suggestion of an occult relation between man and vegetable."[22] The kingdom of death lies in the darkened grove and the shadow of the mountain and below the earth. We see it in the flush fields, the wild waters, and hidden in the eyes of the young. It is nature. All around and yet so often unseen. So, we build the temple—the theatrical and imaginal space—of the "unseen one." There, in those social spaces, our performers, often without even realizing it, dance and sing for *this* god: plays in theaters, hymns and homilies in churches, art in museums, music in concert halls. Tragic art in particular provides the intense light by which foul objects are made beautiful.[23] Not by translating all fearful phenomena into a framework of more palatable theories or forcing them into our most recent scientific grammar but by translating ourselves to those events—acquiescing to their alien hieroglyphics—in order to see, without fully comprehending, what truly comprises the hidden world around us: *violent and strange beauty*. Such surrender is how we become graceful.

We complicate matters, however, when we stray from veneration and humility. If our understanding or use of tragedy becomes too abstract or conceptual—or too confused with our own individual circumstances—we risk losing our reverence and corrupting the play instinct. "The word 'tragedy,' theories of tragedy (assisted by arguments about those theories and about what does and does not fit them), and the plays we call tragedies are—like this essay—benign (though futile) efforts to deny the existence of tragedy."[24] Tragedy belongs to indefinition. We have only an imperfect cartography with which to set its provisional boundaries, boundaries it loves to disdain. Only evasive constructions remain. As much as we crave the security of continuity, it is never certain. Long before the nineteenth and twentieth-century existential prophets of unreason took rationality, theory, and systems to task, Shakespeare outlined the indefinable tragic world: *King Lear* upends all expectations to produce the darkest, most unforgiving of Shakespeare's plays.[25] Like the old question of being, tragedy—as ontological engine and curse—cannot be fully and finally answered.[26] This helps explain why we have princely fools and foolish kings. Presidents and prime ministers.

"Nothing will come of nothing. Speak again."[27]

By its impartial and universal reception, the nothing nihilates everything, but, according to Nietzsche, that is no reason to be nihilistic: "To stay cheerful when involved in a gloomy and exceedingly responsible business is no inconsiderable art: yet what could be more necessary than cheerfulness? Nothing succeeds in which high spirits play no part."[28]

This high art of tragedy venerates the dying fertility god—that enigmatic symbol of nature and the irrational that the Greeks called Dionysus—and signals the highest mode of affirmation; not negation, lament, or revenge. Not nihilism: *life eternal*. Ever recurring. That is, tragedy indicates (in an ontological sense) and testifies to (through dramatic performance) life's seasonal resurrection and reordering, which, maddeningly, requires death and disordering. Or, all tragedies are ultimately expressions of the very god to whom they are dedicated, the dangerous dancing symbol of nature:

> He is the suffering and dying god, the god of tragic contrast. And the inner force of this dual reality is so great that he appears among men like a storm, he staggers them, and he tames their opposition with the whip of madness. All tradition, all order must be shattered. Life becomes suddenly an ecstasy—an ecstasy of blessedness, but an ecstasy, no less, of terror.[29]

Tragic Imagination. What is the tragic imagination? As tragedy designates both the ontological engine and the curse of being, as well as the human spectacle venerating that engine and performing the curse publicly—blind engine and *epi-engine* of art, nemesis, and imprecation—so too does the imagination similarly signify a fundamental and subsidiary mode. Coleridge, effectively misreading Kant, provides the most well-known example when he speaks of imagination in primary and secondary terms: the primary imagination is a fundamental (or metaphysical) characteristic of consciousness bringing us into communion with the very creative powers of nature (or God), while the secondary imagination is principally reproductive and does the sort of suppositional and representational work most often associated with that faculty. The primary imagination operates for finite minds as a repetition of the "eternal act of creation in the infinite," while the secondary echoes and esteems that productive power; it nevertheless finds itself "co-existing with the conscious will" and therefore is more bound by human limitations and failings.[30] We are apperceptive beings connected (imaginatively and organically) to all life and all creation, on the one hand, and deviceful creatures of fancy and fault, on the other. Simply revisit the old stories: the Promethean gift of stolen fire and eating of the tree of the knowledge of good and evil, as well the exilic sojourning price paid for the deed and the resultant necessity of lifelong toil—that is, the need to apply the stolen gift, to justify our ontological or divine trespass. And so even though the secondary imagination indicates the smaller apportionment and stage, it is also the more easily recognizable aspect wherein we find the most applications of imagination: regardless of the actual conditions and limitations of our life, we can, to greater and lesser degrees of possibility, *imagine* things being one way or another. The secondary sense of imagination therefore plays into many accounts of captivity and liberation. Capture the imagination and you capture the very possibilities of existence.³¹ What is the meaning of revolution or salvation without the dream of being otherwise? Of a new or old or better or different or nearly forgotten way of life? Not just molds and patterns of thought but the mythic seduction of captive ideologies and the restless power behind any hope of escape. The imaginative veneration of the tragic revelation, however, simultaneously admits both captivity and escape, returning us time and again to the path of possibility, which we find ever intersected by contrasting powers. This is the tragic triple crossroads: the moment wherein possibility becomes generated at a chiasmus of opposition, driving us both away from *and* toward a unifying identity. Or, fate and destiny caught in unresolvable conflict with a subject seeking liberation.

The tragic cast of imagination primally and spiritually connects us to the Dionysian expression (or revelation) of being and endows us with the power to recreate that connection through tragic art. Every cast of imagination—which encompasses both the primary and secondary modes of imagination—connects us to some original expression of being (prior to any identity) and the consequential (and contextual) dramatic stance we take in response to that expression. That is, styles or genres. Earlier it was claimed that tragedy is life as it is. This is also true (or has the potential to be true) of the other imaginative associations with the various expressions of being (as difference) that subsequently produce art. Each authentic style keys into something universally native. Even if historic and cultural particularities occlude this nativity, universal sentiments *as sentiments* provide sufficient evidence. An affective substrate grounding (and often belying) the motives and deeds of conscious beings. *Dasein*. We are affective arrays of and for the plural expressions of being. And yet, tragedy seems to occupy a special place among the dramatic arts due to it hitting on the lowest and darkest underpinnings of being—and hence all beings—as well as nature's grandest counterpoints. The other styles have the potential to move in and out of this "special place" when they transgress their usual boundaries—boundaries set only by the imperfect conventions arising from those original expressions of being—to offer profound meditations, commentaries, and critiques of the themes most often associated with the Dionysian: death, fate, spiritual pollution, the nature and legitimacy power, hopeless love, impossible obligations, divided selves, and so on. In a word: *freedom*.³² That is, the manifold problem of freedom. A freedom, however, seldom known today. Not mere liberty within social, political, and economic affairs—liberties often chimeric—but a radical style of being fashioned from our ontological doom to be free under any and all circumstances. The dark wisdom we learn from Sisyphus, Silenus, Oedipus,

Antigone, Ophelia, Desdemona, Cordelia. Again, not because they teach us explicit "lessons," but because they, through poetic indication, show us, in matters most defining and indefinable, the way things truly are. The way they have always been and the way they will always be. This is, arguably, the oldest education and the underlying seduction of *the heaviest weight*.[33]

We see the question of freedom stir pronouncedly in individuated tragic motifs—with and against which the tragic hero wrestles—but everything and everyone stands in the balance. It is ultimately not all about the protagonist (enter a reformulation of the problem of hubris).[34] And while freedom, as an essential constituent of the form, falls within the distinct purview of tragic art, its correlates and kin can, as we have said, effectively appear elsewhere. The problem of freedom *can* show up anywhere, but it *always* shows up in genuine tragedies. We will therefore restrict our scope to the singular expression of being we name tragedy. My hope is to offer an anatomy, however gestural, of the tragic imagination and its dramatic art—specifically through Emerson's *Nature* and Shakespeare's *King Lear*—so as to rediscover some of the most remarkable angles on questions of freedom, questions timelessly emanating from all well-executed tragedies.

Something, however, has happened to the tragic imagination, something prompting our dual consideration here of Emerson's tragic philosophy and Shakespeare's tragic drama. In broad strokes, the works of contemporary imagination fail to elicit, and cultural appetites seem no longer to desire, prolonged and performed meditations on the tragic, which most distinctly denotes our understanding of the ontological engine. There is no affirmation of the mysterious relation between life and death, of particular things to the totality of things: "At the bottom of all things, there is only one force, always equal, and ever the same, which slumbers in plants, awakens in animals, but finds it consciousness only in man—the Will."[35] Our culture cares little for the revelations of Dionysus or their contemporary equivalent. The society of the future peopled with naive consumers and monstrous consumers of the naive, both playing out the ancient epic of force.[36] Either end of the equation—commander and commanded, owner and owned, oppressor and oppressed—held captive by a deficit of genuine subjectivity. An emptiness sadly devoid of contemplative disinterest.[37] All political movements and revolutions only serving to attempt to win the war or to reset the board: still, the game continues and our strategies of victory simply reflect whatever self-deceptive responses *seem* most to mirror our own ever-pressing concerns—normally apprehended today merely ideologically, economically, and psychologically—about our deficit, or possible deficit, of power. And in a society that uses (if not *is*) the marketplace (itself no longer a *place*, but a ubiquitous and active *presence*) to appropriate all concerns—even and especially those deeply existential ones—which transfigures all concerns into competitive offerings of amusing, tranquilizing, and self-justifying commodities unable to truly alleviate the reasons for those concerns (or address their intricately enmeshed correlates), the negative consequences emerge as pathologies. These pathologies, created by the empty systems and powers of force, can now only be treated by an increased intake of the products and behaviors of the very system that gave birth to them.[38] Everything now requires therapeutic treatment—in the form of something that can be bought, never freely given—because a vapid conception of happiness and the justification for that happiness at any cost has become *everything*. "Thus is tragedy abolished."[39]

That which pushes all life forward—often as a multiplicity of instinctual drives and social energies—cannot pause and reflect upon this development. It does not tarry of its own accord. It carries on with or without us. No "cure" exists for cosmic forces and there is no "antidote" for human instincts and passions (if we indeed wish to remain human). Only as discrete subjects, however, capable of contemplative thought and reflection—a possibility to be discovered and won—can we quietly pause our own affairs and interrupt our own interests to attempt *thought*.[40] Only we can attempt to *make use* of thought.[41] Only we can act.[42] Only we can take time to do this as a venerable activity, as a baptism of and for life lived. And only we can neglect this possibility of participating intentionally and creatively in the tragedy of being, or, by neglecting it, become, like all unreflective life caught and pushed by nature, simply casualties of the ontological engine. Victims of the curse of being.[43] Martyrs in need of scapegoats. Until, in time, even victimhood, poor surrogate for genuine subjectivity that it is, becomes a vestigial signifier for a host of relations and events registering as senseless. We then, at best, seem like some jumped-up matter dreamed-up by being to be its strange and transitory hostages. Delusional prisoners. But only for a few moments, only appearing for a line or two in the unauthored and unabridged novel of being.

This catastrophic prelude to the decline of the tragic imagination only lightly sketches the sociopolitico-economic-technological conditions of the West—the full array of force's techniques—which have, as their crowning accomplishment, engineered an unending global pandemic of cultural narcissistic nihilism and objectification of all being: the most real product of the indiscrete ménage à trois of *capitalism* (the perversion of profit and the exaltation of unnecessary consumption as necessary and good), *enlightenment scientism* (the creation of a disenchanted world still clinging to the delusion of certainty), and *pragmatism* (the over-privileging of efficient outcomes as the only legitimate and successful outcomes). This threefold iatrogenic sickness has become so insidious that even to acknowledge some variation of it now strikes us only as jeremiad, romantically pastoral, cynical, and as better suited for prefaces and afterwards.[44] Untimely warnings now seem perennial. Books seem ridiculous. The inevitable decline in meaningful and sane civic participation in the second half of the twentieth century heralded only the most discernable beginning in recent times.[45] We have become ever more alienated in the name of freedom. We have become habituated to prefer virtual approximations of activities and associations to actual activities and associations. Mediatized captives who believe that, in spite of everything happening around us, we somehow still live in the finest of times. Not merely a benignly reclusive bookishness and socially deferential disposition opting to minimize any sense of risk in life, which we might find to some degree in any given period, but the increasingly inevitable erasure of all legitimate risks. No one can live dangerously or vulnerably. No more tragic indefinition. Now the tragic imagination finds only disastrous introductory moral lectures—one to which Tate's sanitized *Lear* served as but a prelude[46]—in a world, ironically, without moral measures or time for lectures. And so, our reading here of Emerson and Shakespeare together marks an attempt to rehabilitate the tragic imagination and offer redress for its decline.

Emerson as Philosopher. The use of Shakespeare for this project needs no justification. His name has become synonymous with works of imagination and great tragedies. Writing about Emerson, however, is another matter. Undeniably an influential figure in American culture, intellectual history, and poetry, he nevertheless does not enjoy a wide embrace among the philosophical or theoretical community. It is our intention to treat Emerson as a philosopher, however, who did indeed develop a distinct philosophy filled with insightful questions, provocative claims, and a profound understanding of the unique challenges and possibilities of American society. The crux of the hesitation to regard him as a philosopher rests primarily on the absence of any systematic treatise in his corpus and his apparent disinterest (or lack of facility) in making traditional arguments subject to accepted philosophical criteria. And Emerson's own journals lend support to this hesitation.[47] So, on the one hand, while largely "philosophical" in orientation—that is, he addresses long-recognized philosophical topics and questions—there remains no way to overcome completely this objection as his essays do not utilize any requisite argumentative procedures. He rather simply "essays." He asserts and pivots and invites. He uses lists, questions, allusions. But he does not argue.[48] On the other hand, the philosophical tradition contains many unsystematic and performative thinkers whose writings do not contain traditional arguments—figures who, to some degree, straddle the literary and philosophical divide.[49] Additionally, he gave "University Lectures" on philosophy at Harvard in 1870 and 1871.[50] While we should not simply throw open the gates for any thinker we wish to treat as a philosopher solely due to it suiting our own agenda or prejudice to do so, we should at the very least recognize that philosophical methods and styles vary greatly, from philosophy's ancient origins to its contemporary practice. If for whatever reason, however, some readers cannot bring themselves to read Emerson as a philosopher, then the appellations "essayist" or "thinker" should suffice. Of importance here is our intention to develop Emerson's transcendental philosophy as a tragic philosophy that we will harness to offer an interpretation of Shakespeare's *King Lear*.

Overview of Chapters. Chapter 1, "A Silent Fool," offers a reading of the opening scene of Shakespeare's *King Lear*, in which we examine how Cordelia's silence creates the conditions for shame. In addition to exposing her father's madness, the space of shame created by Cordelia's silence opens up the possibility—the "foolish" possibility—of becoming sensitive to beauty and, subsequently, retrieving the order of love undergirding all meaningful social bonds. We then turn directly to Emerson in Chapter 2, "The Riddle Is an Elegy," in order to lay the groundwork for a sustained reading of Emerson's *Nature*. Surveying selected moments from Emerson's life, we explore how his personal losses provoke his grand attempt to theorize nature and answer the *Riddle of the Sphinx* (the problem of the world). We also present a provisional account of Emerson's transcendental philosophy as a philosophy that is responding to a tragic world in which the illusions that largely comprise our existence—in terrible concert with force and power—must be confronted and overcome so that authentically intuited ideals born of reason and imagination might guide us through our sufferings and uncertainties. Here we move to Chapter 3, "The Perpetual Messiah," to offer a sustained reading and explication of Emerson's major work, *Nature*. Beyond unpacking the prevalent concepts and themes of the work, we endeavor to read it as a manifesto that elevates its basic assertions and questions through differential repetitions. The effect is both exhausting and exhilarating. Through this series of revelations—which are essayed, not argued—Emerson performs a drama of self-recovery that ultimately arrives at the conclusion that a childlike counter-wisdom is necessary for the perennial retrieval of the *Riddle of the Sphinx*, a genuine attempt to understand the world and to freely participate in it. Having sufficiently developed Emerson's philosophy, we take up *King Lear* in Chapter 4, "Wiles of Innocence," and offer an Emersonian reading of it. In addition to certain themes that we explore at length—vision, suffering, love, foolishness, nature, *nothing*—we find that Emerson's tragic art of elevation into awe in *Nature* becomes in *King Lear* a drama of forced descent into cruelty. While forced descent to some degree appears as a regular feature of tragedy, it is noteworthy here because no strong case can be made for a degree of agency, however illusory, theoretically capable of staving off the collapse to come. The world is tragic, not merely the plot surrounding the protagonist. In both the artistic and psychological senses, a *relief* is needed and comes by way of the performed representation of the tragic. *King Lear* thus becomes, arguably, the darkest of Shakespeare's tragedies. Nevertheless, its "lessons" for us arrive as admonitions to liberate the tragic from mere fear and pity, and to restore an ancient, if not secret, admonishment to become graceful and joyful, to rediscover the instinct to play. In the concluding chapter (Chapter 5), "A Fool Speaks," we first review the previous chapters, then discuss festivity and sacrifice in relation to tragic drama, and finally offer something of a palinode for Chapter 1. We see that while the social and political prospects of silence ought to be recovered and practiced, there ever remains those times in which truth must be spoken and injustices confronted. The hope is that our loving silence lends a prophetic potency to our voice in those moments in which circumstances require us to speak.

Caveat Lector. This work employs a voice of invitation—and inclusive "we"—and often alternates between gender pronouns. This reflects both a stylistic strategy and a philosophical commitment: the community of the book should endeavor to be both distinct and open. The interpretation of texts within the humanistic tradition should be welcoming of difference and invite disagreement, and its inclusive charity should forerun its exclusions and criticisms. Further, in addition to our use of and reliance upon a selection of the expected relevant primary and secondary literature related to tragic drama, Shakespeare, and Emerson, it may benefit readers to know that semi-regular references, usually footnoted, to existentialism (Nietzsche), phenomenology (Heidegger), critical theory (Marcuse), post-structuralism (Deleuze), and philosophical anthropology (Clastres) occur throughout. Ideas from Simone Weil and René Girdard, important thinkers difficult to categorize, also helped to clarify certain themes. And as is often the case, footnotes tell a story of their own: a genealogy of scholarly debt, debate, and omission. In any event, the intention behind this particular configuration of thinkers and theories rests with harnessing a conceptual lexicon well-suited to developing continentally informed interpretations and claims for contemporary readers of Emerson and Shakespeare, especially for those who have not read them together. Hopefully, those who have ignored Emerson as a serious thinker or neglected to read Shakespeare philosophically will find themselves tempted by the proceeding chapters to reconsider those oversights, especially in light of our aspiration here to retrieve and rehabilitate the tragic imagination.

Acknowledgments

An early compulsory exposure to a handful of plays by Shakespeare and perhaps a poem or two by Emerson left me with little more than an abstract appreciation for either figure prior to graduate school. Midway through my master's degree, however, as I read ever more primary and secondary sources in the humanities, I began to feel the weight of a wider intellectual world more acutely, prompting me to devour books at a rapacious pace. Each week I would carry away tall stacks from the university library covering a wide range of subjects. It was during this time that I took up a selection of Shakespeare's major tragedies. A few years later I would go on to read Shakespeare's sonnets, *A Midsummer Night's Dream, King John, Measure for Measure, The Winter's Tale,* and *The Tempest*, with polymath and poet Fred Turner, who saw these works as inspired meditations on the nature of time, economy, and beauty. Prior to those seminars and conversations, while still attending divinity school, I took a course on the history of religion in America with Mark G. Toulouse wherein I had my first substantive, although still brief, encounter with Emerson. We read *An Address* in its historical context and though Emerson immediately intrigued me it would take almost fifteen years for that charm to grow into a genuine research interest. Shakespeare, however, due in part to Fred's infectious bardolatry and my doctoral program's emphasis on interdisciplinarity, appeared in my work much earlier, first only briefly in my dissertation, then taking center stage in my first book, *The Ethical Imagination in Shakespeare and Heidegger,* which reflected as well the influence of my mentor and friend, the continental philosopher and Heidegger scholar Charles Bambach.

After exorcizing my preoccupation with Heidegger's phenomenology, at least for the time being, Emerson began to occupy more of my reading and thinking. The astonishing rhetoric of his essays had left such an impression on me over the years—*Self-Reliance, Friendship, Circles, The Poet, Experience,* and *Culture* in particular—that I found myself increasingly incorporating some of his more memorable and provocative lines into lectures and conversations. These developments resulted in a decision to teach a course on American

Transcendentalism, which, to the delight of some students and the chagrin of others, largely became a sustained engagement with Emerson's *Nature* and a selection of his major essays. Our discussions affirmed and cemented my interest. It was around this time, as I began to consider my next project, that my good friend, Jill Drouillard, encouraged me, thankfully, to continue staking out my own territory around philosophical readings of Shakespeare. So, in 2019, I started looking for, and finding, thematic connections by which to read Shakespeare and Emerson together, and to do so in such a way as to contribute something novel and interesting to their respective bodies of literature. And while a number of philosophers and critics have admired both writers, there was, with the exception of approbatory and suggestive remarks by Bloom, Cavell, and others, no sustained book-length engagement of the two figures together. Add to this narrative my supportive partner, Christine, surprising me that Christmas with the lovely 1883 fourteen-volume edition of Emerson's collected works and the die was cast.

———

I want to recognize Amanda Ballard, John Macready, David Utsler, and Abdal Malik Rezeski for reading and commenting on an early draft of this book. I doubt they realize how much their questions and suggestions improved the work or how genuinely grateful I am that they would give freely of their time to do so. The members of the Shakespeare and Philosophy Reading Group, *A World Elsewhere*, which I organized back in the summer of 2011, also warrant acknowledgment. Those conversations, particularly with Jared Bly and Philip Day, equal parts rigorous and enlightening, if occasionally clumsy, helped spur me to continue interpretating Shakespeare's plays philosophically for the next decade. My sincerest thanks as well to those current and former students at the University of Texas at Dallas who have comprised the Philosophy Reading Group: Emma Tharp, Anastasia Zaluckyj, Will Truong, Abhinav Thummala, Macklin Fanning, Eloisa Aguirre, Vyom Raval, Chaz Holsomback, Raymond Hein, Anja Sheppard, Patricia Mathu, Cal Nelson, to name only a few. At one time or another in the past five years all of these remarkable young people have joined me in reading and discussing a great variety of theoretical and literary texts that contributed both directly and indirectly to this work. As we read thinkers like Nietzsche, Weil, Marcuse, Clastres, and Deleuze, they endured my excessive references to Shakespeare and Emerson. I would also like to thank Ben Lima, editor of *The Athenaeum Review*, for inviting me to publish an abbreviated essay version of Chapter 1, "A Silent Fool: Cordelia's Subversive Silence in *King Lear*," in the journal's winter issue, 2021. After its publication I received encouraging remarks, most notably from Thomas G. Palaima of UT Austin, whose gracious recognition of and comments on the work came during something of a personal nadir and were thus greeted with much gratitude. And, finally, many thanks to Liza Thompson at Bloomsbury for her enthusiastic reception and support of this project.

1

A Silent Fool

Not long before her death at the age of thirty-four, Simone Weil, in one of her last letters, reflected on a production of *King Lear* she had recently attended:

> There is a class of people in this world who have fallen into the lowest degree of humiliation, far below beggary, and who are deprived not only of all social consideration, but also, in everybody's opinion, of the specific human dignity, reason itself—and these are the only people who, in fact, are able to tell the truth: All the others lie.[1]

She tells us that this class of people are "fools."[2] No one listens to them because they have "no academic titles or episcopal dignities." In drama we often relegate the spoken truth of fools to the satirical and ironic, their silent truth to the regrettable and naïve.[3] Not simply *truth*. The truth about the way things really are—a truth silently lived or publicly spoken—loses its irresistible and essential qualities when received through the register of foolishness when foolishness remains antonymic to wisdom (or at least what passes for wisdom). History and the wide field of arts and letters give us many fools of fate subjected to the world in and of force—*force* being that which "turns anybody who is subjected to it into a *thing*"[4]—a world represented not only by institutions and systems of power but by prevailing values and ideological undercurrents. This is the iron bar comprising conformity, practicality, and good sense, under which the citizens of all late-capitalistic and overdeveloped nations must pass, precluding dangerously foolish lives, foolish pronouncements of truth, and foolish silence before all manifestations of power. This bar ever lowers in inverse proportion to the need for fools to walk upright. Their relegation to the category of "fool," which attempts to rob them of the truth of their witness, especially by silencing them, nevertheless still contains liberating possibilities: power can be drawn out and exposed. In silence things must be what they really are. This foolish quietude—*elected* or *forced*—indicts power and disrupts the world of force.

But what do we do with such indictments and disruptions?

We should see them as tools for subversion.[5] In those very encounters with persons behaving or speaking in a manner that power judges as subversive (or even simply nonconforming) to its desires, it must, as the force driving it demands, victimize those unruly subjects through identification within the particular domain of that power, whereby those named (or classified) become contained within that system of intellectual or political enclosure allowing power to display, conceal, sentence, and pardon as suits its self-perceived purposes. In those encounters, concurrent with power's prerogatives, that truth—in adopted silence *or* forced silence, by foolish affect *or* consignment to foolishness—testifies against power's judgments. Time will, of course, make fools of us all before the end. Still, in the moment of being named criminal, rebel, subversive, deviant—*fool whatsoever*—the genuine subversion that might shake the social world reveals its efficacy. Shakespeare makes this terribly clear in *Lear*.

Aside. Everything is made to function as a game to power—to those in power—albeit one that distorts the play instinct driving it. We have all endured people who possess great skill at ruining games. Beyond the interpersonal and anecdotal, this claim becomes more defensible when we observe that matters of law are matters of contest comprising their own rules and criteria for winning.[6] Whatever somber and mythic origins politically organized power claims in order to legitimize itself—some seductive antecedent to the story of the state, some narrative for this or that community or shared identity—the mechanisms by which it exercises its will and realizes its designs remain essentially a matter of disfigured play. In this regard, *Lear* only makes explicit what otherwise remains implicit in any political display or organizational use of power. A fixed game in which everyone forced or beguiled to participate—whatever their causes or commitments, *whether they know it or not*—loses. Only force and power and the illusions they sustain win.

The king has grown old. He tires of the affairs of state but not of kingship's privileges. His *destiny* rests in his hands, his *fate* in the hands of his daughters. Here we find the formula of theatrical tragedy: the force of fate rises up against destiny's desires.[7] Events and conditions set the stage for truth to reveal itself and to be roundly denied. Except by madmen and poets who affirm *nothing* or "weakness" and who see the truth of the situation. Except by lovers now and again who have grown foolish by their love. Except, in *Lear*, by a few faithful servants and children hooped together with their lord by unbreakable bonds of duty. Shakespeare gives us Cordelia as such a fool, as well as the Fool,[8] and later, in a most interesting way, Edgar as Tom o' Bedlam.[9] Here we will only consider Cordelia's foolishness as presented in the play's opening movements.

In abrogation of his monarchical responsibilities, Lear decides to divest himself of the worries burdening his great privileges in order to face his end in merry revels and repose.

> To shake all cares and business from our age,
> Conferring them on younger strengths, while we
> Unburthened crawl toward death.[10]

To live out his life as a king without responsibilities, Lear intends to divide his kingdom among his three daughters and their husbands (including whomever Cordelia will wed). Three daughters who, once invested with his political power, become for him, like those ancient daughters of necessity, the triune forces of fate. In *Macbeth* these forces appear supernatural and outside of the family dynamic, though not entirely outside of a recognized, if still ambiguous, role within society. While substantive differences mark out Lear's daughters from Macbeth's witches, the two groups play a structurally similar role within the social dimension and lifeworld of the eponymous characters: neither of whom will in fact turn out to be the true tragic hero. Even in the age of Shakespeare, even now, it is, whatever shape it takes, always a "god" who plays that role (*both* the ultimate symbol of irresistible force and drives *and* simultaneously their atoning redress). All the famed figures of the tragic stage are "mere masks of this original hero, Dionysus."[11] Through the illusion of a free decision (and the delusion of a wise decision) Lear "creates" the circumstances by which he will have no authority to exercise his will or power to indulge his wants. Like Oedipus, he ironically enacts his own curse.[12] Though it is possible that Lear thinks himself to be acting beyond his own interests with a politically shrewd move that would see the old kingdoms of England, Wales, and Scotland restored to something of their former independent status, he is yet driven by the fate of force, which works through all mechanisms of power and self-will.[13] Though the wisdom of age or even a hint of sanity might advise him against this course of action, as well as the game excusing it, he sees no danger. And even if it were not this particular issue of exchanging responsibility for leisure, the tragic conjunction of fate and destiny would undoubtedly find another instance in which to insist that there be a reckoning, a reckoning that would, of course, lay the groundwork for the next crisis.

Again, as the original author and judge of the game—but only as ironic enactor—Lear believes that all will, quite naturally, go well. And why not? His division of the kingdom will arguably please more citizens with territorial identities than it will displease, and his investiture of rank and rule converts his beloved children into his patrons. They will become the powers of the realm(s), surely only adding additional gratitude to their love? Undoubtedly, they and their husbands will make fine regents and will fulfill their filial duties to their father and former king? And even *if* Lear were none too sure about Goneril and Regan, he could always count on his youngest and most beloved daughter, Cordelia, with whom he originally planned to live: "I loved her most, and thought to set my rest / On her kind nursery."[14] But, strangely, as we well know, she refuses his game. Why? And why does Lear react with such incredible rancor anyway? The shadowed corners of the mind hide all manner of monsters.

The game:

> Tell me, my daughters—
> Since now we will divest us, both of rule,
> Interest of territory, cares of state—
> Which of you shall say doth love us most?
> That we our largest bounty may extend
> Where nature doth with merit challenge.[15]

A love test. At first blush, Lear's game seems innocent enough. Each daughter giving a small speech proclaiming her love for him. A little whimsical, sentimental fun dressed in formality. He is, after all, about to give them his kingdom, the least they could do is say a few fine words. The older daughters, whatever their aspirations, take to the game and play it to maximum effect.

> **GONERIL** Sir, I love you more than words can wield the matter;
> Dearer than eye-sight, space, and liberty;
> Beyond what can be valued, rich or rare;
> No less than life, with grace, health, beauty, honor;
> As much as child e'er loved, or father found;
> A love that makes breath poor, and speech unable;
> Beyond all manner of so much I love you.[16]

Regan follows and concurs with her older sister, notably adding:

> Only she comes too short, that I profess
> Myself an enemy to all other joys,

> Which the most precious square of sense possesses,
> And find I am alone felicitate
> In your dear highness' love.[17]

Eloquent exaggerations which, as long as no one draws attention to their substance and scrutinizes them, no doubt pleases Lear. Accordingly, after Regan and Goneril's love pronouncements the king gives them their share of the kingdom. All proceeds swimmingly for everyone. Except for Cordelia, who, between the two speeches, quietly reflects:

> What shall Cordelia speak? Love, and be silent.[18]

and after Regan's speech adds:

> Then poor Cordelia!
> And yet not; since, I am sure, my love's
> More ponderous than my tongue.[19]

Her love and silence presage that which is to come, the preliminary drawing out of the unnoticed and unconscious forces at work in the game. Her depersonalized response creates space wherein the drives at work in and through each of the participants can uncomfortably show themselves. In but a few moments, *nothing* and *silence*—not Cordelia herself—will bear testimony against all the players. That is, it creates the conditions by which they must bear testimony against themselves. What will this testimony tell us? Lear's actions and demands: riddled with taboo energies and want of self-possession. Her sisters' professions of love: filial impiety masked in adoration. Those who speak the truth or for truth's sake refuse to speak: love's vulnerability and duty's foolishness.[20]

Finally, her father turns to her—"Now, our joy" and "Speak"—and the engine begins its rumblings. She gives him his due.

CORDELIA	Nothing, my lord.
LEAR	Nothing?
CORDELIA	Nothing.
LEAR	Nothing will come of nothing, speak again.
CORDELIA	Unhappy that I am, I cannot heave
	My heart into my mouth. I love your majesty
	According to my bond; nor more nor less.
LEAR	How, how, Cordelia! mend your speech a little,
	Lest it may mar your fortunes.
CORDELIA	Good my lord,

> You have begot me, bred me, loved me; I
> Return those duties back as are right fit,
> Obey you, love you, and most honor you.
> Why have my sisters husbands, if they say
> They love you all? Haply, when I shall wed,
> That lord whose hand must take my plight shall carry
> Half my love with him, half my care and duty.
> Sure, I shall never marry like my sisters,
> To love my father all.[21]

Cordelia offers a succinct explanation of her refusal to participate, for to have remained absolutely silent about her silence would seem too ungrateful. Her refusal indicates an affirmation, not a renunciation: she loves her father.[22] She has and will happily give him everything due him. Everything and only that is due him. A hyperbolic expression of filial love makes a mockery of her genuine love and appreciation for him. Her sisters do not mind at all. Lear's game, which invites—demands—such exaggeration, subsequently inverts reality, albeit not in a revolutionary or liberatory way. Those who would lie to accomplish their ambitions receive the rewards rightly reserved for those who would, in an ideal world, speak the truth, while those who would speak the truth receive the judgments usually reserved for those who lie. All because silence exposes the lies concealing the secret truths of the players and of reality. What are these most unknown, guarded matters?

Aside. There are three orders of silence that might better situate us to our analysis here: *existential silence, aesthetic silence,* and *mystical silence.* Undoubtedly, these are not the only ways to think about silence, nor are these orders or modes restrictive, excluding each other when observed or performed, but these distinctions can nevertheless assist us in developing a clearer picture of what silence indicates and makes possible. First, Heidegger tells us that "keeping silent" is an essential possibility of discourse. It is often the case that "talking at great length about something covers over and gives a false impression of clarity to what is understood."[23] We regularly find those who should be listening talking instead and those who should be inquiring answering. At the same time "he who never says anything is also unable to keep silent at any given moment."[24] Heidegger makes a distinction here between idle talk and genuine speech, and between simply not talking and silence. While genuine speech and silence are essential to discourse—discourse being the "*existential-ontological foundation of language*" that articulates the "intelligibility of being-in-the-world"[25]—idle talk and simply not talking cover over or avoid discourse. "Authentic silence is possible only in genuine discourse. In order to be silent, Da-sein must have something to say."[26] Existential silence is part of an authentic comportment or stance toward a free existence with others. It is co-constitutive with true discourse: silence is only possible with discourse and discourse is only possible with silence. We can only really be silent when there are relevant words available to us and we do not use them because we are listening. And we can only really speak when we have silently listened to others and to being itself. If we wish to communicate authentically and productively with each other, to know ourselves honestly, and to become whole beings within a community of other beings, then practicing existential silence is necessary.

Second, aesthetic silence signals our capacity for awe and shame, the conditions required for beauty to arrest us or by which something becomes beautiful. In Book VI of Virgil's *Aeneid*, the Sibyl becomes possessed by the god, Phoebus Apollo. She transforms and her voice and countenance become charged with his divine presence:

> She cried, "Aeneas, are you praying?
> Are you being swift in prayer? Until you are,
> The house of the gods will not be moved, nor open
> Its mighty portals."[27]

And then something even more remarkable occurs:

> More than her speech, her *silence*
> Made the Trojans cold with terror, and Aeneas
> Prayed from the depth of his heart.[28]

In the original Latin Virgil used *conticesco* for silence, which in addition to "falling silent" and "cease speaking," means "to become still." The oracle, when inspired by the god, can speak all sorts of wondrous things: prophecies, ominous warnings, divine wisdom, mysteries of the afterlife. And she can become still and fall silent as well. The admonition to pray followed immediately with silence—"which made the Trojans cold with terror"—suspends the spoken words in the dreadfully calm air of divinity. This empowers the words. The heart grows defenseless under the spell of silence evoking a profound sense of shame. Or "terror." Awe. Aeneas urgently begins praying and petitioning. Poetry best exemplifies this aesthetic silence as what poets remain silent on in any given line of poetry more effectively allows what is said to radiate with an intensity of meaning seldom found in prose. And that this mode of silence elicits shame—a deep sense of incongruous self-reference, of being insufferably exposed by and alienated from what is most desired—alerts us to the humility and sense of mortality required to encounter beauty. If there is no shame inducing silence, then the sublime power of the beautiful cannot reach us.

The third type of silence gives way to truth. It lays the path for its arrival. In the ancient world there were cultic initiates who, after much training and long preparation, would observe the mystical order of silence to gain access to the greater and final mysteries. In that transcendent moment the reception of truth was immediate and entire. This could only occur after the privileged few had learned to shed the common associations surrounding the nature of knowledge and all the argumentative clutter obstructing it. When it comes to this mode of silence, as well as whatever wisdom we might find in closely related mythological presentations, we discover that truth, at least the truth attained by mystical silence, lies outside of the grasp of ordinary discourse.[29] Unimaginative banality cannot enter here. Of course, "true statements" can be uttered after a fashion in everyday conversations and arguments can touch upon truth, but they are more often than not "merely correct" or "seemingly sensible" accounts. The truth given voice in silence and received in silence, beyond even the truths contained in the richest myths, touches upon a wholly other plane of possibility. It is, from the standpoint of ordinary human existence, so secret and so strange that all arguments must be halted and abandoned so that it can simply and profoundly be what it is and be received for what it is. These initiates would be guided through stages of instruction utilizing ever more esoteric myths, symbols, and rituals. They were religious performances and meditative abstractions that readied the mind. Only when prospects had completed their rigorous preparations would the use of various pedagogical tools and the reliance upon intelligible representations cease. Only then, when their souls had been cleansed of all empirical contingencies and habits of belief, would they be able to receive the revelations hidden in absolute silence. In such moments, at the threshold of perfect knowing, on the verge of being subsumed into *nothingness*, reason, newly purified, was liberated from its embodied and sensible limitations and reunited with the divine *lógos*. What was most strange now becomes most familiar as a transcendental act of remembering.[30] In this ecstatic state truth could arrest them and the order of the cosmos be known: all things became one.

Now, concerning the first and arguably most immediate matter disclosed by Cordelia's silence in response to Lear's love test: the king, whatever his other merits, comes to us unfree for his own end—hence his unwise abdication in order to die "unburthened" and free of care—indicating an approach to truth from marked deficiency. He possesses no clear disclosure of his innermost fears or understanding of his darkest desires, he thus has no way of attaining anything resembling authentic resolution in the face of old age and death. He cannot act as whole person. He might indeed have many fine and kingly qualities, but, like all other captive players correctly called "protagonist" (principal mortal sufferer) or wrongly named hero (of divine parentage) caught up in the tragic engine, his faults facilitate his susceptibility to the hidden energies steering all unreflective life. "As flies to wanton boys are we to the gods; / They kill us for their sport."[31] The most apparent consequence of Lear's self-disclosive limitations: truth remains for him something subject to his impaired—or overly *personalized*—understanding of those drives that constitute him, precluding any full—or adequately *depersonalized*—account of the way things really are. The way people, places, and things are driven to be, which in turn reveals the proper and improper objects of acceptance and refusal. The naked soul alone can see the world of force and bear silent witness against it.

Aside. When considering truth, we should surrender any claims to a metaphysically "objectivated" state or emanation of being. There is no pure, universal Truth as Plato and others have contended. Even if or when we concede something like "transcendence"—going beyond the usual limits of experience—every desire for and account of "the truth" signals an expression, contains a signature, bears the stamp of time and place. Nevertheless, we can still acquiesce or aspire to the quiet possibility we each possess of simply *letting things be what they are* and of demonstrably *giving a pious, critical, living account of the way things are*. The unenviable and treacherous task then lies in giving an account of truth that does not leave us with an empty metaphysical notion or merely another perspective among an ocean of perspectives. Rather, something in accord with both nature and ourselves; something extraordinarily capable of helping us to make sense of the world *and* of luring us, arresting us, placing provocative demands upon us. This is why truth is of a higher order and of a finer quality than facts. For truth received in silence and conceived in testimony exposes everything for what it really *is* and for what it *should be*. Especially quiet testimony. And we are always either free or unfree to be claimed by these proclamations of truth. We are never neutral before them. In those encounters, truth reveals how subordinated we are to force and power, how caught up in the spell of illusions, how trapped by the habits of belief. It reveals a profound sense of proportionality between all things. We become decentered. Our lives and world must then be reconstructed in accord with truth.

Bereft of sufficient introspection, caught up in invisible inner wars, Lear's failure to achieve self-mastery—as existential acceptance of what is necessary, political liberation from what is not necessary, and the creation of new ethical imperatives for what is possible—necessarily relegates his response to Cordelia to the overly personal and profane. He finds no home in trust and possibility. He cannot abide silence. He is unable to "hear" the truth of silent testimony about the way things are. In the world of power and force, someone must always be doing or saying something. Never *nothing*. The Fool: "Sometimes I am whipped for holding my peace."[32] As a consequence, he cannot slow the fate of force or mitigate against the world of power. *Nothing*'s ultimate authority hovers at the edges of his kingdom. For now, all remains pre-reflective force incapable of genuine compassion. Goneril and Regan capitalize upon this predicament and artfully though gracelessly handle truth as a "moveable host of metaphors."[33] Indeed, lies of a lesser order become the truth. Is this a necessary illusion lasting as long as its persuasive force and explanatory strength allow? It would seem so. Until the untimely inconvenience and disruptive nature of *nothing* and silent witness—presented by beings' tragic fools—shatter such illusions. Often at the expense of their lives.

To consider the second matter brought to light in this scene, we must recall Lear's disproportionate response to Cordelia's appeal to *nothing* and silent refusal to participate—at least in the way his deficiency expects—in his love contest.

LEAR	But goes thy heart with this?
CORDELIA	Ay, my good lord.
LEAR	So young, and so untender?
CORDELIA	So young, my lord, and true.
LEAR	Let it be so! Thy truth, then, be thy dower!
	For, by the sacred radiance of the sun,
	The mysteries of Hecate, and the night;
	By all the operations of the orbs
	From whom we do exist and cease to be;
	Here I disclaim all my paternal care,

	Propinquity and property of blood,
	And as a stranger to my heart and me
	Hold thee, from this, for ever. The barbarous Scythian,
	Or he that makes his generation messes
	To gorge his appetite, shall to my bosom
	Be as well neighbored, pities, and relieved,
	As thou my sometime daughter.
KENT	Good my liege—
LEAR	Peace, Kent!
	Come not between the dragon and his wrath.[34]

Like Polixenes' turn in *The Winter's Tale*, wherein his wife, Hermione, quite suddenly and unexpectedly, becomes the focus of his jealousy and mania, Cordelia, also seemingly inexplicably, finds herself fallen from most beloved daughter to despised object. Lear, pre-Christian pagan that he is, calls on the sun, the night, the goddess of magic and witches, upon all heavenly bodies which might bear witness: Cordelia is no longer his daughter. He belittles her appeal to the truth in the process: "Thy truth, then, be they dower!" She will be to him as a parent-devouring barbarian. Her honest and plain account of her love for him—and refusal to exaggerate her love for him—produces such a powerful and disruptive reaction that we are left wondering: What has caused this wrathful dragon to emerge? From cherished and endowed to despised and disowned in but a few lines. We do not need to speculate too wildly to discover an adequate subtext contextualizing Lear's erratic behavior.

The rage Lear shows toward Cordelia's reverent silence—probably present in long-standing patterns of behavior—evinces a response to an unresolved fear of abandonment and a dangerous level of insecurity surrounding rejection, more than likely the result of some deep trauma regarding his wife's absence, as well as, perhaps, his own mother's. The missing mother (or mothers) in the play, the demand not only to be loved but admired to excess by his daughters, and the uncontrollable animus displayed toward Cordelia after her apparent failure to fulfill this confused demand, makes a compelling case for Lear's unconscious desire that Cordelia (primarily) and her sisters (secondarily) play the role of wife and mother.[35] This is not the only instance in Shakespeare where we find daughters cast in the role of forbidden love objects. Or of love objects becoming curse objects. These flirtations with incest taboos steer the action onward into ever more destructive territory. As Mark Taylor describes such behaviors and the desires driving them:

> Consciously or unconsciously, sometimes both, Shakespearean fathers dread no circumstance more than the loss, to other men and to maturity, of the daughters whom they desire for themselves; and this desire, both impermissible and inadmissible, expresses itself in very strange behavior—in acts that are arbitrary, selfish, irrational, violent, cruel. The combination of dread and desire that occasions these acts designate incestuous feelings; hardly ever overt, these incestuous feelings manifest themselves through sublimations, compensations, and displacements.[36]

The "incestuous feelings" compelling Lear and other Shakespearean fathers do not often show themselves directly, providing room for ambiguity and doubt. These figures have been socialized to compensate for these strange desires by undertaking less overtly catastrophic activities. Yet, flashes of irrational cruelty—unjustified doubts, unprovoked rebukes, inappropriate games—indicate the pernicious effects of unaddressed underlying forbidden desires. Here, Lear's mercenary reaction to Cordelia so clearly breaks from the usual defense mechanisms redirecting those taboo energies that we are left with little doubt as to the catalyst for his disavowal of her.[37] A course of action ultimately stripping him of everything valuable and leading to a perfected ruination.[38]

Aside. Being laid bare, stripped of every accoutrement, title, dignity, possession, hope: tragedies poetically and dramatically rehearse this infinite repetition of returning to the earth on the earth's terms. Even the gods must heed these laws:

> Be silent, Inanna! It befits the ways of Hades;
> raise not your voice, Inanna, against Hades'
> customs:
> crouched and stripped bare, man comes to me.[39]

The ancient Sumerians returned the dead to the earth "crouched and stripped bare." Allowed to exit the world only as they entered it, naked and small. It was a ritual imitating the life cycle. Even the great Inanna-Ishtar must divest herself of all amulets of protections and royal styles and silently subordinate herself before the powers representing death and *nothingness*. Similarly, the Christian idea of *kénōsis*, or "self-emptying," shows Jesus divesting himself of his full divinity in order to descend into the world and live as a man:

> Let this mind be in you, which was also in Christ Jesus: Who, being in the form of God, thought it not robbery to be equal with God: But made himself of no

reputation, and took upon him the form of a servant, and was made in the likeness of men: And being found in fashion as a man, he humbled himself, and became obedient unto death, even the death of the cross.[40]

The tragic engine of being—displayed here as a divine recital of the humbling aspect of the life cycle and the underlying occult unity of all things—plays out in unending repetitions of denuded multiplicity inexorably returning to, and thereby honoring, the phenomenon of life unfolding into death, death refolding into life, being become *nothing, nothing* being.

The last aspect brought to light by these speeches tells us something both about Lear and the structure of tragic drama: the enginery and its parts require winding up. The stage and pieces must be set, even if we enter in medias res. The conditions for restoration in the play—which includes elected divestment of some essential aspect of identity, order, or place and the possibility of repossession—must first be laid out, slowly come near again, flirt with success, and inevitably fail in the end. The people, places, institutions, cultural practices, and values constituting the particular world of the play find themselves narratively compelled to reveal their hidden dynamic structures and spiritual characteristics in order for the tragic god—symbol of unconscious force, its many drives *and* the atoning countermovements—to explicitly and publicly strip them of their illusions of reality, most importantly the illusion that their elective divestment of what is necessary was ever truly elective or that it ever really happened.[41] What are our choices before the powers prompting them? Before biological imperatives and societally compelled behaviors? Most decisions arrive as ex post facto rationalizations for our participations in the formula of force. (Along these lines we could read almost all of our positions and arguments as justifications after the fact, revealing, in part, reason's tendency to equivocate on our own behalf. The canny capacity to retroactively vindicate our will and our actions, our role in the formula of force. Perhaps reason itself—or any of its recognized uses—frees us from *nothing* but honesty?) The nature or use of reason notwithstanding, the reliable dreams and historical aspirations upon which human reality bases itself will end, all hidden motives known or knowable within the drama will come to light. Even Iago, famous for his refusal to explain his motivations in the end, still tells us of his jealousy and reveals his racism in the opening scene of *Othello*.[42] The tragic engine does not simply address itself to the superficial, it strips all and lays bare what is most personal. We too find ourselves stripped of our secrets in time. In this denuded world the old illusions will no longer suffice, and new or revised ones become necessary. "The art of our necessities is strange, / That can make vile things precious."[43] And precious things vile. The world must drip with *pathos* and bleed with loss while hope unsettlingly lingers. Through this process the particular and discrete becomes general and universal. Something essential about reality must now arrive so that we might accept and venerate it or reject and condemn it. And do so in order that possibilities and impossibilities might be affirmed.

Here, Lear's game shatters the previously functional illusion of healthy love existing between father and daughters to reveal what the nature and destiny of the actual relations dictate: good and evil will become unfixed and words unreliable. The community of values—whatever they are—will always disintegrate in time.[44] Love detaches from life and affixes itself to death. Only *nothing* remains trustworthy. Epic or intimate, it simply and sadly takes an exaggerated instance to remind us. In this way, Lear's contest of love speeches functions as ironically foreboding funeral orations. Not encomiums inflated and false (Goneril and Regan) or even honest and true (Cordelia), rather revelatory eulogies. His children curse him and themselves with their speeches, adumbrating the ruin to come. Though Lear is the subject of these fine false words—as if composing elegies—he has not yet received a "proper burial." He will become something like a specter or revenant: until the end of the play he will have no real life, no real death, no home, no tomb, no means by which to actualize his projects or possess the objects he desires. He will become a towering figure of rage and dark poetry, simultaneously a phantasmal figure incapable of living or dying, one ultimately "condemned to a pitiable existence."[45] Until, through its tools of love and time—*suffering*—the tragic engine fits him for his end. It makes him, as it makes all of us, in an ultimate sense, *khrēsimos*: useful, serviceable, good.

The tragic world, especially as Shakespeare presents it in *Lear*, might lead us to believe that some violation of what lies at the center of any world structure, behind all attraction and repulsion—the order of love (*ordo amoris*)—has fallen into a state of disunity. While tragic drama highlights those moments wherein fate and destiny drive characters to become caught in seemingly unresolvable conflict, it is also true, in a more fundamental sense, that tragedy venerates an underlying unity in all things. That is to say, an actual ontological disunity is impossible. In a Heraclitean sense, the cosmos certainly presents itself to us in a state of disunity, as if constituted of rifting forces, as if the universe constantly dissents. But to believe that this conflictual state signals something "wrong" or "unjust" is largely a Christian idea, in which tragic "disunity" or "dissolution"—the violation of the *ordo amoris*—is the very thing to be repaired. In this view, fate (force) and destiny (will) ought to be aligned, the order of love (right willing) and the order of the world (right understanding) must achieve harmony. The humanistic sciences, in their own way, share this aspiration, replacing spiritual depravity with primitive ignorance. Yet tragedy outlines and particularizes the way things truly are. The order of love quietly remains an undergirding possibility, a hidden power within the mindless world of force, unless cultivated and allowed expression through different modalities or relations.[46] An important aspect of the tragic engine lies in pitting the mindless *and* mindful modes of love against one another as part of time's perfecting mechanisms, making the players ready for their end.

Why is love so important to tragedy? It appears near the heart of almost every tragic drama. Its powers are primal and revolutionary. It touches everything that matters. Or, more accurately, love allows for things to be meaningful whatsoever. We cannot improve upon Emerson's sentences here:

> The introduction to this felicity [love] is in a private and tender relation of one to one, which is *the enchantment of human life*; which, like a certain divine rage and enthusiasm, seizes on man at one period and works a revolution in his mind and body; unites him to his race, pledges him to the domestic and civic relations, carries him with new sympathy into nature, enhances the power of the senses, opens the imagination, adds to his character heroic and sacred attributes, establishes marriage, and gives permanence to human society.[47]

At critical moments love is always personal. But its role in the structure of relations comes before and after us, it transcends us. We can, of course, always locate its subjective genesis in particular instances and relations, but then, once we have entered into the "enchantment of human life," we find ourselves "revolutionized." We are carried away and brought into a new (and very old) reality. Seized in the center of our being by love, we become united with others, drawn into new ethical possibilities; our senses gain aesthetic enhancement, imaginations expand, we receive divine qualities, true partnerships emerge, and the human world gains the semblance of permanency. It does all of this, however, precisely by transcending the particular (going beyond the merely personal or subjective) and transporting us into the universal (apprehending something depersonalized or metaphysical). We succumb to love at first in a very personal way only to have it take us, however momentarily—for world-destructive and reconstructive purposes—far away from ourselves. In order that we, by way of abstraction or idealization, can find a sense of proportion and measure outside of our own experience (however imaginary the whole thing is). Whether we understand it as terminating in objectless contemplations or meditations upon *nothing*, love contains the potential to take us out of ourselves, temporarily freeing us from force's otherwise irresistible formula, so that something else can be discovered or encountered. An idea. To accomplish this liberation, we need silence.

"Good as is discourse," Emerson writes, "silence is better, and shames it."[48] And earlier, in *Self-Reliance*, he tells us, "I like the silent church before any service begins, better than any preaching."[49] Discoursing, conversing, teaching, preaching, protesting, debating, all manner of human speech and conveyance of ideas and problems present us with useful and potentially productive encounters, but silence born of love or prudence in the face of certain impossibilities or uncertain ambiguities—"zones of opacity and incommunicability"[50]—asks of us something more difficult than the articulation or defense of our beliefs. The truth of (our) love and the power of (our) testimony against injustice and madness serves the "imagined" structure of the world that arrests us and—through our quietude—helps to create the conditions of shame by which the "real" structure of the world can be brought into the starkest of contrasts with the world we desire.[51] Not merely an idiosyncratically wished-for world but rather a distinct, if outwardly unprepossessing, world of full and free participation that is "always to come," for which the dialectical drama—fictionalized as tragedy or concretized as history—sets the stage beyond the limitations of the purely personal and communal contemplative realms. We might easily dismiss the radicality of silence to meaningfully strive toward these ends, yet we would only do so if we have already conceded the measure of meaningful work to quantifiable criteria that inevitably reduces all ideas and projects to a material conditionality unfit to evaluate transhistorical projects and commitments. Peace advocates, witnesses bearing silent testimony against oppression and violence, intentional communalists, ordinary folks in ordinary times invisibly participating in the subversion of reality: "fools."

Cordelia is such a fool. With her silence in *Lear*, as in any fictional or historical account, we find no guarantees, only more danger. Her father becomes unhinged, her sisters opportunistic. Her silence, which appeals to *nothing*, compels force and power—in whatever particular form they express themselves—out into the open. In the open we find them stripped of illusion and pretense. Force and power cannot just be, they cannot simply linger. All those caught and subordinated by them must always be busy. Yet, now, though it may take a few acts and scenes and a few more devastating turns, their chief agents can no longer hide among the banalities of life and within the usual administrative movements that so often occlude their insensitivity to the order of love and the freely imagined world to come.[52] They will be seen for what they are. They will perish under their own weight and by their own designs. They will disquietedly and gracelessly enact their own curse. Though they have no choice but to become fit for their end—which is the very reason for the tragic engine—they will never attain the satisfaction or peace of a joyous tragedy.[53]

2

The Riddle Is an Elegy

Both Shakespeare and Emerson offer us a view of the tragic world. Shakespeare builds it by way of events, circumstances, characters, atmosphere, and most effectively through haunting lines of poetic language itself. Not language disassociated from particular experiences or intentionally abstracted from any context, interchangeable with indifferent symbols, as if divorced from a speaker or scene, rather how certain lines linger with us long after we only half-remember who spoke them or why. In recollection or random encounters, the lines seem to have escaped their usual delimitations and connotations, and now exist as fragments, adages, aphorisms. Wandering alone, as it were, these haunting lines—or any interesting, remarkable, or important lines exquisitely rendered in service to tragedy—become instantiations of wisdom and sources of authority. Since we do not normally commit entire books or plays to memory, fragments become emblematic. We wrestle with them in particular. We cite them. "All minds quote."[1] Seemingly self-contained, as if possessing their own context. On such occasions as when we find these nomadic, self-reliant lines returned to the text from which they came, we encounter a mixture of gravity and scandal. A strange surprise that "at home" they, like us, actually appear less familiar.[2] In tragedy, the ordinary communicative function of language falters under the weight of previously unknown or disproportionate personal registers and phenomenal polyvalences. In the downward movements of the tragic world—*katábasis*—connections are not so easily made or made clear; they rather hide in misapprehension or become lost under the circumstances.[3] We grieve that conditions have changed simply by being revealed for what they are not: reality. "Dream delivers us to dream, and there is no end to illusion."[4] Meanings find no adequate means of expression, only incomprehensibility before both the naturally irrational and the inhumanly rational. All the usual actions taken by all the usual characters and writers—taken by us—do not, in the tragic elegies of being, reveal what is truly possible, rather only the inconsequential fate of all players trapped within the world of force. "Thou'lt come no more, / Never, never, never, never, never."[5]

Often thought to champion a purely positive philosophy of self-determination (*autárkeia*) Emerson joins Shakespeare in painting a world of perennial loss.[6] Believe no promises of better days to come, he tells us, because "nothing can bring you peace but the triumph of principles."[7] Yet this triumph indicates no promise of material or political actualization before the world of force and its machinery of power, rather only the inward possibility of self-overcoming (*Selbstüberwindung*) through the cultivation of equanimity (*apátheia*). He aims at something other than usurpation and the replacing of one villain for another: ourselves. This assertion, which we will revisit as this chapter concludes, clearly reveals Emerson's tragic sense of life, the mortal contours of which both establish and disrupt his theory of nature. Like a boundary that must first be set or recognized before it can be transgressed or moved. Or a circle drawn around another circle. He gives an enthusiastic account of this impossible aspiration—heeding and overcoming and affirming affectual life—in his first major work, *Nature*.

In 1836 Emerson published *Nature*, giving us his attempt to wrestle with an ancient enigma: "There sits the Sphinx at the road-side, and from age to age, as each prophet comes by, he tries his fortune at reading her riddle. There seems to be a necessity in spirit to manifest itself in material."[8] While Nietzsche would later link the riddle and the Sphinx to a treacherous interrogation of philosophy's perennial "will-to-truth,"[9] a journal entry from Emerson in the summer of 1835 tells us that this idea of a perpetual quest to solve the "problem of the world" came from his younger brother, Charles, with whom, we should note, he shared a close and powerful bond. The origin here is important because Emerson so idolized his brother that the quest and his brother's fate were bound together. For Emerson, their relationship had become the archetype for friendship:

> We are associated in adolescent and adult life with some friends, who, like skies and waters, are co-extensive with our ideas; who, answering each to a certain affection of the soul, satisfy our desire on that side; whom we lack power to put at such focal distance from us, that we can mend or even analyze them. We cannot choose but to love them.[10]

Friends and loved ones are "co-extensive with our ideas." As we said earlier, love appears near the very heart of tragedy. Our formulation of ideas, our approach to the riddle, whatever we might pretend, does not occur dispassionately at the outset. We come to great questions upon the backs of our moods and in the context of our relationships, and we only shed them temporarily. We set them aside as a performance, slowly, and usually only after the fact in the account we give. Like learning to pause, to measure proportionately, to apply a principle. An uncanny process usually involving no small amount of effort. And beyond habits of hesitation and contemplation, the stripping process—as a recital of the humbling aspect of the life cycle and the underlying occult unity of all things—whether elected or forced, ever remains one of the chief characteristics of the tragic engine, of things being made fit for their end. We therefore find that the riddle, the act of taking it up and attempting to answer the problem of the world, always drives the action of the tragic drama of understanding. The desire to solve the riddle seems philosophy's recurrent *nóstos*. Whatever we think we have learned of the cosmos and ourselves, our human and natural sciences remain tied to the world's tragic movements. In truth, the riddle turns—ever returns—upon those very movements.

And Emerson was no stranger to misfortune as in childhood he lost his father and two siblings. The sorrow, sadly, does not stop there. In April of 1836, the year of *Nature*, Charles, his beloved brother and closest friend, became ill and his health quickly deteriorated. He is gone by early May. This is a mere two years after Emerson's brother Edward had died of tuberculosis. Devasted, Emerson became adrift, ashamed at being alive: "Night rests on all sides upon the facts of our being."[11] Somewhat ominously, he already had tragedy on his mind, as he and Charles had read *Antigone* and *Electra* in Greek the previous year. Although Emerson would occasionally serve as a Greek tutor, a majority of the reading fell to Charles as his Greek was superior. His younger brother noted how enamored Emerson was with "the severe beauty of the Greek tragic muse."[12] Tragedy—the sublime annihilation essential to tragedy—had in fact been on his mind long before revisiting Sophocles or Charles's death.

Emerson's first wife, Ellen Tucker, also suffered from tuberculosis and had long suspected her life would end early. Her poor health, however, did not stop them from marrying. By all accounts Emerson adored her and, like Charles to friendship and fraternity, she became for him the model image of the tragic love object. His Beatrice.[13] Everything perfect bound to impermanence.[14] Everything good lingering only a little while with us before rejoining the timeless realm of idealized memories, exaggerated sympathies, life-affirming oversights.[15] The reason why principles, though never divorced from our affairs, must stand over and above our circumstances. Emerson and Ellen married in the fall of 1829, and she died in February of 1831. She was nineteen. As man and wife, they enjoyed a cycle of the seasons together and but a moment more. The tragic sense of life then overtook him:

> Will the eye that was closed on Tuesday ever beam again in the fullness of love on me? Shall I ever be able to connect the face of outward nature, the mists of the morn, the star of eve, the flowers and all poetry with the heart and life of an enchanting friend? No. There is one birth and baptism and one first love and the affections cannot keep their youth any more than men.[16]

Emerson had already been struggling with his faith. His prolonged engagement with Hume's skepticism, the many developments in biblical scholarship coming out of Europe, German Idealism and Coleridge's account of it, and his own deeply personal and difficult reflections upon the doctrines of the church: now the death of his beloved in whom he had placed the hope of a life rounded out. A complete, if conventional, life: gone. Less than two months later Emerson would return to Ellen's grave and exhume the body so that he might lay eyes on her. Mad with grief he could not fully accept her death. Where had she gone? Her life, her spirit? Whatever his wounded motivations and afflicted rationale, in that moment Emerson began taking his first steps toward a "second birth."[17] How does one accept life's misfortunes and failures and go on? Say yes? Even in the face of death, to affirm life as Ellen did with her dying words: "I have not forgot the peace and the joy."[18]

Aside. Emerson resigned his pastorate in September of 1832 and boarded a ship to Europe on Christmas day. He fled his losses and uncertainties and sought something elusive and transformative in the old world. He met a few of his intellectual heroes, Carlyle, Coleridge, Wordsworth. He visited ancient sites and famous cities. He took in the art, the architecture, the people, the manners. He attended lectures. It was at moments incredibly stimulating and enlightening, but ultimately disappointing. With the exception of a powerful moment at the Jardin des Plantes in Paris where Emerson found himself overwhelmed with the feeling of connectedness to all life—"I am moved by strange sympathies. I say continually, I will be a naturalist"[19]—the trip would largely confirm his earlier conviction, a conviction only temporarily shaken by sorrow, that the old world possessed no better minds capable of taking the measure of the world than the one nature endows to all men.[20]

These great losses spurred Emerson along a new path. A difficult path to a new church of the individual and the much older church of nature. A new American spirituality. Others ought to be loved and cherished and conversed with, but, in the end, "one must go alone."[21] He would in time come to leave behind naive beliefs about the mythic aspects of religion and the afterlife—that is, he would take the mythic *as mythic*—for mind and body belong together. There is no offensively simple duality. All metaphysical ideas, if they are to be good ideas, must also be material ideas. Material here meaning organic and natural in the "highest sense."[22] Not merely the Kingdom of God as an inner reality of inorganic psychic life, but rather as a charge laid upon each person of every generation to retake possession of the earth by endowing it with great purpose, significance, and use. To transform the meaning of the laws of a dying world into those of a living world by accepting the unity of those laws in everything that is. To cultivate what the American philosopher John McDermott called a "spiritual liver" capable of metabolizing and synthesizing the facts of our existence.[23]

Emerson does not advocate for the direct transformation of the tragic world into some idealized picture of a gay cosmos. The task of the great soul—as creator, as thinker—is to see the beauty of the tragic world. To understand positionality, timing, staging, the mysterious metamorphoses required for a shining moment to be what it is. It is to become a person who begins anew every day: "glowing and strong, like a morning sun emerging from behind dark mountains."[24] To discover for themselves that the dying and failing of things provides the very conditions of beauty, of love, of new ideas. Of old ideas rediscovered. Not as reminiscences of the eternal or infinite, but as temporally grounded and arising from finite perspectives that allow for determinations about anything in the first place. In this way the riddle of the world sings its own synchronal palinode. It gives its own answer or redress—which might entail incommensurability with direct formulation—in the very asking. The sorrowful or pious questioning into the enigma itself reveals the grateful upsurge of life perpetual. The elegy of being is the hymn of being. As *Nature* demonstrates, Emerson learned this early and never forgot it, even if, as some argue, *Circles*, *Experience*, and *Fate* grant us superior articulations of this elegiac hymn. His tragic anamnesis: "I learn geology the morning after an earthquake."[25]

And we should not take the personal aspects of Emerson's life as the only events threatening to alienate and undo him, the only happenings provoking radical change in his thinking. The social crises of the times in which he lived also presented divisive challenges. America found itself changing. As economic and material conditions developed, so too did the broader social and political climate. A unique American ecology began to take shape. Having long lived under the cultural influence of Europe, a pressing need to find their own voice and ethos fell upon American thinkers and artists. Tensions, long in the making, began necessitating release. A grand transposition signaling the forging of a new national identity. The concerns of developing a uniquely American intellectual spirit and artistic voice notwithstanding, the progressive minds of the nineteenth century—inheriting the as yet unexhausted revolutionary energies of the eighteenth century—began pushing back against all manner of social injustices: abolition of slavery, women's suffrage, radical (liberatory) educational theories, humane working conditions, challenges to unchecked industrialization, and capitalism. We also find them abandoning orthodox interpretations of the Bible, questioning the meaning and practice of communion, fundamentally reformulating beliefs about salvation and heaven, as well as the nature of revelation, of miracles, the divinity of Jesus, and the very idea of God. The layers of complexity, if not impasse, resulting from growing polarization on a host of social issues—in which the order of the world could no longer be sustained in accord with prevailing practices and ideological shifts—indicates but one half of the "priming power" confronting America.

Simultaneously, in order to progress along Enlightenment and Industrial lines, society seemed in danger of becoming not simply conventional, but "mechanical." Everyone exchanging—or made to exchange—the fullness of life lived in the context of a community for a socially managed atomic existence ordered to perform societal functions. No thinking, no questioning, no development of authentic self-culture. The romantic rebellion against enlightenment quantification and excessive rationalization at the expense of both quality and intuitive reason—or, how a person dies for the sake of categorization and control—heavily influences Emerson and the other transcendentalists. And yet so too do recent scientific discoveries and the optimism accompanying great technological advancements. They were not simply naive or reactionary renouncers. The transcendentalists walked a path between many opposing sensibilities. Not a path of modesty or moderation, rather one open to wherever their conscience dictated and imagination permitted. They demanded no universal agreement among themselves, only the conditions by which to live self-determined lives. They were only bound by elective spiritual aspirations and a few insistences: divine immanence, the intuitive perception of truth, a rejection of external authority.[26] Many undertook progressive social projects—Alcott's Temple School, Ripley's Brook Farm, Brownson's work anticipating Marx, Fuller's advocacy of women's rights, and so on—while others, like Emerson, primarily sought the intellectual freedom provided by solitude. While we often find a social radicality tied to the transcendental temperament, the emphasis on self-culture tended to make formal alliances and partnerships with reform movements difficult, at least for Emerson. He found official group affiliations generally distasteful. It worked against self-culture. To adhere to a platform or a creed of some sort represented the very conformity he wished to escape. Self-trust dictates distrust of any subordinating power that does not come from within, from reason emanating through rehabilitated instincts, especially as it relates to moral judgments and stances on sociopolitical matters. Though highly opinionated and progressive in his journals on all manner of social issues—treatment of Native Americans, woman's suffrage, property rights, immigrants and immigration, U.S. imperialism, and so on—under normal circumstances he was publicly no topical commentator:

> I do not often speak to public questions;—they are odious and hurtful, and it seems like meddling or leaving your work. I have my own spirits in prison;—spirits in deeper prisons, whom no man visits if I do not.[27]

But Emerson, like the other transcendentalists, had always stood against slavery and supported its abolition. And yet he had never formally joined the abolitionist movement and he rarely had complimentary things to say of those who engaged in direct political polemics. This somewhat passive support, however, changes after Margaret Fuller's death in 1850 and the passing of The Fugitive Slave Act two months later. With her death Emerson lost his "ideal audience" and a friend who, more so than any of his other famous interlocutors, simply "gave him more."[28] She pushed him to make his idealism an expressly lived philosophy. The new law, which required the return of slaves to their owners—even if they had escaped to free states—when taken with the loss of his friend, infuriated Emerson to a degree no one expected. Emerson could not comprehend how modern lawmakers, people presumably able to "read and write," could pass such a law. He believed the institution of slavery poisoned everything it touched. It was a vile social relic. He swore publicly that he would not obey it, and he used his considerable platform and all of his rhetorical powers to denounce slavery and those who defended it. It reminded him of the avenging element of the divine in Greek tragedy, which he associates with nature:

> Slavery is disheartening; but Nature is not so helpless but it can rid itself at last of every wrong. But the spasms of Nature are centuries and ages, and will tax the faith of short-lived men. Slowly, slowly the Avenger comes, but comes surely. The proverbs of the nations affirm these delays, but affirm the arrival. They say,

"God may consent, but not forever." The delay of the Divine Justice—this was the meaning and soul of the Greek Tragedy; this the soul of their religion.[29]

A singularly inhumane social practice distorts the weight and passage of time upon Emerson's conscience. And while his thought never becomes more daring or passionate than we find it in *Nature*, it does in time gain refinement and more moments of restraint. Yet it also gains a few harder edges, more selective ambiguities, cedes more agency to fate, and shies away less from social concerns. Still, Emerson's philosophy never acquiesces to moderation or despair.[30] His theoretical commitments of 1836 remain essentially the philosophy of his later works. If anything, that the tragic element becomes more pronounced in later works allows us to revisit *Nature* with a compass better suited to navigate its terrain.

We must therefore resist the common temptation to read *Nature* as simply offering a theory of nature at a secure remove. It shows us what a manifesto for thinkers looks like: no overt call to particular political action, no new economic theory, no dissolution of old institutions. And yet, in Emerson attuning himself to the question of the world—trying his fortune at reading nature's riddle—no politics, no economics, no institutions remain safe. The Sphinx is the "father of dread" and "the strangler." She curses with drought and famine. If we address ourselves to it, we must become ready to die. Or to win. Something will die either way: and yet the mystery of the world regenerates for every generation. It returns. "Our life is an apprenticeship to the truth that around every circle another can be drawn; that there is no end in nature."[31] Answering the enigma offers but temporary "relief" from the tragic curse. A moment for the triumph of principles, "like a morning sun emerging from behind dark mountains."[32] And yet it is only a moment. As the moment passes, we realize the cycle never ended. The path between opposing positions and views, as Emerson walks it, is, however, a revolutionary track leading to the chiasmatic riddle of being in the first place: the intersection of fate and destiny. Again, the temporal and finite positionality of a particular life staged within the broader drama of life. This *metaxical* way does not simply amount to philosophical moderation. The thinker is *daemonic*. The role requires becoming reacquainted with the primordial danger of being alive in the world—as only a being capable of deep loss and radical veneration can be—and makes moderation and ideological conformity impossible: "Beware when the great God lets loose a thinker on this planet. Then all things are at risk."[33]

Why? Because "all is riddle, and the key to a riddle is another riddle."[34]

The circumstances of Shakespeare's *Lear* also speak to a shift in material and social conditions. The English Renaissance occurs at a time of transition from feudal aristocratic and medieval ecclesiastical structures governing all aspects of life to a new world dominated by commerce and the proto-atomization of personal relations.[35] Failed conspiracies notwithstanding, the English experienced no overnight revolution or immediate alteration of social relations. Their view of the world, if not their philosophy, arose within the nascent *and* mature anxieties produced during a prolonged evolution pregnant with promise. Still, the only guarantee was uncertainty. With the exception of the clarity surrounding commercial concerns—the motivation to compete and turn a profit—the age-old institutions and the values they safeguarded no longer provided the sense of continuity, community, or purpose they once did. And the new trends in ideas—humanism, scientific method, greater parliamentary power—were as yet unproven. What characteristics does art take on during such a protracted interval?

Directly or indirectly, art always reflects the conditions of life within a culture. In uncertain times it draws even more deeply from the anxieties and fears and secret hopes of its audience. A great work of art, if it does anything, represents an age. It educates us about a people, about their world, their affairs and concerns. If we consider it a truly great work among great works, it becomes transpersonal, transhistorical, achieves the possibility of universal *resonance*.[36] It then not only tells us about the lives and worlds of others but educates us about ourselves. These works come to play a part in the fashioning of our own identity. Shakespeare gives us several such works, and *King Lear* can easily be counted among them. In it we find the uneasiness associated with succession, accompanied by changing political dynamics and economic realities, as well as the tension existing between old and new values being worked-through theologically, philosophically, and creatively. The nihilism present in *Lear* expresses the inarticulable and unresolved questions about human nature and society—about the cosmos itself—in an age characterized largely by its indefinition: helping to explain the remarkable popularity and prescience of Shakespeare's tragedies. How can judgments and evaluations take place when the values required to make them have become unfixed?[37]

Positions and metrics must, of course, be created out of the proving ground of lived uncertainty within a particular context. The at-hand material enacting a return to essential concerns about the human life drama. A new repetition of the oldest fears faced with philosophers' minds and poets' pens. Shakespeare's characters serve as his conceptual personae allowing his audience to try their fortune at reading the riddle of the times, at answering the enigma of being. We do this, if we choose to, when we invest ourselves in the perfectly failing agency of those for whom "the time is out of joint": Oedipus, Antigone, Hamlet, Lear, Macbeth, Lady Macbeth, Emerson, Nietzsche, and all those who—theoretically or theatrically—find themselves face-to-face with the problem of the world.

Literature and philosophy have given us many ways by which we might approach the riddle: an uncompromising portrait of the world, a complete and explanatory system or a rejection of theory in favor of existential attunement to primal moods or fidelity to the earth and our uncanny nature or a search for the underlying order of reality or even irony or absurdity. For Emerson, attempting to give an account of the riddle and a possible solution speaks to a recurring and inveterate task. He lays out his program and biases in his introduction to *Nature*:

> Our age is retrospective. It builds the sepulchres of the fathers. It writes biographies, histories, and criticism. The foregoing generations beheld God and nature face to face; we, through their eyes. Why should not we also enjoy an original relation to the universe? Why should not we have a poetry and philosophy of insight and not of tradition, and a religion by revelation to us, and not the history of theirs?[38]

Emerson does not despise institutions for their preservation of old and interesting ideas, but he does detest the loss of honed intuition, of original insight, of novel theories, of self-trust—of self-culture inspired by pre-Christian self-discipline (*áskēsis*)—in favor of assuming that the most important and remarkable ideas have already found their way into the libraries. It is not a matter of being one or the other, old or new, rather an "also" that leans heavily toward an authentic and creative relationship to nature.[39] Schools and churches must not simply safeguard the works of the past, they must teach their students and encourage their congregants to leave those works behind: to read the book of nature for themselves, to know God directly without doctrinal mediation, to see life as the ultimate grammar and dictionary, to attune themselves to the world and write their own books. Why? "The books of an older period will not fit this."[40] Each generation requires its own account. How could we ever "enjoy an original relation to the universe" if all we did was read nature through the theories of others? Our capacity to experience nature as it is cannot be colored by blind adherence to the ideas of previous ages. Intellectual and spiritual retrospection that subordinates *will to power*—as *will to ideation*—to old fidelities unhelpfully unburdens us of this work. We develop no purchase of our own, no perspective, no predilection or overpowering necessity for creation. Even if the penultimate objective lies in overcoming *will to power* and transcending the self through contemplative means—to pause and disrupt the world of force—the preconditions of doing so always lies in the accumulation of power born of self-trust. "Power is one great lesson which Nature teaches man."[41] To learn it, however, we have to reorient ourselves toward nature: "Worship must he learn."[42] How do we learn worship in relation to theories? Circumspection in philosophy? Especially when our opening move is refusal to accept the venerable creeds and systems handed down to us as having the final word? To love and learn from great books while demurring at the thought that they are unquestionable or final? "Books are the best of things, well used; abused, among the worst."[43] We have to begin another way. As Heidegger reminds us, "Questioning is the piety of thought."[44]

Emerson continues:

> Undoubtedly we have no questions to ask which are unanswerable. We must trust the perfection of the creation so far, as to believe that whatever curiosity the order of things has awakened in our minds, the order of things can satisfy. Every man's condition is a solution in hieroglyphic to those inquiries he would put. He acts it as life, before he apprehends it as truth. In like manner, nature is already, in its forms and tendencies, describing its own design. Let us interrogate the great apparition that shines so peacefully around us. Let us inquire, to what end is nature?[45]

If we read this naively, we might think Emerson assumes that all of our questions will find fit answers, that every interest will terminate in objective explanation. We might forget the lesson of *Circles* (or the eternal return) and think the riddle solved. This brings us to a critical—and nuanced—aspect of Emerson's metaphysics and epistemology. Emerson believes in a transcendent idea of nature that unifies all beings. It conditions objects of knowledge and all possibilities of experience. This is a retroactive conditionality taken as a priori. And yet, nature *is* its material contours and operations. It is only through our own sensible understanding—born of our own delimited and delimiting condition—that we might approach the idea of nature in any satisfactory and liberating way. That is, in a fashion utterly transparent and vulnerable, we can work with and through our limitations of thought and experience to arrive at their outermost boundaries, at our most authentic possibilities of understanding. In that spatially and temporally verging dimension of thought—*imaginatively considered*—we might transgress the sensible limits of possibility in order to enter into a depersonalized unity of all things: the very idea of being or nature or the cosmos. An encounter with "divinity" now becomes realizable. This ideational unity is only a possibility of imaginative reason when it is approached through our own attuned subjective encounter with phenomenal nature or our own euphonic reading of an existing theoretical account or artistic representation. Though Emerson champions the first approach, either can enable us—in the realm of thinking—to shed the delimiting constituents of the subjectivity that we were required to attune and harness in the act of approaching a creative theory in the first place:

> Standing on the bare ground—my head bathed by the blithe air and uplifted into infinite space—all mean egotism vanishes. I become a transparent eyeball; I am nothing; I see all; the currents of the Universal Being circulate through me; I am part or parcel of God.[46]

Our historically situated "consciousness"—our allotment of "reason," our culturally circumscribed "imagination," our apportionment of and talent with any of the "faculties" we might employ in thinking through the formation and play of concepts—must locate the latent potentiality of a unified idea residing both within and beyond our own inner resources (thus the absolute imperative of self-trust). This initially and provisionally "speaks" as the intuition that guides or lures the constructive project, drawing us into what is essentially *nothing*, but what returns to us as the *synthetic a priori* idea of nature or being. It is *as if* it were ever gathered together and waiting for us. Whatever idea we receive, even the most unfamiliar, perplexing, and orphic, we find it *as if* already "ordered" or "given form" by reason. Perhaps we could consider it along the lines of the Stoic's generative principle of the cosmos (*lógos spermatikós*), working in and through all things? As *if*.[47] A way of overcoming, by merging, the classically separated realms of the sensible (or phenomenal) and the intelligible (or noumenal). Though unsurprisingly often reminiscent of German Idealism, the reintegration or unity of spirit and matter he presents arrives not only in the key of the Stoics but of Spinozan monism. It runs parallel with Feuerbachian contemplative materialism (an appellation like transcendentalism that originates with pejorative intent) and, arguably, anticipates Deleuzian transcendental empiricism. That is, a rich account that ultimately overcomes—or strategically *evades*—the reductive division between varieties of idealism and materialism. We could, and probably should, simply call it *Emersonianism*.[48] Whatever we name the method, the final field of play we find arrives as the strangely familiar country of an immanent God. The language of ideas that waits for us as we quietly, and quite erotically, contemplate the music and movements of nature. That which we ever trace in being's retreat before thought.

Looking for emendations, if not theoretical alternatives, to the "paltry empiricism" in vogue at the time,[49] Emerson turns to Coleridge's romantic reception of Kant's transcendental idealism: "It is asserted only that the act of self-consciousness is for us the source and principle of all our possible knowledge."[50] And "The primary Imagination I hold to be the living power and prime agent of all human perception, and as a repetition in the finite mind of the eternal act of creation in the infinite I AM."[51] Or, to let Emerson speak for himself:

> The soul is the perceiver and revealer of truth. ... Revelation is the disclosure of the soul. ... Let man then learn the revelation of all nature and all thought to his heart; this, namely; the Highest dwells with him; that the sources of nature are his own mind, *if the sentiment of duty is there.*[52]

There exists no "objective knowledge" as such awaiting discovery through "correct methodology," and we will discover no "universal ideas" *outside* of the human enterprise that constructs and welcomes them. However spurred on as he is by Plato and Plotinus and related accounts, Emerson is no simple idealist.[53] Truth neither abides upon a metaphysical plane nor a fiction of fancy. He offers us something else, a compelling synthesis of both ancient and nineteenth-century predilections: a tragic account approached through temperament.[54] We only see and think through the lenses our moods allow, and our theories will never touch upon the eternal and unchanging (the unnamed prior to ideation). "Souls never touch their objects."[55] Our essays toward knowledge or truth must nevertheless be tried. They must be articulated and manifested through a creative, generalized, depersonalized account—within a new or revised set of laws or principles—that excises all previously restrictive appeals to that initial subjective experience. In a sense, we ride and trust our attuned temperaments to an imagined plane wherein an ideational unity relieves us of the subjective limitations of our temperaments to reveal a universal end. An aim. A reason. Although we can only approach it this way, the riddle of the world cannot actually be solved by one person's uniquely bemooded experience or novel notion. A mere concept, however remarkable, cannot change our world and efficaciously carry us forward. How then? Unless an account of the experience or a developed notion or a well-formulated concept has *become* an idea approachable by anyone anywhere willing to think in accord with that idea. Unless the account has become transhistorical. Unless the work has manifested a remarkable "universality." Or, perhaps more accurately, all of our beliefs and biases that form our determinatively coherent (or incoherent) theory of the world, which we always already carry with us and which prohibits new ways of encountering nature, must first be stripped from us through crises, honest discourse, or spiritual practices, in order that we might become capable of encountering a true and truly transformative idea. This is a wondrously traumatic affair. Ever afterward we attempt to recreate it or give an account of it. We fashion theories and portraits of the world based upon it. We try to lure others with a philosophy or vision based upon an encounter that they themselves have not yet had. We try to provoke it or make it seem necessary or simply most helpful. A theory or work acting as friend, rival, an engaging and querulous stranger. It is all notions and concepts and arguments, all themes and imagery and styles. The theatrically tragic element here—the perennially performed echo of the ontological engine—is that this imagined universality is transitory. The book or poem or theory attempting containment: even more momentary. Its language and devices and sensibilities age much less gracefully than the idea itself. The Beautiful, the Just, and the Good have aged better as the enduring quarry of philosophers than any particular articulation or expression of beauty, justice, and goodness. And yet: "Everything looks permanent until its secret is known."[56] Until the riddle is provisionally answered once again through the necessary array of illusions.[57] The idea of nature in the highest and holiest sense must be encountered again and again by others, and new accounts given of it. Our confidence in the explanatory power of the idea we discover through creation will, like all old gods, inevitably diminish and fall away. Yet we can still marvel at their grace or daring or former power: Plato, Descartes, Spinoza, Kant, Hegel, and others. We can compose new paeans, future elegies.

Shakespeare's *Lear* abandons any semblance of possibility for truce or balance or restoration between human society and the world. For Emerson, creative portraits and attuned conceptualizations work toward a unified idea that allows us to affirm nature without denying its tragic architecture. By doing so, this affirmation participates in a perennial activity that maintains the imagined world structure upon which institutions and social practices stand—through trying our hand at the riddle. With Shakespeare, however, in the tragic worlds he composes from *Hamlet* onward, we receive no such illusion of stability. Prior to the turn of the seventeenth century, we only find tragic events, disastrous decisions, flawed personalities. But with *Hamlet* the image of the world darkens.[58] Perhaps one of the reasons *Hamlet* runs the longest of Shakespeare's plays rests with the writer wrestling not only with characters and plots but with a poet contending with the world. He searches earnestly but in vain for the language to restore symmetry, to resurrect the dead (which he arguably does not find for another ten years with *The Winter's Tale* and *The Tempest*). This theatrical presentation of indefinition upends the medieval and early modern senses of an ordered creation, mining the uncertainty of the age—perhaps of life lived honestly in any age—and aligns the Shakespearean tragic world more squarely with Sophocles than most of his contemporaries. Even the works designated "comedy" during this last period emit pervasive insecurity and highlight complex relations. Everything has become thesis resistant, argumentatively fragile, and balanced on the thinnest of tenets. Now a truly comedic outcome is simply luck. Agency counts for much less than it once did.

Shakespeare's tragedies after 1599 no longer arrive principally as cathartic portraits of flawed protagonists, for individuals—however towering, introspective, capable—become decentered personas and the tragic dramas "inescapably social."[59] The theatrical evolves to represent the ontological and social conditions of life with more fidelity. As powerful of a witness to and against the formula of force as Cordelia is, no one holds a position of pause and refusal long enough in the tragic world to allow them to offer up a theory or vision of the world capable of healing it, both due to the limitations of individual agency and to the more essential truth that the dramatic world is, strictly speaking, not "sick," rather only in or out of accord with the ideas that ground society. And not only the dramatic world, for all the arts to some degree, intentionally or unintentionally, cannot help but express what is happening within and between the manifold dimensions of human life. The most sublimely traumatizing works—tragedies—seem to arise in such times as when *we do not know how* to be in accord with the world or what the world even means. Yet, amidst all the precarity of times wherein values have become fragile or lost, the desire to dwell in accord with something solid and true, pits otherwise unwilling agents against those who pine for advantage or have fallen through the insubstantiality of society's moral ruins. We are reminded here that while tragedy only signals one of several theatrical modes, it is nevertheless the ontological state of affairs. It offers the most monstrously marvelous account of human life. And our opinions on the matter matter little. Our romantic or pragmatic or dogmatic attempts to undermine or turn or ignore the tragic vision and account go nowhere. Even if a philosophical theory offered an anti-theory or an artistic vision allowed for silent testimony indicting force and shaming power, there would still be no final overcoming of force and power, only ever temporary cessations of institutional mechanisms and ephemeral spaces for spontaneous expressions of love. Pure moments of freedom. Other plays attempt this liberating movement of love through forgiveness, but forgiveness as accomplished by and bound up with penance.[60] Repentance (as sincere sorrow and committed action) by the forgiver must overtake and replace penance (as a mere act of abasement) by the offender for true restoration to take place. Prior to Shakespeare's theatrical world advancing into the tragic umbra at the turn of the century, Portia, in *The Merchant of Venice*, exemplifies one beautiful flirtation with this possibility—"the quality of mercy is not strained. / It droppeth as the gentle rain from heaven"—still the "aggrieved parties" appear unable to realize their own wrongs. They do not yet realize that they comprise co-constitutive positions in the procedure of aggrievement. Mercy remains only a weapon for justice. It is not until Prospero in *The Tempest* that Shakespeare makes his way to a language capable of renouncing will to power and will to revenge through the restorative possibility of forgiveness free of penance, wherein the wizard suspends his own revenge plot and chooses love and mercy:[61] "I'll drown my book"; "This thing of darkness I / Acknowledge mine"; "Be free, and fare thou well"; "As you from crimes would pardoned be, / Let your indulgence set me free."[62] All justifications fall away under the quiet lure of love. And yet, before Shakespeare had found his way to forgiveness, the tragic world of *Lear* precludes any sustained mortal agency to abate or pause for long, much less restore. Even Cordelia finds her way back into the formula. We witness the inevitability of social dissolution.[63] The end contains as much promise for the future as *Antigone*: "For mortal men / there is no escape from the doom we must endure."[64] Nature and the gods are not venerated—only invoked for rage or self-justification—and the ideas upon which social order stands falter under the weight of those same unreflective "natural" energies driving life toward death. Unless nature becomes an idea for veneration, unless it becomes "divine." Not a mere concept or dogma or set of concrete conditions defaulted to for justification or reductive explanations. Edmund's invocation of nature can help us make this explicit, if only as a negative example.

> EDMUND Thou, nature, art my goddess; to thy law
> My services are bound. Wherefore should I
> Stand in the plague of custom, and permit
> The curiosity of nations to deprive me,
> For that I am some twelve or fourteen moonshines
> Lag of a brother? Why bastard? wherefore base?
> When my dimensions are as well compact,
> My mind as generous, and my shape as true,
> As honest madam's issue? Why brand they us

> With base? with baseness? bastardy? base, base?
> Who, in the lusty stealth of nature, take
> More composition and fierce quality
> Than doth, within a dull, stale, tired bed,
> Go to the creating a whole tribe of fops,
> Got 'tween asleep and wake? Well, then,
> Legitimate Edgar, I must have your land.
> Our father's love is to the bastard Edmund
> As to the legitimate: fine word—'legitimate'!
> Well, my legitimate, if this letter speed,
> And my invention thrive, Edmund the base
> Shall top the legitimate. I grow; I prosper.
> Now, gods, stand up for bastards![65]

Edmund's soliloquy here has received much attention from commentators. Many read this as Machiavellian cunningness or as approximating a Nietzschean *will to power*. "He who cannot obey himself will be commanded."[66] Edmund's invocation of nature and his indictment of custom additionally underscore the ancient distinction between custom (*nómos*) and nature (*phýsis*), a distinction sometimes retrieved in order to justify an unscrupulous opportunism. The division and disagreement between custom and nature, however, cannot rest on reductive claims that exclude their shared origin in human theorizing. Both require, among other things, interpretation and conceptualization—necessitating imperfections belying the limitations and biases of the human condition and its cultural contingencies—even the laws we call "natural," which appear as fundamental features of the cosmos, and, more glaringly, the laws we call "customs," which seem merely features of the social world we have constructed. Now, once the imaginary foundation and play structure of human law (positive law) becomes known and subsequently insecure due to resting principally upon habituations and beliefs (habituations and beliefs inevitably revealed to be incommensurate with, if not contrary to, one another), an Edmund or an *Übermensch* or an existentialist or an anarchist or a poststructuralist—a villain, a hero, a rebel, a poet, a theorist of difference—can undertake projects inaccessible, if not unthinkable, to most everyone else. The clear lines distinguishing these responsive "roles" can become equivocal. What separates Satan from the Messiah from the sadistic antihero turns upon the grievances and sympathies present in their portraits (as well as within those for whom the portraits were painted).[67] "To be great is to be misunderstood."[68] This nomadic fluidity of undertakings and identifications results from: (1) electing to see positive law as arbitrary and nonbinding for those who possess the will, sensibilities, talents—*power*—to act in accord with their own nature rather than conform to a socialized persona; (2) rejecting the claim that any essential sense of "nature" exists prior to its conceptualization or entrapment in theorization and social praxis (particularly as it relates to "human nature"); or (3) refashioning the language and lens by which the delimiting aspects of life (derived from natural or positive law) are approached or received in such a way as to become capable of rehabilitating the possibility of fundamental *and* novel encounters—with "Socrates, a temple or a demon"[69]—resulting in critical projects capable of liberation and the creation of an authentic identity.[70] *I* becomes *other*, *being* is *difference*, *univocity* returns to *multiplicity*. "He is to convert all impediments into instruments, all enemies into power ... He will convert the Furies into Muses, and the hells into benefit."[71]

Yet, for all his ambition, insights, and demonstrable gifts, Edmund fits neatly into the role of villain. If we did not know what was to come, we might imagine ourselves rooting for him as we would any underdog: "Now, gods, stand up for bastards!"[72] But Shakespeare does not compose him in the life-affirming shape of the overman, nor does he grant him the spiritual largesse of the Emersonian great man. Edmund certainly rejects the intrinsic legitimacy of customs that would curtail his own projects and he praises nature as a goddess, but even Nietzsche speaks of the *Übermensch* learning to love without pity, learning to die (and thus live) without *ressentiment*, learning the nauseating wisdom of Silenus and affirming life in the face of that wisdom. In accord with a non-moralizing sense of truth and a fidelity to the earth—what is most "natural"—the transhuman (*Übermensch*) creates new values in order to *overcome* nihilism, not to enact it as Edmund does. And the Emersonian "great man" and "over-soul"—early spurs and models for Nietzsche's overman[73]—must, in addition to learning how to love in a higher way, learn to restore what has been taken and lost; he must come "into the arms of fallen men" as he "pleads with them to return to paradise."[74] By "heroic encouragement" he holds others to their destiny, to their own great purpose.[75] Not to use and abuse them for his own gain, which is no true gain. One of the chief revelations of nature, Emerson tell us, is the discovery of the "NOT ME" that constitutes me.[76] As John Lysaker formulates it, Emerson, like Kant and Fichte, sees no immediate access to our own nature; we rather "encounter ourselves in our encounters with what we are not."[77] This revelation arrives not as purely theoretical knowledge, but as something deeply felt and intensely imagined, something arousing a responsible relation and sense of duty toward that which is *not me*, toward the *other*.[78] Not dictatorially imposed from without but awoken from within by an encounter with multiplicitous nature.

The "plague of custom" that deprives Edmund the opportunity to exercise the full array of his human powers must indeed be answered with power—"Life is a search after power"[79]—but an incredibly, if not incredulously, peculiar power, as a deep silence sometimes indicates, which can only be *won* from out of the mindless drives of nature, which can only be *rescued* from out of the calculative mechanisms of societal force. The unwise motivations that busy us with self-negating agendas and the lazy habits that keep us from meaningful ventures—both of which make quietude nearly impossible—take time and effort to unlearn. And it seems foolishness and weakness to those still ordered about by force and amused by its distractions. Edmund soliloquizes but finds no deliverance without or within, until the end, when it is, perhaps, too late. If he, however, had discovered a reason to practice stillness and silently mused upon *nothing*—*nothing* (that is) distinct from the instrumentally performed noisy nihilation of the world, *nothing* (that is) *otherwise than being*—then he might have prepared himself for a god to lift him from out of the formula. He could have found himself arrested. Like a poet overcome by voice. For nature to arise as such an assisting goddess—to become "divine"—it must first, in the manner we described earlier, *become an idea*, an idea capable of reaching back and bestowing upon him what society ever conspired to take: the very desire, whatever the conditions of life, to take up the riddle of the Sphinx and by so doing to change an unchangeable world. To change an unchangeable world by way of a theory that imperfectly and provisionally grants to us and to others a new vision which ignites a revolution in praxis. Again: "Beware when the great God lets loose a thinker on this planet. Then all things are at risk." The rare power to create under conditions (almost always) precluding creation for all participants.

The tragic reading of *Nature*—the chronic riddle it retrieves—which we are attempting to develop here alongside *Lear*, finds a disquieting fulfillment with Emerson's masterstroke, *Experience*:

> An innavigable sea washes with silent waves between us and the things we aim at and converse with. Grief too will make us idealists. In the death of my son, now more than two years ago, I seem to have lost a beautiful estate—no more. I cannot get it nearer to me. If tomorrow I should be informed of the bankruptcy of my principal debtors, the loss of my property would be a great inconvenience to me, perhaps, for many years; but it would leave me as it found me—neither better nor worse. So is it with this calamity; it does not touch me; something which I fancied was a part of me, which could not be torn away without tearing

me, nor enlarged without enriching me, falls off from me, and leaves no scar. It was caducous. I grieve that grief can teach me nothing, nor carry me one step into real nature.[80]

Emerson's decision to mention his late son without developing a more substantial portrait of loss or of honoring, in some recognizable way, a level of decorum related to mourning, and, further, to cast grief into such impotent contrast with "real nature," has prompted many to focus on the psychology at work here, often labeled dissociative. Either Emerson, not unlike Lear, was unable to acknowledge the discrepancies between his life and thought, as well as between various claims made in his work, *or* he, not unlike the Fool, could note with savage irony all apparent discrepancies while he, not unlike Edgar who merely wore madness deceptively as he lovingly led his father to "the cliff," held the conviction that no essential discrepancies existed.[81] More succinctly stated, either Emerson could not address the death of his son in a meaningful way or there was no reason to do so. We will not pursue either of these readings directly. Perhaps if we considered dissociation hermeneutically instead of psychologically, we might think of a manner of reading without the usual associations and expected references. Something seems to be unintentionally missing or intentionally occluded. Or, put another way, a form of misreading. Or even, how things elude us when we go to give them definition.[82] Many possibilities might open up with such hermeneutical maneuvers, especially for those attempting an original exegesis or novel theorization. And while this interpretive approach and the psychological disorder of dissociation can both generate insightful speculations, let us nevertheless set them aside in order to consider the passage above in light of what we have already said about Emerson's overall project in *Nature* and its tragic underpinnings.

First, though this aforementioned passage, and *Experience* overall, seems to present us with discrepancies within Emerson's life and thought, it is, upon careful consideration, better read as an evolved reiteration of the foregoing analysis. What appears as a denial of the disclosive nature of moods previously championed is in fact a mature confirmation of their disclosiveness. It is what they disclose that has changed for Emerson. *Experience*, appropriately titled, offers a less eclectic, somewhat more sober or world-weary account of moods than the one given in *Nature*. In short, our moods reveal our reliance on illusions. That is to say, they disclose the necessity of illusions. The much-needed portraits of existence or worldviews upon which our emotional lives turn. Upon closer inspection, however, we discover that some part of our being always seemed to know better than to believe completely that things were the way they had been framed for us. And yet we feel helpless to act upon those repressed suspicions. It requires an uncanny faith or remarkable "self-trust." From these quiet suspicions we can work toward provisionally and temporarily shedding the inauthentic self that requires these illusions in order to partake of an original communion with nature. Unadorned, unarmed. We, whatever we essentially are, emerge from that encounter restored, whole, free of illusions, reequipped with depersonalized insights, possessed by *ideas*. At least one idea. At least for a time. Still, before this series occurs, the self and its moods and its experiences must first be obeyed— not reacting to the most obnoxious feelings and impressions, rather acting upon the gentler spurs of the quieter suspicions speaking through and under them—before they and the self that bears and is born by them can be overcome. Communion with divinity requires a conversion. Then a tempered and useful enthusiasm can embrace fate and give an answer to the riddle.

Let us note this development as explicitly as we can. Prior to this "transcendental experience" or "conversion," and even afterward to varying degrees and intensities, we suffer from conformity to the contingent cultural views and societal practices in force that curtail or preclude confidence in our natural intuition, the "voice of our true self," which, before any fundamental encounter with *nothing—the tragically otherwise of nature*—is only able to speak through our temperamental reception of moods and experiences in the language of the illusions and metaphors that our world allots to us. Such habits of thinking and living provide us with an approximal and simulated sense of self that is, we learn, an affective ruins we cannot yet fully trust.[83] The self we wear is still too caught up in the enginery of inessential things, too forced and ordered about. To advance before the more primal powers of the possible hid in *nothing* and to see the illusions for what they are, or what they try to hide, requires a life of intellectual and ethical vulnerability—a "spiritual life"—that many, if not most, find impossible. And yet if we can somehow heed the quiet call of *nothing's* possibilities and accept our illusions as illusions and attune our affectual selves to the tragic *difference* of nature whispering those possibilities— which have heretofore only arrived for us as reactions molded by the world of force and its institutional mechanisms—then, if we are fortunate, we will find ourselves carried into those unfamiliar regions of silence and stillness wherein the individuated identity of the old "self"—that menagerie of masks mistakenly taken as our own private person—is temporarily set aside as our true being, delivered over to this *nothingness*, dissolves into the unity of being, which is the very idea of being *otherwise*, of being as *difference*, of not being a "thing" at all.[84]

Rather, a life.[85] As belonging to life. And death. The idea of nature can now be seen as the unending repetition of a ceaseless multiplicity, of a generative-destructive *nothing* that is the origin and destiny of being. To catch sight of the idea of nature is to transcendentally experience a "virtual simulation" of the peace waiting just up ahead for all. No more separation, no more partial identities, no more contingencies. "I am nothing; I see all."[86] Social and professional considerations notwithstanding, it is no wonder why Emerson originally published *Nature* anonymously.

These transcendental encounters with nature—the *idea of nature* fashioned by reason upon the silently generative plane of *nothingness* we imaginatively welcome—that persist within us as a possibility and outside of us as a destiny, provoke a radical shift in perspective as we return from those moments transformed and equipped with rehabilitated instincts to guide ourselves through the illusions of existence. Any rigid distinction between inside and outside, any inflexible separation between I and other, any unyielding difference between ontology and ethics become problematized and reformulated. Or they vanish altogether. The troubles and challenges of a sorrowful life adjust in proportion and value commensurate with the vantage gained from the illusion-nihilating perspective of destiny. Not pessimistic resignation but life affirmation through reorientation in accordance with the idea. What perhaps began as mere sensuous appreciation or intellectual curiosity spurred by ignorance or lucky caprice or suspicion becomes a deep-seated wonderment before what is:

> But when the mind opens and reveals the laws which traverse the universe and makes things what they are, then shrinks the great world at once into a mere illustration and fable of this mind. What am I? and What is? asks the human spirit with a curiosity new-kindled, but never to be quenched.[87]

As a result of this new vantage—of being a fragment imaginatively and momentarily returned to its proper place like a lost line of poetry returned to its poem—our relationship with others and with ourselves change. Our senses of connection and loss and importance and relevance all reorient. Our emotional register does not close or dissociate, it opens more fully:

> The name of the nearest friend sounds then foreign and accidental: to be brothers, to be acquaintances—master or servant, is then a trifle and a disturbance. I am the lover of the uncontained and immortal beauty. In the wilderness, I find something more dear and connate than in streets and villages.[88]

Emerson realizes that particular relations, temperaments, class status, talents, and weaknesses are all a matter a chance. From the unliberated view, accidental adornments. Given and taken away. In the lexicon of a heightened perspective, however, these relations and the intensity of those relations become fated. Our very desires too. Even fighting fate only arrives as an option doled out by fate. To whom is it given to do so? Who heeds the quiet under-voice of being? Who does not? Cannot? Why? To what lengths are any of us willing to go to change ourselves or, to the degree we can, our situation? To endure loss? To move beyond it?

> I shun father and mother and wife and brother when my genius calls me. I would write on the lintels of the door-post, *Whim*. I hope it is somewhat better than whim at last, but we cannot spend the day in explanation.[89]

Our second remark comes as a consequence of the first: there is a direct line between Emerson and the stoics.[90] That ancient account would locate the cause of suffering not in unfortunate events themselves but within an un-rehabilitated inner life, with how we relate to and find ourselves disposed toward the world. This is why Emerson says grief teaches us *nothing*. He grieves that grief teaches us *nothing*. Its madness so intoxicates us and, if done well, can prove cathartic and healing. Still, in itself, from the vantage of depersonalized *nothingness*—"I am nothing"—grief gives us no access to the universal idea of nature; it instead traps us in our own limited experience.[91] "I am a fragment." In lingering there we demonstrate our failure to have discovered, accepted, and taken responsibility for those things most truly ours (our rehabilitated drives and reorganized relations), and we confuse them with what is not ours at all (drives fashioned by the world of force and disorganized social relations). Quite simply, we neglect what we must attend to and try and fail to exercise control over that which we have no power. Our loved ones die. Our beautiful moments pass. They do not belong to us. We have yet to cede providence. We have not accepted that everything is in accord with the divine *lógos* that orders all things to be what and how and where they are. Living life without this basic level of acceptance makes suffering inevitable, if not the default pattern of our existence.

Is a modern stoicism articulated in romantic language the end of Emerson's philosophy?[92]

Aside. As noted in our preface, tragedy signals the curse of being. Emerson connects the apprehension of a depersonalized unity with this curse:

The Indian who was laid under a curse that the wind should not blow on him, nor water flow to him, nor fire burn him, is a type of us all. The dearest events are summer-rain, and we are the Para coats that shed every drop. Nothing is left us now but death. We look to that with a grim satisfaction, saying There at least is reality that will not dodge us.[93]

However fine or stirring, gentle or disruptive, the emotional register of life—prior to an affectual conversion before imaginary *nothingness* and the unity of the idea of the *not me* (*difference*) that is nature—leaves us captive and subject to the world of force and its imperatives. We are ordered about in every way. Unless we acquiesce to the curse of the ontological engine and shed our fragmentary selves to become, if but for a moment, *nothing*. Unless we apprehend the reality "that will not dodge us." This is the strange, quiet power working through us, whereby, in our immanently cursed existence, we become our destiny. We return to ourselves free to take up our adornments and relations and illusions for what they are and what they indicate. An implication of these indications: "If my wife, my child, my mother should be taken from me, I should still remain whole."[94] Millennia earlier in Epictetus' *Enchiridion* we find: "Did your child die? It was given back. Did your wife die? She was given back."[95]

Nature's complex tragic portrait of the world in the manner of a poetic-philosophical manifesto, as Barbara Packer keenly observed, shows Emerson at his most "exuberant and inventive," displaying a "speculative boldness he never afterward surpassed."[96] And, I would argue, while his "theory of nature" never lands concretely or clearly upon an extractable thesis, the boundaries it nevertheless establishes, such as they are, are ones that he—even in transgression—never escapes. Thankfully so. In the works that follow *Nature* his writings continue to explore the landscape of thought and phenomena, social institutions and habits, and he gains admirers and detractors, and, most terribly relevant here, he experiences more losses. The passages earlier on do not signal an orthodox stoic resignation, rather they testify to how exuberance, in time, becomes "bewilderment, exhaustion, and despair."[97] And yet life must be lived. The sense of proportion that philosophy and experience teach so well. While unorthodox in articulation, the consolation does touch upon the timeless. Personal grief and suffering do not themselves lead to universal ideas or truth. They are "shallow." The depth of our own being, if surveyed only through our own suffering, become hollow before the infinite idea of being. That is, if suffering moods were the beginning and end of philosophy's disclosure, then the revelation arrives counterfeit. Not only the sorrows, the sublimities too. Emerson desires more of them and yet knows that there is no foolproof guarantee: "I am very content with knowing, if only I could know."[98]

As Emerson wrote *Nature* in the shadow of death, so too *Experience* takes shape under the cloud of his son's passing. Waldo Emerson—"Wallie"—died of scarlet fever at the age of five only two years earlier. "I seem to have lost a beautiful estate—no more. I cannot get it nearer to me." He talks immediately of property and the loss of property. He tells us that such loss "does not touch me" and that it "falls off from me, and leaves no scar." He has given us difficult lines to wrestle with but infinitely less difficult so than to live with. He and his son and their circle of loved ones were not abstractions or figures in an equation. He lowers the veil usually separating a life from its polished works. In the letters that follow his son's death Emerson appears to have become "reduced to a stuttering and helpless repetition. 'Farewell and farewell, my darling my darling, my boy, my boy is gone. To Margaret Fuller he wrote, Shall I ever dare to love anything again?'"[99] Emerson's devastation is utterly understandable. What is more deeply humanizing and joylessly relatable than the loss of a darling one? And yet, must we reconcile these unguarded biographical points with what he says in *Experience*? No, of course not. Why write books and essays or make art if all that matters comes out in our private disclosures? But they do, in this instance, help us appreciate the humanity behind the words and the finer texture of their moment. They expand our account of them. Without conflating discreet biographical details with reasons, it seems natural to consider them as we wonder why certain undertakings were undertook. We can try to understand those difficult lines better as we take up the elegiac riddle for ourselves, doing so for reasons that our own biographies will never fully answer.

―――――

Shakespeare's tragic world does not accomplish what Emerson's manifesto and later essays realize. His *nothing* does not yet present the same possibilities. "Nothing comes of nothing." The curse of being has not yet been acquiesced to through the grammar of forgiveness (though Edgar and Edmund try) or the unity of the idea of nature ("The wheel is come full circle!"), so restoration and freedom for one's destiny remain withheld from the characters. It remains true that there is no escaping the engine that makes everyone and everything fit for their end, but the players fight an impossible fight because they know no other way forward. Few characters in *Lear* clearly realize that the world of force directs their actions and reactions—Cordelia in the opening scene and the Fool (who were both probably played by the same actor in early productions of the play[100]), as well as aspects of Edgar as Tom o' Bedlam—thus we get only a little silence and a few good jokes. We might add Gloucester, the unnamed servant at the close of Act 3, and even Lear, but only imperfectly and at certain moments, and only when it is, from a narrative or theatrical perspective, too late to matter.

Everyone's inconsolable sorrow and grief at the end and all attempts to make things right altogether fail. This is the "gift" of the world wherein and when the characters, like us, exist as mere fragments, deployed for deplorable sport in a game that means nothing but its players believe it means everything. They take the illusion of sorrow as reality and cannot love and live free of it. In the end, everyone left alive grieves. Edmund attempts to reverse his faithlessness with truth and penance, but it is too late and penance cannot wind down the engine. The "reward" of the game's players is dealt out equitably in death and sorrow without recourse of exchange or amelioration. Only the unbearable weight of dark illusions laying upon parents and children previously too involved in their own superficial pursuits and pre-reflective reactions remain. If only the riddle could have been taken up or the grammar of forgiveness learned earlier—if only the idea of nature and the order of love, born of the *nothingness* (difference) "behind" being (identity), had been radically accepted and allowed to arrest and transform anyone—then they could have had some hope of another resolution. Another ending. Had only the tragic world allowed it.

> **KING LEAR** And my poor fool is hanged! No, no, no life!
> Why should a dog, a horse, a rat, have life,
> And thou no breath at all? Thou'lt come no more,
> Never, never, never, never, never!
> Pray you, undo this button: thank you, sir.
> Do you see this? Look on her, look, her lips,
> Look there, look there!   *Dies*
>
> **EDGAR** He faints! My lord, my lord!
> **KENT**   Break, heart; I prithee, break!
> **EDGAR** Look up, my lord.
> **KENT**   Vex not his ghost. O, let him pass! he hates him much
> That would upon the rack of this tough world
> Stretch him out longer.
> **EDGAR** He is gone, indeed.
> **KENT**   The wonder is, he hath endured so long.
> He but usurped his life.

ALBANY	Bear them from hence. Our present business
	Is general woe. (*To* KENT *and* EDGAR) Friends of my soul, you twain
	Rule in this realm, and the gored state sustain.
KENT	I have a journey, sir, shortly to go;
	My master calls me, I must not say no.
EDGAR	The weight of this sad time we must obey;
	Speak what we feel, not what we ought to say.
	The oldest hath borne most; we that are young
	Shall never see so much, nor live so long.

Exeunt, with dead march[101]

3

The Perpetual Messiah

In the last chapter of *Nature*, entitled "Prospects," Emerson writes that "Infancy is the perpetual Messiah, which comes into the arms of fallen men, and pleads with them to return to paradise."[1] Some read Emerson's concluding movements as palinodal, as seeking "to atone for his divisive theorizing earlier."[2] The "Emersonian dialectic" often shifts between "visionary aggression" and "pastoral union" without ever tarrying too long in either direction, but the end of *Nature* strikes certain readers as landing on a "rapt vision of redemption," minimizing or even sabotaging earlier unresolved tensions.[3] They see a loss of the book's earlier scintillating oscillations between edge and welcome, which work together to generate his signature equivocations, whereby he leaves the reader with provocative pronouncements and evocative ebullience but no argument. Those thesis-resistant alternations and evasions, which endear him to his admirers and exasperate his critics, cease at the end of *Nature* as Emerson seems to land wholly and artificially on a vision of universal messianism. It is *as if* his method of approaching the idea of nature in an original way—the most apprehensible and sustained task of the overall text—cannot adequately resolve itself in a manner consistent with the style of his thinking and writing up until that point, whereby he finds himself forced to fabricate an affected finale. It seems as if he fell back into an old habit from which *Nature* had only seemed to be breaking, namely, ending the book like a sermon: "The end of all preaching is to persuade men to become good."[4] Despite the skepticism or embarrassment that many scholars feel about persuading their own readers in such a perspicuous way toward such moralizing ends, especially those who wish to adopt a critical distance and deploy methodological objectivity, Emerson nevertheless firmly held to the conviction that it was the "primal instinct and duty of the human mind to look with a sovereign eye of hope on all things."[5] This means that all intellectual endeavors are essentially ethical endeavors. He was not thinking and writing merely for himself. He tailored his lectures and essays, like his sermons, for the common mind: his aim was to convince, not prove. Formal logic and systematic approaches then as now appeal to few within society. Such tools and procedures *as* tools and procedures are in and of themselves beneficial, but taken alone or immoderately utilized they cannot accomplish Emmerson's agenda. When it defaults to epistemic-centric problematics, Emerson, like other nineteenth-century iconoclasts Kierkegaard and Nietzsche, had "little patience with modern philosophy."[6] He instead followed the advice given to preachers of his time that ideas were to be "developed through implication, allusion, and *indirect directness*."[7] His role as a presenter of questions and persuader of positions was to survey as many vantages as possible, begin from the periphery, and slowly circle inward toward the heart of the matter.[8] Even in his most mature works, works masterfully displaying the dialectical transpositions of a tragic thinker, he rarely failed to part without an encouraging word.[9]

Aside. In our roles as readers and teachers of philosophy and literature, what do we have to say whenever we find someone suffering, say a student, a friend, a stranger? Someone marginalized or oppressed? Someone experiencing social injustice? Do we take up our professional tools and procedures and lay out arguments and textual truths indiscriminately? Diagnostically? Do we offer up facts and syllogisms pertaining to all parties involved? Both oppressor and oppressed? And though they seem to weather them like easily-painted-over graffiti, do we shout revolutionary sentences burning with dangerous possibilities at institutional edifices? Do we say and do only what particular moments ask of us? Assuming, of course, that we can read the moment for what it is. In not so pressing moments, slower moments of solitude, how do we proceed with our intellectual work? Do we set life aside and organize our research and our questions and our conclusions around rational principles? Or perhaps around principles of communication aimed at dispassionate discovery and informing the informed and the rationally dispassionate? Or do we join with others caught up in the epic of force and its machinery of power in order to find a way forward? Do we abrogate the voice of a personal perspective seeking its limits and associations and truths in exchange for a formal air of unprejudiced analysis that only arrives at conclusions already largely dictated by the evidence selected or the principles applied? Or do we own and check and measure our biases against the questions that life itself and the lives of others demand of us, speaking honestly and with as much art and conviction as we can manage? Ultimately, really, are we trying to help anyone understand the world better? To see it for what it is? To help them acquiesce to what they most are and actualize who they could become? To transform themselves? To become free? To play their part in changing the world? To live a dignified life? A life at all?

———

Still, how? How could Emerson enter the unending cycle of the tragic world with *Nature* and exit in a way that honored that repetition? As with most of his writings, everything seems to flow instinctively, even the sudden jolts appear native under the polish of revision. And yet how could he represent an endless repetition when endlessness in representation is impossible? We are left wondering whether Emerson, as a writer of magnificent poetic intuition—arguably better expressed in his prose than in his poetry—had no choice but to will an affirmative, if not a transformative, ending into being were his undertaking to provoke his readers to do anything more than admiringly add his little book to their collection of little books or, worse, read it as merely an artifact of his findings:[10] "Books are the best of things, well used; abused, among the worst."[11] The best of things being to get people thinking their own thoughts in an inspired way.[12] The worst being to occlude that possibility. He thus begins with soaring claims and relatable propositions, then moves into the more difficult territory of presenting and navigating the burden of our ruined spiritual condition necessitating an original and rejuvenating reunion with nature: "enacting a performative drama of self-recovery."[13] But the drama, as a tragic aspect of the recurrent festival of the wise—the drama of understanding—always revolves around a curse and a secret that is to be piously acknowledged, courageously cured or solved, and ecstatically celebrated. And nature itself *is* tragic and we seem but tragic actors upon its stage and cycle of scenes. So then, what are we to do with Emerson's theory and its concluding messianic uplift?

While we worked through *The Riddle of the Sphinx* in Chapter 2—an expression succinctly thematizing the essence of Emerson's endeavor—we will still be well served by performing a reading and rehearsal of *Nature* to "see better" how and why Emerson ends the work the way that he does.[14] We will not, however, perform such a robust rehearsal of *King Lear* in the following chapter, though we will attempt a thematized *Emersonian* reading that explores its tragic frontier; a frontier which, as previously noted, reveals an evolution in Shakespeare's plays, a development indicating a retrieval: theatrical tragedy dramatizes the socially dissolute world and nature's ontological *indifference*, not simply a deeply flawed protagonist or series of catastrophic events. Our recitals of these two works—thematized and otherwise—will, ideally, make it possible for each work to "explain itself" and suggest its own significance and conditions for conclusion.

———

Aside. We cannot read a text or a work without some consideration of (1) the context in which it arises, (2) the internal structures or cohering (or incohering) logics implicit or explicit to it, and (3) an awareness of our own biases and agendas as interpreters. There is always a story behind the story, a particular manner and arrangement by which something is done, a biography behind our decisions to read something and to read it in a particular way. Our scholarly analyses and discourses often hinge on the first consideration, exploring and unpacking and connecting selected aspects of genealogical data situating a work. This is the default mode and expression of research within most of the humanistic sciences. The second consideration also finds a home in academia, wherein a certain challenging or recondite work (or problem or topic or argument) requires slow methodical examination and explication of its internal workings and construction: Kant's *Critique of Pure Reason*, Hegel's *Phenomenology of Spirit*, Heidegger's *Being and Time*, Deleuze's *Difference and Repetition*, Levinas's *Totality and Infinity*, and so on. This approach usually relies on some version of the first but does not necessarily rehearse those findings outside of the scholarly apparatus as the intent lies with examining the internal architecture and sense of the work itself. All reasonable exceptions conceded, the various forms of the third consideration—hermeneutical, psychoanalytical, existential, historical material, and so forth—do not usually appear conspicuously in either of the first two unless to do so provides a rhetorical or argumentative advantage. Nevertheless, conspicuous or inconspicuous, all works bear a biographical agenda. We might, merely as a point of order or for ease of entry into a paper or a book, disclose some prejudices and personal interests up front, but only strategically and usually succinctly: "Let me put all of my cards on the table." Otherwise, such things seem better left to private conversations and conference confessionals between sessions. Or, occasionally, the third consideration comes as a conceit granted to established figures or asserted by those who have elected not to concern themselves with the illusion of impartiality or the delusion of objectivity—"journalistic remarks" interspersed throughout or comprised entirely of "strong misreadings."[15] Of course these considerations or approaches regularly interpenetrate and condition one another at a basic level of scholarly interpretation and argument, yet we can still distinguish these approaches and temper (or modulate) our expectations so that we might beneficially participate or *play along*. True for both charitable *and* critical interpretation. True for taking a text, especially a text about a text or several texts, on its own terms. And yet, what are we to do then with Emerson—or Nietzsche or Heidegger or Derrida or Foucault or anyone else—who sets out to bypass (or deconstruct and diacritically reconstruct) the first two considerations and focus on the third? That is, whatever voice or method they appear to harness, it really comes down to how it all stands and falls with them as interpreters. How do we read thinkers who provide us with highly intuitive and idiosyncratic accounts? Emerson's pointed thoughts on a passage from the scriptures, Nietzsche's brief remarks on Shakespeare, Heidegger's expansive reading of van Gogh? Or artists themselves? Especially ones of original vision and symbols and syntheses? How do we successfully unpack William Blake or Paul Celan or analyze Joseph Beuys or Cy Twombly? What even constitutes a good reading? Common tendencies found among the more interesting, important, and remarkable interpretations of rich and abstruse works provide their own criteria for what amounts to "good reading."[16]

A good reading attempts to do one or more of the following: *provoke* readers to think or to see something they have not yet thought or seen, demonstrate the *necessity* of offering the interpretation, prove *helpful* to readers seeking entry into a conversation if they participate with the analysis. Writers can openly disclose what makes their theories provocative, necessary, or helpful, or they can simply exhibit one or more of these qualities in the manner by which they develop their arguments or organize and unpack their claims. An interpretation of or theory about a work only needs to hit upon one of these virtues to recommend itself to us, but clearly hitting upon all three—a bit of writing that is provocative, necessary, and helpful—provides readers with the opportunity to have a truly meaningful encounter. It challenges us to see something new, places an imperative upon us to reconsider settled matters, assists us in unearthing something hidden or not easily accessed. Plato reading reason, Emerson reading nature, Kierkegaard reading Christendom, Marx reading capitalism, Nietzsche reading the Greeks, Heidegger reading being, Weil reading Homer, Illich reading schools, Deleuze reading difference, Greenblatt reading the material surround of Shakespeare's life; we can certainly quibble with any list of examples provided, but the influence of such readings upon our own reception of what we choose to read and consider cannot be easily set aside. Certain figures, texts, methods, and accounts lie in wait for any reader in the humanities who undertakes the vocation of scholar.

If great works are the enduring mirrors many take them to be—if we feel we should read them because they contain something indispensable to a conversation we wish to join or if we notice that generation after generation returns to them to find or redefine themselves in and through them or to take them to task and hold them accountable—then asking what they disclose about us as readers in the times in which we live becomes an imperative. If the theory of the world recurs in the form of an elegiac riddle, then the topics, claims, repetition of motifs, and the outlay of action and speech in those works considered emblematic of tragedy—theatrical or theoretical—should, in some way large or small, consciously or unconsciously, contribute to the revelation of the engine of being. Put another way, if the perennial endeavor to give an account of the world and our place in it is or is best thought as an enigma—as a "dark saying" requiring intuition and imagination to see what is hidden within the question itself—then the theoretical and artistic works that attempt to solve it will to some degree represent that enigmatic structure not simply overtly in arguments or images but within the arrangements, styles, themes and inner relations of the works themselves. They will bear the tragedy in their bones. The selection of topics, the number and setting of scenes in an act, expositions, repetitions, actions, silences, entries, exits, voice and the relation of voice to mood, mood to reason, reason to experience. As ancient riddles hide their own solution in their construction and language, so too the riddle of the tragic world—the occult unity of all things, the machine that makes all of nature's constituents fit for their end, the strange relation of fate to freedom, the mystery of the generative *nothingness* that is the *otherwise* of being—gives us, at the very least, an outline of the secret architecture housing the answer.

Our reading of the riddle, as we find it in *Nature* or *King Lear* or somewhere else, must draw out this hidden solution—a solution that might solve very little of what we hope it will—and do so in a way that tries to be provocative or necessary or helpful. Again, hopefully.

———

Introduction. As we earlier distinguished ontological tragedy from the human drama that performs tragedy, we should not conflate or confuse specific tragic events and accounts with the tragic itself. Despite how we usually employ the term, "tragedy" does not indicate that something specific has happened to this or that person or family or people. It is not a disaster, defeat, or setback. While commemoration speaks to a certain characteristic of the tragic dramatic festival, the tragic itself is not a discrete historical event or mythological series of events occurring a long time ago or yesterday. The engine of being is itself built of *difference*. Not static identities. *Nothing* causes tragedy. Causal explanations, particularly in the mechanistic sense, derive from, and are perhaps necessitated by, force and its often-seamless association with power. Force and power in nature appear much like time and time's effects: "And nothing 'gainst time's scythe can make defence"—except acceptance and the promise of life to come.[17] We cannot, therefore, lay the tragic nature of our existence at the feet of any particular aspect of modernity, nor the catastrophic effects of causal explanations upon the head of the Enlightenment or the atomization and professionalization of human life (though these latter developments are certainly problems warranting romantic rebellion and transcendental redress). Such developments signal only innovative expressions of the tragic epic of force. We can attend to and refuse this tragic drama, but tragedy itself, ontologically considered, is not something we can fix. *It is the way things are.* And Emerson's ending does not deny this. Clearly neither does *Lear's*. They rather obliquely retrieve from antiquity the true conditions of nature and our humble, if strategic, performance in perpetuity of and before it. A fearful admiration for wondrous being. An undeniable weakness before force and power. An air of awe before *nothing* and of welcome before *nothing's* expression through *difference*. The reflective wish to surrender misdirecting desires in order to accept the unity of being and the necessity of *nothing*, life and death, blessings and transgressions. Transformed, the hope remains that these desires return to us and we can say *no* and *yes* in authentically strange ways. Even and especially as the world falls apart around us.

Remembering this helps us to read Emerson more decisively, to join his sentences and paragraphs and pages together in a project portraying reality and liberation. A project we can only understand if we recognize that Emerson never stopped being a preacher at heart. Though his thinking would mature with weightier claims and more suggestive ambiguities, he possessed a vision of his true vocation early on. In the fall of 1832, not long after losing Ellen and shortly before setting sail for Europe, Emerson resigns his pastorate and shares the following with his congregation:

> I am about to resign into your hands that office which you have confided in me. It has many duties for which I am feebly qualified. It has some which it will always be my delight to discharge according to my ability, wherever I exist. And whilst the recollection of its claims oppresses me with a sense of my unworthiness, I am consoled by the hope that no time and no change can deprive me of the satisfaction of pursuing and exercising its highest functions.[18]

Though his personal losses had become insurmountable and as a matter of conscience he could no longer formally perform the liturgical duties required of him, Emerson intimated that no change in circumstances—or titular profession—would "deprive [him] of the satisfaction" of not only continuing to pursue preaching the spirit of the gospel (as he understood it in each phase of his thinking) but of developing it to its highest expression. Not content simply to have transmitted the good news to the likeminded and officiated the sacraments to congregants eager to receive it—"preaching to the choir"—Emerson would transform the Christian gospel into transcendental philosophy, compose its manifesto, and take it to the wider world. At first anonymously, then unreservedly.

The "Introduction" to *Nature* gives us a clear set of propositions, some appearing as entreating questions. Emerson is interested in an original relationship with nature. A personal and intimate connection with *erotic* undertones. The term "erotic" here signifies the basic and organic lure for some form of congress particular to the needs and desires of liberated—or would be liberated—subjects who must act and associate from a total and centered place of being whereby they can express themselves polymorphically without repression or redirection due to social mores about perversity or deviancy.[19] In an Emersonian sense, this erotic relationship with nature carries no restricted sense of pertaining strictly to the genitalia and sexuality, rather it implies something else: erotic love's power to bridge the divisions between its individuated aspects as well as between those individuated aspects and nature itself as a whole. It is an overcoming of the separation of universal and individual extremes by abandoning ourselves to the primal lure that exists between us and between all bodies.[20] In this way, *eros* testifies to an undergirding possibility of, and deep-seated drive for, a primal unity. This is eroticism as fundamental life-affirming expressions of reconciliation between ourselves and others, between nature and ourselves. Or, the *ordo amoris*.[21] Stated negatively, it is a will against alienation, which is so often the cost of life lived in conformity with civilization's demands in order to extract its compromised promises.[22] Emerson wants to deconstruct the ordinary approach to great ideas, books, and social practices. No more measuring our life and thought solely against history. Imitative and retrospective life: groping "among the dry bones of the past."[23] Living in absolute deference to and in uncritical imitation of the intellectual biographies and spiritual insights of the dead do not free us for our own lives and our own erotic union with nature and the divinity it emits (or with which we endow it). Such excessive backward facing ruins all living generations. We must therefore exchange absolute deference to the past with an erotic abandon to nature and our relationship to nature now.[24] "The sun shines today also."[25]

Understanding the erotic drive behind Emerson's philosophy helps situate us to his belief that all science has the aim of finding or adding to the construction of a theory that restores us to ourselves by restoring us to nature.[26] Again, *nature as an idea* articulated in transcendental philosophy. For Emerson, transcendentalism (a historical variation and emendation of idealism) insists on "the power of Thought and Will, on inspiration, on miracle, on individual culture."[27] And all of these are "natural phenomena" because they all occur within and through nature. Miracles must be "one with the blowing clover and the falling rain."[28] Accordingly, this theory at which all sciences aim is not merely a theory of unity in a long history of theories of unity. That characterization fails to convey what is at stake. It is rather the perennial desire for the idea of nature—in the most sublime sense—which, if apprehended, is offered or gifted back to others as a "true theory," a compelling creative "portrait," some account whatsoever: an answer to the riddle of the Sphinx. The test of its truth being "that it will explain all phenomena."[29] It will in some way reveal the hidden unity and enchantment of affiliation existing between all things. A visionary theory that (erotically) illustrates the connectivity born of the alterity signified in the *not* of the *not me*. Though Emerson states it as a negation, the *not* of the *not me* testifies to the acceptance of the *difference* or *otherness* that is given: "nature and art, all other men and my own body."[30] We do not own these things. And even though what we do "own" was "freely given" to us by nature—what is inwardly most ours in terms of thinking and willing—we must nevertheless win the finest expression of those gifts not by struggle but by acquiescence. This restores us to the *not me* from which we found ourselves separated and allows us to become—by returning to—the *other*, the *difference*, the *nothing* from which our existence sprung. A pure being as *becoming*, prior to any identity, a manifold unity prior to any existential or psychological fragmentation. In this process of restoration, we become most ourselves as differentially undefined and unindividuated beings always already found in the non-negating *not* of the *not me*. Such indeterminate freedom of being intoxicates and delivers us not only into an epistemological abyss[31] but an ethical one as well.[32] It is marvelous and terrifying. We keep learning how much personal and collective work remains: no great theory will ever arrive as the last and final theory of theories that accomplishes this for everyone, everywhere, for all time because "permanence," Emerson tells us, "is but a word of degrees."[33] And because "anything love [*Eros*] finds his way to always slips away."[34] All other specialized theories of the various sciences carry us along, playing useful but limited regional roles: each discipline and area in its own way participates in the rounding-out and furtherance of this recurring drama of understanding. Unless, of course, we cease performing the drama in preference to something else.

———

Aside. If it were unclear, this ontological distinction—me (or any particular being) and the *not me* (or everything else or nothing as no particular thing defined in advance)—is merely a temporary illusion that Emerson finds both "necessary" and "insignificant." Why? Though we are woven into it, none of us own the material and material circumstances of our embodied existence as biological beings (with biological needs and powers and limits) thrown into a social existence (with socially constructed wants and rights and restrictions) in quite the same way that we possess the agency and possibilities associated with our own allotment of mental, imaginative, and spiritual life. We can fight and dream and conspire together in countless ways. And this is why the distinction between the me and *not me* is "insignificant": we share in that agency and source of possibilities that are not circumstantial and which allow for full and free participation in this life with others.[35] We could here assert that such *freedom*—as we find it in these dimensions of life (mental, imaginative, spiritual)—is a precondition for any struggle for social, political, or economic *liberation*. We have to be essentially free in order to be able to refuse, to resist, to think, and to do otherwise. (If we could but learn *to forgive* and become free.) Yet, why is the temporary illusion of the ontological distinction also "necessary?" In short, the organizing power of the mind walks us through the trials of a separated existence and the tribulations of individual or private minds allowing the tragedy of life to be wound up so that it can, like the final revelations of an ancient mystery or secret gnostic teaching, disclose that the essential order of the world is always already erotically united in the *not* of the *not me*. Nothing—as pure difference, as true otherness—lies behind and within and out ahead of all nature, of which we are all essentially a part. We simply, though necessarily, lost sight of this original unity as we were habituated to a socialized existence requiring ever more justifications to misconstrue this unity and the means of individuating it. Like a story unfolding in manageable portions and not simply uneventfully concluded. Or a puzzle game that must be played. Or time experienced in moments and seasons instead of all at once. "Now, the world would be insane and rabid, if these disorganizations should last for hundreds of years,"[36] or if we never had them in the first place to work through. And so, this process of recognizing ourselves as distinct from what is not ourselves and the subsequent overcoming of ourselves as those recognizably separated selves in order to be restored to what is not us as what is most essentially us: an unending call to communion and the play of life.

Nothing. How to begin? In the first chapter of *Nature*, Emerson tells us that we need solitude to undertake this task of apprehending the idea of nature and of being restored to the unity that the idea both makes possible and is. Not only withdrawing strategically from society but also from our routine retirement to our books and those solitary activities explicitly provided by society. We must go to nature itself, silently witnessing all of its "envoys of beauty." This call to return to the natural world in an unmediated and personal way conveys the most recognizably romantic element in *Nature*, yet it is nevertheless an important starting place—aside from the introductory entreaty to reject retrospective relations and insights in favor of discovering and creating original ones—if we are to arrive at the desired destination: restoration of what lies within us to that original unity.[37] In our current ruined state, into which society educates us, we find all-natural objects in themselves inaccessible. The mind must open to nature's direct influence and receive these envoys of beauty, but, for the transcendental or ideal project, we must also recognize the limits of such receptions by way of sensible experience alone. We are more than mere sensible beings, more than aggregates of experience, more than bundles of relations. We are thinkers, theorists, poets. We are ourselves ideas. Approached solely by way of sensible experience or impressions—especially when those impressions have been schooled and habituated in advance—nature will always conceal the full array and depth of its secrets. These secrets remain undeliverable through the reception of the sensuous surround when the sensuous surround is the only manner in which we consider nature and when that manner is mediated by socialized concerns and old habits of thought. That is, the lack of true thought. We must therefore find another way to nature in order to avoid extorting from it what it does not freely give us in sensible experience alone. Here Emerson distinguishes between two senses of approach and reception of nature: "the integrity of impression made by manifold natural objects" (resulting in the secret idea of nature as a unity) and nature as seen and used by socialized beings with material needs and concerns (resulting in the well-known categorization of nature as useable resource). Emerson writes:

> It is this which distinguishes the stick of timber of the wood-cutter, from the tree of the poet. The charming landscape which I saw this morning is indubitably made up of some twenty or thirty farms. Miller owns this field, Locke that, and

> Manning the woodland beyond. But none of them owns the landscape. There is a property in the horizon which no man has but he whose eye can integrate all the parts, that is, the poet. This is the best part of these men's farms, yet to this their warranty-deeds give no title.[38]

Most everyone readily accepts the division of nature into nations, states, counties, municipalities, private and public property, places of learning, worship, play, commerce, the taxonomic division of life into kingdom, phylum, class, order, family, genus, specie—sectors, categories, subdivisions, *uses*. A world organized as such conditions the charming landscape and everything arising within it to be received as lumber and farms and furs and postcards and commodities whatsoever—into information and profit. It is the woodcutter's world and, more fatally, the businessman's fiefdom. Yet when the poet or the philosopher or we ourselves, when so comported, have an eye for the transcendental unity of nature as an idea, these divisions are overcome, recontextualized, and returned to us—*transformed*—as both ours and not ours. Me and *not me*. The bit of lumber is returned to the tree, the tree to the landscape, the landscape to the sensuous surround of being. No institutional authority can issue such a deed of ownership and surprise, only the apprehension of the idea of nature. Otherwise, all else comes to us through the lesser illusions of division, the insalubrious delusions of private ownership, and the deceptive beliefs about profits of the lowest order.

If we can apprehend the idea of nature as the poets and poetic (or ideal and tragic) philosophers do, then we can replace our superficial sense and utilitarian use of nature with one derived from "the spirit of infancy."[39] Not the unadulterated innocence of childhood before any concepts and complexities entered life or some pre-theoretical way of being in the world dealing *exclusively* in myths of what is given, but a theoretical romanticism—whether we disparagingly call it contemplative materialism or approbatively name it transcendental empiricism or historically frame it as American transcendentalism—that grants the mature possibility of a *second naivete* that restores us to nature (as necessary parts of it) and by which we see and relate to nature anew (as essential participants). To lay it out procedurally: we must first become sensitive to natural impressions in a deeply personal way (things as individually beautiful); we then, perhaps with practice and in stages, are able to abandon ourselves entirely to those impressions so that we can become *nothing* ("I become a transparent eyeball; I am nothing"); this total *imaginative* immersion into all sensible impressions temporarily suspends our individuated sense of self (along with all of our learned privatizing inclinations); finally, the suspension of our fragmented sense of self allows for the unifying power of reason to think—that is, cognizably, to receive and gather in a preparatory and generative way—nature as the *idea* of nature *as if* it were always there waiting for us to discover it through such imaginatively conditioned uses of reason.[40] We then return to ourselves forgiven and whole, having caught something of the mysterious "occult relation between man and the vegetable."[41] We see the world anew and find a renewed place in it.

Emerson transitions here to posit four uses of nature: commodity, beauty, language, and discipline. Each of these corresponds to Chapters 2 through 5 and indicates an ascendency of importance. We should note that while Emerson employs the word "use," he has more in mind than its usual pragmatic connotations. When we practice or participate in these uses our material existence does indeed "profit" in various ways, often in the manner that ordinary conventions champion or assume, but these uses—from a higher vantage of nature as an idea and human life lived in response to that idea—open up more profound and meaningful modes of profitability. Areas of life usually unaddressed if not constricted by subordination to economic and political spheres, wherein all use and profit can only be understood in service to those spheres and not life itself. And so, with these challenges to our everyday understanding of nature in mind, we will read each use as an *ascending stage* of insight into our original relation to nature.[42] Proceeding in this way means that the status of our relation to nature must, as mentioned earlier on, undergo a transformation, if not existentially or spiritually, then at least performatively. We therefore begin in a place of relative familiarity (*commodity* as the lowest use) and build toward greater unfamiliarity (*discipline* as the highest use, before moving beyond "uses" altogether with Chapters 6 and 7, *idealism* and *spirit*) before returning to our respective situation—the world and ourselves—having been changed by the process. Each chapter heading reflecting a stage that heightens the threat of the total dissolution of the familiar identities and structures that comprise our sense of self and world. And if we endure these ascending trials—largely by assenting to a *non-exclusive* sense of what is already given or *forgiven*—we will return to the familiar (Chapter 8, "Prospects") to find that it now radiates endless tragic energies and runs upon impersonal laws that not only ever destroy the world: they renew it ceaselessly.

―――

Commodity. Emerson begins with the lowest order of use. He tells us that this use of nature arrives most directly and that all people can immediately acknowledge it.[43] This is the shortest chapter and Emerson leaves it to us to reflect upon this particular use ourselves because the catalogue of possible commodifications of nature arrives "endless" and "obvious."[44] One point from this section does warrant consideration, however: a mixed optimism regarding free markets. Early and late, Emerson concedes that material wealth has resulted in the creation of many fine and wonderous inventions that appear to benefit all citizens. "The private poor man hath cities, ships, canals, bridges, built for him."[45] He mentions post-offices, courthouses, roads, books, everyday tools, and so on. All means of travel and communication and contrivance against the elements and disorganization find redress in those institutions and devices commoditizing nature or making nature commodifiable. And not only do the architectures, infrastructures, engines, and tools that wealth creates help us directly by meeting all of our material needs, they also, in part, constitute our social and spatial sense of the world in which we find our everyday existence. We have places to go and activities to do there. We have work.[46] That is, in addition to the spaces, objects, and services that the market-driven production of commodities provides—the market here signifying the totality of social structures and relations that both manufacture "goods" and the desires for those goods when such desires lack intuitive inclination—they allow us to occupy our time "productively" and with "purpose." The problem here, of course, is that this world which generates roads and riches, monuments and shovels, courthouses and books, also manufactures a class of people who do not in fact get to enjoy the fruits of commoditized nature. At least not the first and fairest fruits. It gives us a working class that aspires to procure and own, but, in truth, as a class, they can never fully procure and own since the system of production and profit would end. It gives us, whatever else we might label them, the modern poor in perpetuity. In the lowest degree: "the fools."[47] The ones to whom we never listen. The harvest of material riches actually tends to impoverish rather than liberate. Materially and spiritually. Those that seek such riches do so in as much as they seek the power to enact their designs—which according to Emerson indicates a natural inclination—but the pursuit often turns mad and all that is gained profits only the few.[48] And it profits the few only in the lowest and least helpful sense. If the fruits of wealth will be made available to all, Emerson tells us, then the grand market of the world and its total industry will be justified. Yet, though never fully discarded, we can sense his faith in capitalism's potentiality waning in later years. He voices his ambivalence and hesitation when, in his essay "Wealth" from *The Conduct of Life*, he recalls Goethe: "Nobody should be rich but those who understand it."[49] Emerson tells us that a person is only genuinely rich if *the people* are made rich by that person and that he is poor if he makes the people poor.[50] A path to wealth must be opened for all or the way of capitalism impoverishes everyone and everything it touches.[51] The poor, whatever their sociopolitical standing, suffer material disenfranchisement; the rich, whatever their excessive enfranchisement, fail spiritually (unless the wealthy change the world with their wealth, which would necessarily include changing how wealth is attained in the world). But Emerson hates dictating imperatives that abrogate others of the responsibility to attend to their own self-culture and sense of civic duty. Emerson is no socialist or Marxist. He remains therefore reservedly sanguine about capitalism, but his optimism rests with what it can and ought to do, rarely for what it actually does. And though Emerson does not go as far in his criticism of capitalism as his closest German acolyte, Nietzsche[52]—for whom "industrial culture ... is altogether the most vulgar form of existence that has yet existed"[53]—we would still do well to note the spirit of suspicion and concern for our economic system voiced by America's first public philosopher over a century and a half ago.

Beauty. For those already somewhat familiar with Emerson, Chapter 3 appears familiar territory. He describes the love of beauty as a "nobler want of man" that can carry us up from out of the merely commoditized uses of nature. Beautiful objects and actions can certainly still fall prey to lesser uses, but its transcendental possibilities as an affective reality of inner life—a transportive desire—corresponding to the order (or ordering) of the world remains resistant to total appropriation by market forces and theoretical schemes. He begins by recalling how the Greek word for the world, "cosmos," (*kósmos*) implies beauty, presumably in terms of "beautiful order" or "beautiful appearance."[54] That is, how things come to the eye already pleasantly arranged in shape, color, motion, *as if* all appearances have been composed for us.[55] Emerson goes so far as to say, "There is no object so foul that intense light will not make it beautiful."[56] This reminds us that from the tragic or fate-filled point of view, all things become fit—*become beautiful*—for their end. Whatever appears otherwise is either in the process of becoming fit (which itself possesses a demanding beauty) or the eye of the perceiver sees by a less intense light. To be sure, there are phenomena and relations and objects more beautiful and inspiring than others—and we can for productive argument's sake judge things unattractive—but we should not forget that Emerson believes the universe itself to be beautiful and its grand operations to be beautifying.

Emerson offers three aspects or modes of beauty which, again, like the uses of nature to which it belongs, we should read as escalatory: perception as and for delight, beauty as and for virtue, beauty as object of and for intellection.[57] The first mode primarily registers as the basic aesthetic experience of natural splendor and, secondarily, works of art and other objects of human engineering and conceptualization. "The tradesman, the attorney comes out of the din and craft of the street and sees the sky and the woods, and is a man again."[58] The worker becomes a person again. The deleterious price paid for civilizing professions that demand our prime hours and energies find a spiritual restitution that heals without "any mixture of corporeal benefit."[59] If we want the soul to have a fighting chance, then the long hours of labor that challenge our upright posture must be answered with beauty. Rightly praised for his descriptive genius when it comes to natural splendor, Emerson constructs various scenes throughout his works illustrating nature's beauty and that beauty's enlightening and therapeutic effects. Here he writes,

> I see the spectacle of morning from the hilltop over against my house, from daybreak to sunrise, with emotions which an angel might share. The long slender bars of cloud float like fishes in the sea of crimson light. From the earth, as a shore, I look out into that silent sea. I seem to partake its rapid transformations; the active enchantment reaches my dust, and I dilate and conspire with the morning wind. *How does Nature deify us with a few and cheap elements!* Give me health and a day, and I will make the pomp of emperors ridiculous.[60]

If we can but pause to notice—and notice well—what nature through its beautiful envoys freely offers at any given moment of the day, our misery can abate awhile; we can check the weight of our concerns against the world's proportions, we can feel, if only briefly, divinized. Of all royal favors he might have asked for, Diogenes only wanted Alexander to step out of the sun's rays, which are themselves free. The works of Homer, Shakespeare, Rilke, Sze, Morrison, and Mehretu are beautiful too. If we let them, these works undoubtedly provide us with the opportunity to have powerful encounters with beauty and truth. And yet, the beauty of nature itself changes from moment to moment, from day to day, season to season, always. It refuses to tarry for us. Except in the rarest of instances—*except for Shakespeare*—this makes perfect representation impossible.[61] Art creates beauty and founds truth but, according to Emerson, never wholly enduring and commensurate with nature's sublime living drama:

> In July, the blue pontederia or pickerel-weed blooms in large beds in the shallow parts of our pleasant river, and swarms with yellow butterflies in continual motion. *Art cannot rival this pomp of purple and gold.* Indeed the river is a perpetual gala, and boasts each month a new ornament.[62]

The second aspect of beauty concerns its expression in actions aligned with authentic, enthusiastic, and courageous reason. "Every rational creature has all nature for his dowry and estate. It is his, if he will."[63] Although Emerson, in somewhat typical nineteenth-century fashion, emphasizes larger than life heroic action—"Leonidas and his three hundred martyrs consume the day in dying"— he includes ordinary ethical action as well. In fact, when it comes to this ancient association of beauty with virtue, which he retrieves here in a modified form, the importance of any distinctions between heroic bravery, social responsibility, moral courage, excellence in any undertaking whatsoever, and between discrete, interpersonal, and public acts relaxes. The creative interplay between will and thought that places its trust in our own individual capacity to order and make sense of our lives and our world—as creatures of reason and imagination—and act accordingly is, like the ordering and appearing cosmos itself, beautiful. Or, virtue is the peculiar beauty of human undertakings that attempt to make sense of the world and act in accord with those sense-making powers and inclinations. We are ourselves, in effect, living portraits of nature.[64]

———

Aside. The tragic element of this treatment of beauty, in case we needed reminding, lies with the futility of any human performance that does not ultimately recognize its limits, contingencies, temporality, and death—and subsequently venerates the ontological engine that made it so. Tragedy is, ontologically speaking, the way things are and, performatively speaking, the festival that honors the way things are *and* the ways we hope they will be. The performative expression, though always rooted in the festival, extends—or should extend—to all areas of life requiring recognition of our position before nature. Virtue in all its forms, therefore, can only be beautiful if it is reconciled to our tragic lot. The universality and atemporality of the ideas from which we generate ideals against which we measure all of our concepts and actions are themselves only taken *as if* they were such, and not *as such.*

———

For the third aspect of beauty Emerson again retrieves an ancient notion: the beauty of intelligible objects. Objects of the intellect signal the highest sense of beauty in that we can perceive them—think on and delight in them—in relation to "the absolute order of things as they stand in the mind of God, and without the colors of affection."[65] This is not a strict distinction between empirically sensed phenomena (registered temporally and spatially) and purely intelligible objects (present only a-temporally and nonspatially), rather the *intellection* of all phenomena within some scheme of knowing that takes all phenomena as ideas (unities discretely apprehended), rendering whatever is encountered *as* knowable. And always after a fashion, of course. The very act of naming being perhaps the oldest example. Grammars come to be within our experience of the world in order to organize the words that indicate and speak for phenomena. If we wish an original relation to nature, we do not *begin* with universal ideas removed from this life, ideas providing the cognitive conditions for encountering, categorizing, and evaluating things. We instead use our cognitive, sense-making powers to translate the world into organizable features that stand in accord with principles that arise *within* and *by* the very same process of sense-making and organization. *Knowing* is a drama or a game—an aspect of the recurring tragic festival—that reflects the material and social world in which it arises.[66] We only treat the most transportive and illuminating concepts the drama creates—*ideas* in the grand sense—*as if* they preceded the account we endeavored to give by participating in the dramatic event. *As if always already.* Beauty here, as it pertains to objects of the intellect, indicates the fecundity and regenerative power of certain conceptualizations when they are seen in their relation to the system of knowing (or ordering) as a whole: "without the color of affection." That is, what begins as deeply personal (the reception of beautiful envoys that delight) becomes depersonalized objects of thought that rise to the universally true (ordered knowledge of the whole, or *ideas*). To become liberated subjects, we allow these truths (from which we fashion principles or laws) to occupy privileged positions in our thinking, conditioning all else. These beautiful truths become foundational and restorative. They become absolute. We no longer have to be alone or persist in delusions of epistemological sovereignty because others attend to these truths with us. Because we could not attend to these truths without them. Because we now have, and have always had, a place in the order of things. Even in a tragic world. As Emerson writes,

> *Nothing* is quite beautiful alone; nothing but is beautiful in the whole. A single object is only so far beautiful as it suggests this universal grace. The poet, the painter, the sculptor, the musician, the architect, seek each to concentrate this radiance of the world on one point, and each in his several work to satisfy the love of beauty which stimulates him to produce. Thus is Art a nature passed through the alembic of man. ... Beauty, in its largest and profoundest sense, is one expression for the universe.[67]

And yet, at the end of "Beauty," Emerson adds that beauty is not ultimate.[68] He considers it as an evocative herald of the last and highest expression of being, the final cause of nature: *spirit*. The words "God" and "reason" provide us with other approaches to and articulations of spirit, one mythic, pious, poetic, the other discursive, systematic, cognitive. We will consider this final cause in more detail when we cover Chapter 7, "Spirit."

Language. Emerson develops his philosophy of language along three lines:

1. Words are signs of natural facts.
2. Particular natural facts are symbols of particular spiritual facts.
3. Nature is the symbols of spirit.[69]

As with *Nature* overall, these three aspects indicate escalating degrees of insight into the function and essence of language. The escalating degrees of *use*—commodity, beauty, language, discipline—correspond to intensified refinements of power. And though casual readings of Emerson do not often emphasize it (and he offers critiques of our common assumptions about it), he undoubtedly proselytizes as a minister of power.[70] Redeemed and refined power. His thoughts on language, therefore, give us not only a theory of language as such but a theory of how language advances the full array of our human powers. Now, by his enumerated list we see that Emerson's initial sense of language traces back to our material experience of the world. Not simply the obvious words that indicate physical phenomena or aspects of phenomena—how things are what they are and their shapes, movements, textures, colors, scents, tastes, and so forth—but words expressing grades of abstraction and affectation when we describe our encounter with the world and each other theoretically. We have many institutions of one sort or another that make use of highly abstract, specialized, or technical language: juridical, political, economic, religious, academic, and so on. For example, whatever connotation it now carries, the metaphysical lexicon, as all lexicons, found its genesis solely in humankind's habitation within an empirical realm:

> *Right* means *straight; wrong* means *twisted. Spirit* primarily means *wind; transgression,* the crossing of a *line; supercilious,* the *raising of the eyebrow.* We say *heart* to express emotion, the *head* to denote thought; and *thought* and *emotion* are words borrowed from sensible things; and now appropriated to spiritual nature.[71]

Spirit and the spiritual dimension of things begin with our experiences of the material world. When caught in metaphysical modes of thought relying heavily upon highly specialized abstract language, we easily forget the material origin of words. Nature inaugurates spirit.

The second aspect or elevated understanding of language initially seems to invert what we just established: "Every natural fact is a symbol of some spiritual fact."[72] Emerson argues that not only are words emblematic of natural phenomena, natural phenomena are themselves emblematic in that they ever relate to our state of mind. He describes this relation as a "radical correspondence between visible things and human thoughts."[73] As with Kant's noumenal reality, we cannot access *things-in-themselves* (if *things-in-themselves* even exist as other things exist). We can only receive what comes to the senses in the manner allowed by the structure and operations of our mental life. All conscious beings have a share of and participate in a universally *active* principle, which allows for us to organize our natural facts in accord with it.[74] In both a cognitive and spiritual sense, the state of our inner life, or "soul," determines how we find and relate to the natural world, how we interpret phenomena, how we decipher being. And though mythopoetic descriptions might make use of original (or imagined) spatiotemporal experiences and material demarcations, the universal soul in which we all have some latent share—*lógos spermatikós* or *Reason* or *God* or *The Over-Soul*—does not literally stand apart from us or above us: it is natural too. The clearer the path we have made to this universal capacity—which for Emerson occurs through "simplicity of character" and "our love of truth"—the greater our power to connect our thoughts to their corresponding ratio-spiritual symbols.[75] Lovers of truth can therefore speak the truth. Put another way, affective attunement of our inner life to natural phenomena (becoming sensitive to beauty) allows us to correlate those phenomena to the emblematic structures we have culturally and cognitively been given in order to understand and describe them (becoming liberated subjects). When it comes to language in particular, we paint the world with words. Honed instincts, learned techniques, improvisation with materials. Truth, in this sense, is the creation of an original fidelity. As a negative consequence of this relation between inner and outer life, however, "the corruption of man is followed by the corruption of language."[76] This means that without a renewed inner life words and symbols cannot prompt our understanding or spur our sentiments toward truth because they have lost all authentic and authenticating power. Words then become fraudulent.[77] Their ordinariness becomes unable to free us. They no longer give voice to phenomena, or if they do we cannot hear them. And as we have already seen, we enter this life of riddle-solving already fragmented and ruined. Fallen. When we begin to come to ourselves—begin noticing, asking questions, taking stock—we realize that we have been speaking this contaminated language, a syntax disassociated from the idea of nature as a whole, not united in spirit, unknown to our intuition. Until we set aside old habits of thought, trust our deepest instincts, become sensitive to the envoys of beauty, lose ourselves upon the plane of *nothing*, and, as all original thinkers and poets before and after us, apprehend the idea of nature, we will never lay claim to our most authentic and whole sense of self within the world—*as creators of the world*. Until then, language possesses no magical qualities by which to spell the world and give grace to our experiences and power to our projects.[78]

The third aspect of language addresses the most obvious problem created by the second: "Have mountains, and waves, and skies, no significance but what we consciously give them, when we employ them as emblems of our thoughts?"[79] That is, again along the lines of Kant's idealism and Coleridge's romanticism, do *things-in-themselves* possess any meaning or value or purpose as such beyond what we give them through the process of intellection? Is it only our rational organizing of them into systems of knowing that bestows definitions? Do our words and symbols have the final say of significance? Emerson answers decisively: "The world is emblematic. Parts of speech are metaphors, because the whole of nature is a metaphor of the human mind."[80] The world—as something *knowable*—is a product of consciousness. Without too much difficulty we can imagine the absence of human intellect in the cosmos and concede that the cosmos would persist without noticing our departure.[81] "Imagination dead imagine."[82] Emerson, and other idealists making similar arguments, proposes nothing necessarily absurd here, only that—in addition to our affective disposition determining the timbre of our cognitive or spiritual reception of nature—the world itself is the result of ideation. It is an idea. Nature, being, the world, the cosmos, the universe: each designation bears a discrete and specialized meaning, but the overall sense of nature that each term also indicates, ideationally speaking, is still a culturally and temporally determined product or account of human understanding that has harnessed reason's power to draw forth that image or idea from out of an imagined atemporal *nothingness*. An imaginative, ordering act of the mind considered as a collective phenomenon. The activity of the shared *lógos*. This does not mean that we simply "think up" new realities or "will into being" novel worlds, as though it were all a matter of mental energy and poetic creation. Rather, the world becomes *objectivated* and *real* through the process of its creation.[83] It comes to us as something already concrete, distinctive, and enduring. As "some-*thing*" at all. Whether we approach the world in terms of socially constructed customs and historic institutions ever in tension with nature and natural processes, or in terms of our own internalized mediation between animalistic desire and enlightened desire, we nevertheless always encounter the world as "reality," and the words defining that reality as fixed. Even if we want to fight that reality and evolve its lexicon. But through the process of learning nature's various and ascending uses—commodity, beauty, language, discipline—and our finer, if esoteric, means of expressing those uses—idealism, spirit, prospects—we become capable of challenging all the old habits of unliberated thought and of offering, in their place, all manner of original theories and insights. Emerson, we ought never forget, seeks not only an original relationship with nature but a new occult revelation: an all-uniting theory that makes explicit the otherwise hidden harmonious association between all disciplines and endeavors. And in the realm of language this means that creative correlations of phenomena to forgotten and new and strange emblems for those phenomena can unlock undiscovered dimensions of the soul.[84] That is, a renewed use of language can assist us in becoming transparent to ourselves in relation to the world. The need for this renewed use of language—and of the other uses—compounds as we continually grow more incapable of accessing ourselves in relation to the world and what we do possess of ourselves fails to relate to anything of value.

Aside. Still, how do we talk seriously about *value*—or meaning or purpose or any related notion—when all designations, formulations, systems, all knowledge whatsoever, however embedded and reified they have become, are only products of the human intellect? Imaginary structures made real through time and habituation? Based essentially on *nothing*? Our existence is tragic, but tragic drama, we must continue to keep in mind, indicates a recurring festival that honors nature's seasonal nihilation *and* regeneration. It is our peculiar liberation in joyous acknowledgment of our limitations and agency given to us by fate.[85] Even the power to "fight fate" is, in part, fate's gift to us.

Discipline. Emerson here joins together the previous three uses in such a way as to prepare us to transition from our debilitatingly excessive concern for pragmatic matters and our unhelpful tendency for metaphysical dualisms toward a joyous tragic philosophy of the ideal. He does this by first distinguishing between understanding and reason (a distinction important to many philosophers, perhaps most relevant for Emerson is that Coleridge, following Kant, makes this distinction).[86] Understanding deals with how we receive and organize phenomena. It is the faculty that traffics in empirical data. Our discursive ability to search out differences (as negations) and locate likenesses among the various objects of the senses. The activity of understanding allows us to generate specific associations between things, to assign roles, to outline and enumerate patterns, and to gain senses of proportion and importance in relation to what has already been established. It is the tireless effort in "dealing with sensible objects ... to form the *common sense*."[87] The wise thus possess common sense as a measure of *propriety*, while "the foolish have no range in their scale," or *impropriety*.[88] While the understanding collectively contributes to a common sense of life or a shared sense of reality with others, when it comes to the actual exercising of our understanding it is largely a subjective affair in which we bring the myriad aspects of nature and society together into a formal or informal scheme of knowing. Our intellect's basic power to organize. The understanding is a mixed blessing in that for all the explanatory glories of grand systems of thought it provides, it also makes the unjust demand that things be something other than what they really are in order to fit within the parameters of our designs. In this way, the understanding appears similar to the wonders and limitations of Aristotle's *epistēmē*, Aquinas' *ratio*, and Heidegger's *das rechnende Denken*—all calculative modes of thinking. If we take the understanding alone and read *will* and other forces through it, we are left with a Schopenhauerean (or reductive Nietzschean) view in which nature is made to serve us and our plans.[89] And where we cannot bring it to heel, we let it be or learn retroactively to desire it *as if* we had willed it so. Knowledge then can only be the result of our *will-to-know*. It becomes a mode of domination, a form of power. To be sure, power is ever desirable and Emerson is a prophet of power, but devoid of reason's reach into the abyss of being—the meditative respite before *nothing* that disrupts the tyranny of force—power as knowledge can only be the realization of force acting through us: unconscious drives, creaturely instincts, will to power, and so on. What seems to be most ours—our understanding of the world—is then only the consequence of our subordination to force and its many guises. Put simply, understanding cannot save us.

Save us from what? The ruinous state in which we always find ourselves, fragmented, imitative, unable to face the truth of our situation. Emerson does not offer some dream of an otherworldly heaven or literal latter-worldly resurrection, but the rehabilitation of our instincts, the renewed sense of a united self, the restoration of our original relationship to the idea of nature as a whole. This requires *reason*. In an ancient spiritual mode, reason signals both the necessary counterpoint to understanding alone and the sort of retrieval indicative of *Nature* in general. There is undoubtedly a mystical element in the earliest accounts and technical usages of *lógos*, which should give our modern assumptions pause. Whether a stable and hidden principle behind all things or an active power present throughout nature, unbiased readings of Heraclitus and Plato and the Stoics clearly testify to reason being more than merely "rational" or "logical." It must, however, be affectively attuned to its own possibilities and the intelligible objects it generates piously cherished.

Aside. We should take note here of the use of words prefixed with *re-*. Recognition, recovery, rehabilitation, relation, remembrance, renewal, restoration, resurrection, retrieval, return, and so on. Like the ancient stoics, Emerson, along with Nietzsche and Deleuze, is a tragic philosopher of eternal return, of circles. And Shakespeare's philosophical content, though present in his histories and comedies, manifests most clearly in his later tragedies and romances, when the world darkens and simultaneously widens and folds in upon itself with ever greater indefinition and incomprehensibility—when it recurs in novel ways—when questions then become more fruitful sans solutions and characters eventually cease their concern for certainty. Why worry about being certain in a world that, like ourselves, and in spite of all the institutions and traditions and theories tasked with preservation, refuses to hold still? The use of the *re-* prefix might—like *de-*, *per-*, *com-*, and other prefixes—often only suggest a particular intensification of an idea or an action, but with words like those we have listed here and used throughout, recalling *re-*'s primary usage can illuminate our eventual destination in considering the tragic imagination: it calls something "back to its original place," it is that which "is again," which "comes anew" and "once more." It is a repetition, yet always new. And *re-* also means "against" or "undoing." The repetition, without being a simple negation, also "stands against" what is, in that it is *different*. We can negotiate the messianic element present at the beginning and ending of *Nature* through this restructural approach existing (initially) between phenomena and mental life, and we can open up its possibilities as well with the *difference*—the strange *no-thing-ness* of being as becoming—which ever returns through us and as us in the creation of renewed stances and identities and theories.

Given the central role and sustained emphasis that intuition or instincts play in Emerson's philosophy, it is important to recognize that he, like Coleridge, equates intuition with reason. This means we always already possess the capacity for a certain kind of "perfect knowledge"—or *pure means of knowing toward and for an end*—that is interwoven into the very structure and activity of our consciousness. We do not have to develop and train it in the same manner as the discursive understanding, only rather reclaim it. This reclamation or rehabilitation process, as Emerson presents it, seems more a matter of overcoming certain habits of thought and belief by learning how to let them go than anything else, which, regardless of the degree of our intellectual talents, anyone can do. Hence, though we can locate aristocratic elements in Emerson's thought, he undoubtedly offers a democratic account of instinctual knowledge *through* the faculty of reason. Though our long-standing religious convictions, social demands for conformity, and quotidian habits of thought all tend to conspire to restrict it, reason is nevertheless a universal capacity. Nature has endowed everyone with it. Of course, one of the great misfortunes of civilization remains that though reason ever speaks to us and through us, we, in order to live peaceably with others, learn to ignore its voice. A plight seized upon by various unruly rebels, romantics, and idealists. Being both a universal and universally occluded capacity explains, in large part, why Emerson pours so much passionate rhetoric into challenging convention and encouraging experimentation and self-trust. He wants us to rehabilitate our very soul. By this account, reason does not stand apart from our creaturely drives and desires as a strange and inhuman power, but rather works through those forces and brings them into their fullest and finest expressions when guided by reason. Unlike the immediacy of those drives prior to rehabilitation, however, the voice of intuitive reason only calls quietly. Becoming deaf to it occurs without alarm or effort. Still, as Emerson's transcendental articulation of reason arrives in the partial guise of a romantic response to the aspirations of the Enlightenment, it nevertheless appears to contain much of the often-maligned modern expectation that we all can and should—and eventually will—conduct ourselves in accord with our own share of reason. Reason as *instrumental rationality*. As that which makes all things calculable in advance. Such was and is the grand conceit of modernity that Emerson negotiates (or that we must negotiate when reading Emerson). For all his plenitude of progressive thought, here and there he appears hemmed in by the conceptual language and metaphysical biases of the time.[90] Although a given work or articulation of an idea might achieve transhistorical influence, none of us fully escape the age and *ethos* in which our thoughts are circumscribed. And yet despite these occasional theoretical and linguistic constraints, it remains ill-advised, if not impossible, simply to classify Emerson's thought wholly and directly in relation to any well-defined philosophical school, including the transcendentalist movement he helped to popularize and lead. That is, we cannot simply describe him as a "transcendentalist" thinker and thereby gain clear entrance into his writings. As Emerson himself declared, "there is no such thing as a Transcendentalist *party*; that there is no pure Transcendentalist."[91] While useful for situating him and his philosophy historically, placing too much emphasis on that designation certainly creates difficulties in apprehending him through his own writing. As with other philosophical schools and movements, the assumptions and expectations that certain classifications bear, at best, restrict the meaning of original thinkers and, at worst, cause us to misconstrue them. When we name Kierkegaard, Nietzsche, Buber, Ortega y Gasset, Heidegger, Sartre, Beauvoir, Camus, Fanon, and others "existentialists," anyone who reads them seriously will quickly realize the limited benefit of doing so, as what marks out their differences far outweighs their similarities. In any case, with Emerson's attempt to read the riddle of the Sphinx and solve the problem of the world, reason returns to its ancient and mystical origins, which, in as much as it is a private allotment of a universal capacity, means that it must always be individually recovered and attuned. It is never, as the modern bias often assumes, simply a value-free, a-temporal, objective capacity, even though, as we have already said, we can cultivate a view *as if* such a universal perspective were retrospectively the case: thus, the importance of imagination in accounts of knowing.

Still, what exactly can we intuit by way of reason? What does reason accomplish distinct from understanding? "Reason transfers all lessons [of the understanding] into its own world of thought, by perceiving the analogy that marries Matter and Mind."[92] The transgression long laid at the feet of Plato and Descartes and Kant (although Kant tried valiantly to redeem this sin) wherein mental life or an intelligible realm (or even a noumenal reality) stand apart from the world of the senses is, according to Emerson, forgiven by way of reason's most profound ability to see past the illusion of separation and restore us to the unity of nature. While the understanding divides, apportions, relates, and systematizes within nature's material frame, reason—without requiring the understanding to abandon its activity or relinquish the knowledge it generates—brings those "natural facts" before itself, framed only by itself, upon *nothing else*, and so sees the profit of individuation and separable data as both illusory *and* necessary. Though they essentially *are not*, we need our objects of knowledge *to be*. They are the characters in our drama of understanding, the saviors and scapegoats of the tragic festival of the wise. That is, in order to be known—and as long as we believe it is desirable to know—nature must suffer the violence of our understanding. No longer only the dispassionate instrument reconditioning intuition, now reason itself sees and speaks as the rehabilitated intuition (through a collection of instinctual drives) and works in dialectical accord with understanding's operations, providing us with a way to overcome all the philosophical sins (illusions) originating from that ancient and modern metaphysical transgression (dualism). On its own, Emerson's faculty of reason arrives in the vein of Aristotle's *noûs*, Aquinas' *intellectus*, Heidegger's *das besinnliche Denken*—capabilities or modes of meditative thinking. It is both an immediate (direct) and a slower (patient) mode of thinking. But when considered in contrapuntal harmony with the understanding, our knowledge of the world becomes something else. By reclaiming its originality, it becomes *spiritual*.[93] That is, our knowledge of the world moves to the center of our being, to the meaningful intersection of our cognitive, aesthetic, and social concerns.[94] And this unity in and as variety takes on a divine majesty—an *otherness*—that transcends the lower compromised senses of divided and commodified use, allowing for a new and redeemed sense of means.[95] A means for what? For overcoming itself. An end that redefines all. The *ideal*.

Idealism. Having introduced the unifying power and original possibilities of reason in "Discipline," we begin the transition from the uses of nature to its end. An end toward which "all parts of nature conspire."[96] All parts before (illusory) and after (necessary) nature's unity within or as its own idea. And as he starts to summit the manifesto's final movements and offer his fable—the ruined god's messianic return to innocence that temporarily reestablishes the joyous elements of the tragic world[97]—Emerson feels as though he must once again rehearse the underlying concern manifest in the operations of understanding (sense-making) and reason (receptive intuition): what is the relation of the kingdom of the senses to the empire of the ideal? The relation of the world to the mind? Though harnessed for occasional conceptual clarity and regularly for poetic power, we know from the proceeding considerations that Emerson's world possesses no strict sense of inside or outside. The me dissolves into the *not me*. *Everything is nature*. His transcendentalism does not take nature as existing *in-itself* separate from the metaphor or emblem of nature created for and from it. This means that nature is *both* perpetually recreated *and* indistinct from its own idea. While things whatsoever perish always, the idea of nature, whatever shape it takes in this or that poetry or philosophy, ever persists in thought (as long as there is thought). As much as we would like to resolve this issue, we cannot pin Emerson down here. Take the philosophical instability generated at the intersection of

Neoplatonic monism, Coleridge's dualistic idealism and the German idealism that inspired it, Stoicism, Swedenborgian mysticism, wide readings in the natural sciences, Emerson's own recovering Unitarianism, throw in the heart of a romantic poet, and you have the indefinite formula for an unsystematic (though not thoroughly irrational) philosophy willing to bear its own contradictions (apparent or real) clearly in service to phrases and principles that astonish. When reading Emerson it is as though "we are not to be argued into slow assent but startled into instant agreement by the self-evident quality of each proposition."[98] However satisfying or dissatisfying we find his rhetorical maneuvers, Emerson's unique dialectal movements nevertheless prompt him to take up what he believes remains a problem—a "noble doubt"—for his readers: what and how the senses sense what they sense prior to reason's rehabilitation and restored relation to the understanding. His conclusion is that we find *nothing* behind nature as a final cause that is divorced from our own theorizing. And yet, even though Emerson would gladly dismiss dualism (or solipsism) by authorial fiat, it is mainly because he takes this manifesto so personally that this enigma of thought and experience—the seeming independent existence of nature (all that is *not me*) and the end we create for it through the idea of nature (which originates and is found within me)—still arrives as Emerson's "apocalypse of the mind."[99] As Barbara Packer writes,

> The mind is an uncovering, a revelation of significance; it also may be the consuming fire in whose flames the dross of nature will be burnt up. Perhaps its most significant contributions to the argument of *Nature* is its implicit assertion that the mind is not a place but a process; not an isolated inner space passively receiving sense impressions, but an active power incessantly striving to reveal the meaning of creation.[100]

In truth, though he feels he must wrestle through it, an actual or conclusive solution to this problem remains unnecessary. The problem comes to us as but a repetition of the ancient dramatic performance of thought that continues to this day—taken as theater, stage, characters, chorus, *plot*, an alter to the god, the machinery of the god's arrival (in order to intervene), attendees—in which the entry, exit, and importance of certain problems, be they heroic or villainous, are measured against their historical role in the overall narrative. The problem of dualism arrives as a byproduct of the plot supplied by metaphysical narratives (or systems) unable to absorb their own tensions, much like an unresolvable development requiring an improbable but necessary *deus ex machina*. Whether we accept such strange interventions—one substance, one mind, the necessity of illusions, metaphysical causality, and so on—will, in the end, come down to historically determined tastes or judgments weighed against the renewed intuitions of reason. Or, that a problem—a minor character posing as a villain—can be burned in the fires of thought and let go.[101] It rests with us who seek to synthesize what appears worth salvaging from flawed theoretical systems and to overcome the old habit of accepting unnecessary problems from them, especially when to do so forces us to barricade ourselves against the very benefits those theories have to offer. The *will-to-theoretical consistency* clearly reflects a metaphysical bias for identification predicated upon similarity rather than difference.[102] As Emerson tells us, "With consistency a great soul has simply nothing to do."[103]

Ultimately, we can have ideas *and* materials. We can be compromised of atoms and historically determined social relations *and* enjoy the life of the mind and the ideas and principles (or ideals) it generates. We do not have to choose one or the other. "There is much to say on all sides."[104] That we doubt and undertake to give an account whatsoever can do more than suffice: it can liberate the senses to sense generously and the knowing faculties to think thankfully. In this way, Emerson's "apocalypse of the mind"—as Nietzsche's aphoristic tapestry or Deleuze's differential repetitions—belongs to the recurring tragic festival of the wise. Old answers returning as new questions reclaiming original insights through novel expressions.

It cannot be emphasized enough that taken together with a de facto view of reason as essentially instrumental, the un-rehabilitated instincts, capricious as they appear, will nevertheless always direct us—almost invisibly—toward an absolute sense of reality: *the world of force*. The "real" absolute. Inwardly (*pathos, drives, destiny*) and outwardly (*ethos, forces, fate*) as yet indistinguishable.[105] In our ruined condition, our decisions arrive as rationalizations after the fact that simply apply the lexicon of biases allotted to us by circumstance. By fate. Reason seems only a tool and we but things. The resulting derivative views and alienating tendencies into which the world of force subordinates us—through metaphysical systems *and* unjust social practices—are, in large part, what Emerson's manifesto seeks to overcome. His aspirations for the uses, though particular in each case, nevertheless gesture toward our *creative participation* in an end: nature's final cause. The introduction of his "noble doubt" and "apocalypse of the mind" arrives more as an earnest, critical aid in this decisive transition from uses (and means) to end, and not as any genuinely embedded obstacle of thought. *The burning process that reveals*. Emerson shows us that we can allow ourselves to acknowledge the limits and uses of our understanding and still move beyond them. This acknowledgment also functions as a prolonged hesitation or pause to consider—*to reconsider*—how it is that nature works to free us from the world of force.[106]

Now, to move past these unresolved tensions (tensions still wrestled with in one form or another by many philosophers today), Emerson outlines five theses— or higher "effects of culture"—associated with his version of idealism: (1) nature works with spirit to free us; (2) poetic language elevates reality; (3) beauty and truth are one; (4) the empire of thought renews us and the world; and (5) ethics and religion teach us to accept the unity of all things in nature. Let us briefly unpack them.

First, we find in modernity that any misleading metaphysical assumption, like dualism or a reductive sense of causality, more easily overtakes our thinking whenever shifts in position or circumstance occur.[107] Why? The idea of nature as a whole for which the Dionysian drama of understanding allows has been *exchanged* for nature as a mere spectacle within a linearly progressing (rather than differentially repeating) narrative. Emerson seems to praise this spectacle when he tells us that "the best moments of life are these delicious awakenings of the higher powers, and the reverential withdrawing of nature before its God."[108] That is, we hold nature at a theoretical distance or at an artistic remove. We take it as a grand object and ask for it to remain still as we capture its likeness. But nature ought to be viewed this way only in order to assist our general project, our attempt at a contribution. It does not speak to the way things really are. A more wondrous sense of reality—even and especially a tragic reality—in which all beings and relations substantially participate (even by suffering and dying) can vanish in a moment when taken as a spectacle. Viewing the world as we view a portrait is useful only as long as it is not an expression of a metaphysical belief about the world indicative of our ruined, un-rehabilitated state. Truly taking the world as an image—and not simply framing it so as a theoretical or creative technique—diminishes the world and denies being's expansive unity. And when the world becomes not only an image but a vast collection of ever-moving mechanical or mediated images—when things move and alter around us without pause or substance, we inevitably come to see ourselves as images: *things* frenetically desiring to occupy space in the picture of the world, yet for some inexplicable reason we ever fail to do so. Not only does nature withdraw before God, God absconds with nature's mysteries. We are left only with forceful data; no persuasion or astonishment. And regardless of our level of explicit awareness about the various metaphysical positions undergirding our sense of reality, it is nevertheless due to them that the world so easily appears to change and slip away from us and us from it. And we from ourselves. The conditions of our modern social life and its many mediated relations only accentuate the shift. A century after Emerson writes *Nature*, Heidegger offers a similar analysis: "The fundamental event of modernity is the conquest of the world as picture."[109] Now everything that seems to matter (and much that does not) arises as a confrontation of worldviews, and not as what arrives from an open and receptive philosophical stance or as a dialectical and revolutionary act of creation. To be sure, that we inherit various philosophical and social complications as the result of metaphysical entanglements signals nothing new, but that those complications present themselves as being *pictographic in actuality* is. Not merely the employment of fable or allegory or myth or symbol in the useful presentation of nature as an idea, rather that the idea of nature can (or must) itself only be perspectively apprehended imagistically or formulaically and concretely congruent with nature *and* the end of nature is quite a recent development. Even the methodological prohibition against *bias* in interpretation now only generates a delusion of atemporal *objectivity*. Our sense of world—world as the particular surround of nature and the structures and activities of human life in which we find ourselves—now comes to us as largely composed of images, and as contingent upon technological systems and capitalistic allowances and exclusions. It certainly comes to us today as a cacophony of manufactured images and cultural avoidances all the way down. For this reason, Emerson makes use of examples illustrating the feverish mechanical and commercial pace of modern life—the view from a ship, a coach, a railroad car, as seeing through a camera, as watching a puppet-show—adds to the apparent ease with which we take on new and revised images of the world.[110] Explorations within the context of deeply rooted philosophical, civic, and religious commitments have given way to dalliances in the key of market-encouraged consumer taste-testing. That we try on ideas and temporarily adopt ritual practices as sartorial preferences reveals that they "are no longer contradictory to the status quo and no longer negative."[111] The current interchangeability of ideals and convictions that once undergirded historical protests and genuinely transcendent objectives neutralizes whatever critical and emancipatory power they potentially once held. Though Emerson reminds his reader that he is "only an experimenter" who works to "unsettle all things," it should be obvious that such critical and creative work can only occur within a stable world (even and especially a dangerously tragic one populated with illusions) with explorable frontiers and secure habits of thought that can be challenged.[112] This tells us why aphorism 125 of Nietzsche's *The Gay Science* reads as both elegy and provocation: "What festivals of atonement, what sacred games shall we have to invent?"[113] In any event, the mechanized array of insubstantial views, commodified images, and heartless practices impersonating expressions of meaningful identity have, of course, replaced slower philosophical comportments toward life and ends-oriented theories, especially and not un-ironically the ones with pronounced metaphysical commitments. But it was never metaphysics per se that was the problem, rather only the limitations and the refusal to acknowledge those limitations by particular metaphysical systems that were used to make concrete determinations about the world. No art, all science.

Second, the ideal philosophy goes beyond the use of language to the ends of language, even hinting at the proper end of thought itself, by which genuine thinking begins and for which it endures. How? Empirically minded materialists, whether sensualists or skeptics, arrange thoughts around their experiences (or claim to do so), while idealists and poets (poets being idealists by default) organize and present experiences in relation to thought (as intuitive reason).[114] The imagination here becomes accentuated and fundamental as it signals the principal faculty by which creative theorists and poets accomplish this work. As Kant argued in his first critique, imagination—as a power—determines sensibility a priori by synthesizing it with intuitive reason within the basic structure of reality—space and time—in order to have experiences and knowledge whatsoever.[115] That is, imagination conditions how we receive the world and it draws together the necessary elements for there to be a world to receive (as something knowable). It gathers together what comes before and what could possibly be. It is essentially the joining and generative ground of knowing. Emerson emphasizes imagination as the creative expression of reason upon the material world, as fashioning it in accord with intuited precepts not yet fully disseminated or comprehended.[116] Hence, the "timeless ideas"—like beauty or justice—perennially recur to convey something both strange and familiar, true and not yet true. And when housed in a poetic or philosophical genius—a person possessed of "heroic passion," both sensitive to the world and incredibly intuitive—truths and new possibilities stake shape in works of art and thought. A generation becomes defined or finds itself redefined. Though Emerson understands the limitations of circumstance and fate—of social and natural forces—he nevertheless believes that individuals can marshal history and denominate a people or an age:

> A man Caesar is born, and for ages after we have a Roman Empire. Christ is born, and millions of minds so grow and cleave to his genius that he is confounded

with virtue and the possible of man. An institution is the lengthened shadow of one man.[117]

In terms of agency and freedom, he privileges discrete personhood, ever masked as it is, over any collection of social energies and forces, but without discounting those energies and forces, as he makes clear in *Fate*. Along these lines, as far as Emerson is concerned, there is no greater art around which reality takes shape than Shakespeare's. His dramatic poetry appears so well-intuited and superbly synthesizing that he actually represents a sublime metaphysical problem: *perfect representation*.[118] The particularities of that problem set aside for now, Emerson finds in Shakespeare a "transfiguration which all material objects undergo through the passion of the poet."[119] This ability inverts, recasts, and plays upon the various ways we usually experience the world and our sense of proportion. That is, aesthetic and transvaluative. Shakespeare and all other magnificent poets, artists, and ideal thinkers—creators and thinkers of and for the ideal—heed that latent human potentiality possessed by all and, through their own native talent, cultivated disciplines, and directed drives, learn how to perceive and express the ideal:

> The perception of real affinities between events (that is to say, of *ideal* affinities, for those only are real), enables the poet thus to make free with the most imposing forms and phenomena of the world, and to assert the predominance of the soul.[120]

Until we free ourselves to see and think along with (and not merely in the shadow of) Shakespeare or some other visionary figure—ultimately to see and think for ourselves between the ordinary material and theoretical exclusions—we will remain caught in a prosaic reality that does not freely offer to us the most sublime possibilities of our tragic condition, rather only subordinates us to a limited array of options offered by those institutions and customs controlling our circumstances. The quest for the ideal indicates the adventure of thought toward the recovery of nature's otherness, our strangeness, and of creating new edifices and arguments representing the world as it is and can be.

Aside. If Shakespeare does indeed lay bare the real relations between things in such a way as to reveal how the inner workings of human life (the soul) impress themselves upon—and *as*—reality, then what does this mean for our reading of *Lear*? While we will attempt to develop this in more detail in the following chapter, it should be apparent that Shakespeare does not merely act as a conduit of social energies and reflect material forces at work. Such powers and contingencies indeed play a role in comprising his world and his art. Yet, if we take Emerson's ideal philosophy seriously, then we should see that our own reception of the material and social conditions of late-sixteenth and early-seventeenth-century life in England—if not now—does not best occur by way of objective or agendized interpretations of accounting ledgers, legal documents, and journal entries, but by Shakespeare's poetry itself, particularly his tragic dramas.[121]

The third aspect of the ideal philosophy arises, in part, from the ancient doctrine that beauty and truth belong together. "The true philosopher and the true poet are one."[122] It is an argument rehearsed by the Romantics whom Emerson admires. It also presents something of a pharmacological twist within Plato's own system. By introducing the idea of beauty (as the poetic objective) and placing it in such close proximity to truth (as the philosophical objective)—and seeing them as different articulations or expressions of essentially the same thing: the good (*àgathós*)—Plato opens the door for later thinkers to undermine the strictly abstracted reception of his metaphysics. Although his system sets ideas above the reach of material conditions, by conceding the essential connection between beauty and truth, he tempts more sensuous souls to re-inscribe the superiority of the poetic and pre-Socratic traditions—which Plato had attempted to overcome—over and against their epistemological demotion (if not exclusion). To be clear, Emerson has no desire to deconstruct Plato. He rather simply sees the ancient connection and the Platonic account of it in such a way as to serve his own transcendental articulation of the ideal philosophy. Moreover, for Emerson, "Plato is philosophy, and philosophy, Plato."[123] And between *Phaedrus* and *Symposium* we already have enough erotic allowances and Dionysian disruptions to topple the less helpful aspects of *The Republic*: "Then be quiet and listen … I'm on the edge of speaking in dithyrambs as it is."[124] In any case, the laws of nature that determine how phenomena reveal themselves and how they behave in predictable ways—in as much as ascertaining particular repetitions serve our quest to solve the riddle of nature—actually find their ground in our assertions of something absolute.[125] And more so than the absolute (the established fundamental *identity*), it is the *assertion* itself that indicates faith in the creative act—theoretical or aesthetic—which seeks to apply the otherwise secret truths of an idea (fashioned and found by reason out of *nothingness*) whose depersonalized beauty (simultaneously familiar and *strange*) arrests us within our own deeply personal thought life.

The assertion, in the forms of philosophy and art, sets forth laws that attempt to explain and bind phenomena. As Emerson later writes, "Philosophy is the account which the human mind gives to itself of the constitution of the world."[126] And the activity ends in the absolute. That is to say, the creative assertion that attempts to explain and bind phenomena finds fulfillment in the establishment of an unconditioned absolute grounding all laws and principles.[127] *The idea becomes the ideal.* Hegel's formulation:

> The Truth is the whole. But the whole is nothing other than the essence consummating itself through its development. Of the Absolute it must said that it is essentially a *result*, that only in the *end* is it what it truly is.[128]

For Emerson, the absolute that is established (and taken as ultimate measure of universal identification, including *difference*) only lasts for as long as the laws or principles presented *as ideal*—or *as proceeding from the ideal*—possess the power to arrest us by way of the particular portraits or accounts of nature in which we find them: "There are no fixtures in nature. The universe is fluid and volatile. Permanence is but a word of degrees."[129] In time, we will always grow indifferent toward difference when it is established as a law or principle. When it becomes an absolute marker for universal identity. According to Emerson, we endow nature with these inventions of our intellectual and spiritual life; they are not objectively and universally inhering laws somehow paradoxically existing outside of the very process that creatively discovers them. That is, we discover only what we hid prior to giving it a name. Philosophy can therefore be considered a poetic science attuned to the task of *naming* the world. A task for which silence ever remains requisite.

The penultimate aspect of idealism involves the "elevation" of the soul within its ideational activities. Emerson begins by reasserting the idealist's noble doubt—that apocalypse of the mind—which calls into question the existence of material reality. As ideas themselves take on more privileged roles over and against our ordinary habits of thought and behavior, and as they come to pulse with ever more substantial being, we come to feel as though we but pass through dreams and shadows of a world while our minds tend toward more timeless concerns.[130] An old and not un-ironic tendency among philosophers. Nature, then, might even appear as an appendage to the soul when encountered in the light of the sublime idea of nature. The great metaphysical sin, so to speak, perpetrated upon nature in the name of an "ideal nature" housed (or unhoused) upon an atemporal and more essential plane of thought. A thinker's Olympus, Emerson calls it. This is where we find divinity.[131] Emerson tells us that such thoughts are themselves divine: rehabilitated reason intuiting by creatively participating in the order the world for the festive dramatization of understanding. What has historically often been forgotten, however, is that such thoughts possess only the reality of thoughts—only and yet extraordinarily so. As Feuerbach would provocatively assert just five years later: "To think is to be God."[132] Here Emerson references and alters a passage from *Proverbs* 8, pluralizing the usually singular account of creation: from "I was set up from everlasting, from the beginning, or ever the earth was" to "these are they who were set up from everlasting, from the beginning, or ever the earth was."[133] Whether or not Emerson was attempting his first formal articulation of his eventual universal Christology—that is, we are all Christ when we think and believe as Christ—it is clear that while this speculative realm has historically only welcomed the few, it is open to all.[134] Part of the allure of Emerson comes from the fact that he writes as a democratic thinker who desires to see all people become intellectually aristocratic. He is aspirational. He wants everyone to encounter the divine or ideal nature of things by trusting that they carry the divine nature within themselves.[135] Life's manifold sufferings and insecurities then lessen—by being endowed with purpose or perspective or proportion or plot—by the light of the highest possibilities of thought. In that divine region, wherein imagination works in concert with intuitive reason—prior to understanding—we think along with the gods, as gods. In that region, "for the first time, *we exist.*"[136]

For the final section of "Idealism," Emerson offers an initial sense of what he will further develop in the following chapter, "Spirit." The benefit gained from a philosophy beginning in this region of thought—wherein we find our true existence—is that it allows us to overcome less integrated and disproportionate views, as we often find in conventional religious beliefs and banal ethical practices. The ideal theory reveals the inadequacies of religion and ethics, as they only tend to degrade nature through their respective applications to daily life. Their conceptions of nature, not yet elevated to the ideal of nature, tend to subordinate nature to their understanding without benefit of creative-rational apprehension. "They put nature underfoot."[137] Their accounts and imperatives remain too tied to habits of thought overly invested in either the dogmatic placement and circumscription of the idea of God as an entity outside of nature (religion) *or* of addressing the absolute solely in relation to interpersonal and societal obligations devoid of authentically aristocratic aspirations for either party (ethics). Notions and duties devoid of the *eros* woven into the very structure of all *possible* realities. Truth is then only and unhelpfully apparitional, not of nature or in accord with intuitive reason; justice merely a reflection of historical and current cultural practices, making all universal claims deceptive. Higher culture—self-trusting and self-cultivating—upends these vulgar views so that reality can, in a non-delusive sense, merge with the visionary.[138] Emerson describes the possibility of this union between materiality (historical and physical) and incorporeality (imaginative and ideational) as proceeding from a return to childlikeness.[139] Childlikeness here indicates a progressive emancipatory function of our regressive capacity to *re*-cognize—to know again in a new way—the forbidden and forgotten.[140] For children, the world is concrete *and* flexible, filled with delicious sensations *and* cruel edges, populated with fantastical beings *and* invisible realities. Why else would Heraclitus tell us that "time is a game played beautifully by children" or Jesus that "except ye be converted, and become as little children, ye shall not enter into the kingdom of heaven"?[141] Why would the philosophy of those ancient materialists, the stoics—along with Spinoza, Nietzsche, and Deleuze—so seamlessly and unapologetically possess incorporeals?[142] It is, in Emerson's estimation, prior to unhelpful conventions of thought, "that view which is most desirable to the mind."[143] In retrieving the forbidden and forgotten, reason finds its utmost limits and possibilities and returns to the practical task (in renewed concert with the understanding) of living life in the world. Here, by the rediscovered and now expanded light of reason's original childlike association with imagination, an alluring aspect of ancient stoicism can explicitly arrive to assist us. We can now behold our cosmopolitan connection, one to another, all to a world; a world wherein our differences do not of necessity alienate or marginalize us but is itself the living choreography of the *ordo amoris* around which our differences organize themselves in novel ways through reason's generosity. Emerson's ideal philosophy sees everything that has come before and is now and is to come "as one vast picture which God paints on the instant of eternity for the contemplation of the soul."[144] Not the subsumption of all differences into one totalized thought life, but the elevation of all heretofore sung and unsung aspects of the tragic life drama to the contemplative region.[145] We envision the drama this way in order to turn aside and revise old accounts and to create ways forward within the tragic world. New ways of being. *Strange, other, different.* This aspect or stage of Emerson's transcendental account of the ideal philosophy also "respects the end too much to immerse itself in the means."[146] That is, the aims and hopes of theory ought to be privileged over its particular execution. Otherwise, we risk becoming too dogmatic or too enmeshed in particular habits or methodological commitments that exclude the possibility of revision or novelty. Compassion for others, for example, arises from an end that can and should express itself in a variety of ways. To allow only previously approved ways of expressing love places means over ends and denies creativity and possibility to our ethics, our familial relationships, our romances, our friendships, and our interpersonal life generally. We can, perhaps, here sum up this aspect of the ideal philosophy—this higher stage of self-culture—by stating that it restores our childlike sense of wonder—so flexible in its acceptance and advocacy—whereby nature retains its strange divinity, all persons their irreducible dignity, every action its potential enrichment. All portraits and accounts now liberate their respective patrons and clients (from being only means) through more perfect—ideal—representations (ends approached polyphonically) by resisting all easy subordination to mere understanding (taken monolithically) and domination (as an exercise of unrefined power) through old habits of belief and blind faith in social institutions.

―――

Spirit. With the seventh and second to last chapter of *Nature*, Emerson offers a selective and effective repetition of his transcendental philosophy. And not only this chapter but the manifesto itself ought to be read as an elevating series of repetitions: ideas and claims and questions differentially and dialectically reconsidered and rearranged and repeated. Exhaustion and exultation, along with his signature ambiguity, run parallel right up until the conclusion. Still, while not always known for directness, there do remain a few points Emerson desires to make as clear as his dialectically tense and rich rhetoric allow. He begins this chapter by once again emphasizing a unity in nature that reveals us to ourselves in an original way—who and what we truly are—and that provokes us to redefine ourselves accordingly: "And all the uses of nature admit of being summed in one, which yields the activity of man an infinite scope."[147] The escalatory repetition or winding elevation of uses toward ends that work to unify all parts and regions of experience and thought, and which find pure but imprecise articulation as ideas—from which follow principles or ideals—are, in the highest and final sense, derived from reason and discovered within "God" or the "over-soul" or that which is "not me." When taken as ends and not as means, these articulations or expressions can never be exhausted because the origin from which they spring is itself inexhaustible: *spirit*.[148] While we find in Emerson (and in other iterations of idealism) a certain level of equivocation and exchangeability with all of these terms—God, reason, soul, other—we, nevertheless, find spirit taking center stage here. All other unities that provide ground for some region of our thought life, even the ones taken as most holy (God) or most unifying (reason) or most vital (soul) or most defining and terrifying (other), still only arrive subsequent to spirit. Whether this is due to those appellations carrying more specific connotations or bearing particular limitations, Emerson does not say. And in many ways, as we have already said, they remain largely exchangeable at a conceptual level, which we ought not forget. But he titled the chapter "Spirit" and not "God" or "Reason" or "Soul" or "Other," and we ought not forget that either. For Emerson, spirit—behind which lies only *nothing*—denominates that which animates the universe, the *anima mundi*. Perhaps spirit is a way of imperfectly naming the essentially indefinability of *nothing*? Not that from which we seek to escape nihilation but that which acts as the very ground of consciousness itself? That out of which we imaginatively fashion possibilities of liberation from tyrannical forces? That by which we lay claim to a fundamental freedom for other ways of being?[149] These speculations notwithstanding, it is clear that for Emerson spirit refers both to the highest expression of being for which beauty acted as the evocative herald and to the fundamental principle of life in general (making the association with *nothing* even more intriguing) that is bound only to the task of expressing and organizing itself through the manifold dimensions and processes of nature, which we particularize as world and individualize as self—and realize as *self-culture*. It is a cosmic undertaking and we, individually and collectively, play but our part in it. Our role in the tragedy is simultaneously allotted (nature and society, *phýsis* and *nómos*) and self-authored (self-culture, *áskēsis*). When we employ the religious language of divinity, we appeal to the providential and hopeful aspects of spirit's animation of all creation; when we deploy the language of reason, we concentrate upon patterns and accounts that unify; when we talk of soul or imagination, we address its apocalyptical (revelatory) and generative tendencies. If spirit's herald, beauty—which teaches us to love and worship nature in relation to the repetition of its origin toward its end (which is *no-thing*)—goes unheeded, its irresistible animating force takes on the form of the *epic of force* (which encompasses *everything*).[150] A dictatorial dialectical variation of the tragic life drama in which meaningful participants—even those who seem but fools destined to suffer and die or bear witness to such—find themselves reduced to inessential "things" easily interchangeable one for another. A worker, a student, a constituent, a consumer, a victim, a criminal, a statistic. Emerson's tragic philosophy of idealism—his account of American transcendentalism—resists such reduction by reclaiming the ends for which humans undertake their most essential life-affirming and excusing projects: justice, love, beauty, truth, goodness. These ideals testify to any strange resistance to subordinating classification devoid of life-affirming ends. These ideals can be taken as rationally apprehended, theologically disclosed, imaginatively constructed, and so forth. Emerson here once again takes up a variation of the apocalypse of the mind, believing that the spirit of nature delivers to us, or through us, certain questions that appear fundamental: "What is matter? Whence is it? and Where to?"[151] These questions demonstrate our capacity to create "problems" for ourselves in order to spur and intensify our intellectual and spiritual life by sentencing ourselves to *durance vile*, by undertaking the trials and tribulations associated with the solving of those problems. That is, they are questions posed for solution in the *purification*—or perfection—of the soul.[152] The metaphysical transgression of dualism leads to myths of an existential alienation (myths fully appropriated and harnessed to maximal material effect by the world of force). "We are as much strangers in nature as we are aliens from God."[153] Nature seems to flee from us as prey before a predator. But such discord, such alienation, such predation, comes only from what we elect to carry within ourselves. We have written it, or allowed it to be written, upon our experiences and into our accounts. Do the other creatures themselves feel so discorded and alienated? Emerson's transcendentalism reminds us that we are natural and need no longer feel alienated from nature. And yet, of natural creatures endowed with reason (*lógos*) and imagination (*Einbildungskraft*), we are perhaps *uncanny*, the most terrible and strange and wondrous part of nature, which helps explains our inevitable slide into homelessness, into feeling estranged and forlorn in the world.[154] "A man is a god in ruins."[155] The great irony—if not the great opening movement of the tragedy upon which all other forces prey—is that we are in truth the most worldly and most at home: when we, through original envisioning, reclaim our place in the universe, creating and dwelling accordingly. Recall that the share of nature that we represent—which we *are*—however conspicuously tragic by degrees, is discovered in the "not me" of nature, in the otherness of being. We must lose ourselves in order to find ourselves.[156] And when we do—cycling through various "problems"—we are delivered over to a dignified association with *what is*, a healing sense of proportion, a mind reborn for wonder: vision, judgment, responsibility. Any identifications afterward arise either directly from the essential *nothing* comprising *what is* or from all animating and self-organizing spirit. Either way: unending repetitions and expressions of otherness, difference, and strange *nothings*, whether denominated religiously, intellectually, imaginatively, or left in silence. What we find as we dialectically work our way through the prisons of metaphysical problems—as stages of *apocalyptic gnōsis* or agonistic stations[157]—is restoration to a place of vision and significance that does not, strictly speaking, belong to us but rather to which we belong and for which we are responsible.[158] We become those who tend the commons together. Forever afterward, the question of materiality, or any metaphysically induced problem, takes it rightful place among the curious myths and rhythms of the ancients. If we remain open to them, they teach us about the possibilities and limits of human creation and thought, and the aspirations for life within the boundaries of a shared mind that stretches back to the beginning and forward to the end. Intellection both bound by fate and freed by destiny.

———

Prospects. At last we come to the concluding chapter of *Nature*, wherein Emerson offers one final repetition of his transcendental philosophy. Here the work nears a coalescence and self-adherence which, while we still have no argued thesis as such, provides us with the dialectical parameters of his vision. And as that vision comes into better view through this last repetition we find, surprisingly, the emergence of what is perhaps Emerson's true hope for his philosophy: while his transcendentalism chiefly turns upon (1) an imperative never to accept (or reject) unquestioningly the validity or permanence of any existing belief, (2) the rehabilitation of the instincts (and faculties) in order to apprehend ideas from which we generate ideals, and (3) the desire to see (and create) the world anew in accord with those ideals, the end of his philosophy does not lie with these aspirations alone or with any classical epistemological ambition to acquire wisdom for its own sake: he rather offers a philosophy of power. *Power redeemed and refined*.

How does Emerson arrive at this?

He has claimed that our inquiries—*as inquiries*—into "the laws of the world" and "the frame of things" disclose that the actively attuned mind (which most directly and openly associates with spirit) has always already housed all latent possibilities of discovering universal ideas, however indefinite and strange, and that the reactively veiled mind (which does not directly and openly associate with spirit) has become delimited by the habits of belief popularized by empirical science, in which everything finds itself reduced to the status of an object or a thing, to a mere sensible identity—an equivalency—that serves a role or function, or will be made to do so. The latter describes what Emerson, like so many other keen theorists of the nineteenth and twentieth centuries, wishes to overcome: it is the "torpid soul" awakening to the "undiscovered regions of thought."[159] On the one hand: the truth of the whole (the idea of nature) comprised by difference undergirded by *nothing*. On the other: particularized facts (regions of nature) conditioned by identities determined by material forces. Or, a metaphysical fate that bestows a material destiny *contra* a material fate that precludes a metaphysical destiny. A theoretical game of exclusions and allowances whereby meaningful determinants can only represent the dominant rules in force. In such a world, becoming a "liberated subject" means renouncing careful positions and accepting the reductive demands that, in order to participate in the illusion of civic life, we must choose either a metaphysical (or "religious") or a materialist (or "political") worldview and do so in a time when we do not know how to talk constructively about either in mixed company. Assuming, of course, that we have anything worth saying. And though Emerson is an idealist, he desires, like the *imagined* partnership between reason and understanding, to go through the performance of a reconciliation (or at least an elective nomadism that must recognize the boundaries it transgresses). An ideal philosophy or theory divorced from the many sensuous scenes he and other poets paint of the material surround, whether sweet or cruel or sublime, and of the social world, whether all retrospective or busy or in ruins, becomes an enlightenment nightmare, in which intuitive reason deteriorates into instrumentalized rationality. Its power manifests as rational domination in which the theoretical organization of all phenomena and relations are placed into preapproved classifications and relations. In many ways, material philosophy represents the inevitable result of that deterioration (devolution mistaken for revolution), wherein what is true *can only be true if* it follows from the most pragmatically useful methods of verification available, thus the disenchanted but "divine" status dubiously granted to statistics and the data born of laboratory and informational sciences, as well as the cultural (*die Bildung*) decline of societies whose members feel free to select the statistics and information that verify their individualistic (false) needs in order to justify and excuse their view of the world. Its power finds articulation in social theories and expression through practices that subordinate (or appropriate) all potential opposition into an all-encompassing picture (*Gestell, Weltbild*) of dialectical struggle in which social justice somehow (and somewhat suspiciously) exists without any ideal theory of justice (because rather than force and its related instruments of power, it is, ironically, the ideal theory of justice that is, in large part, blamed for historic injustices).

These are, of course, extreme and uncharitable characterizations of theoretical (or hyperrational) and material (or empirical) positions, yet representative nonetheless of wayward philosophizing become totalizing worldviews, which, according to the cruel efficiency of power's expression, level down all social positions into dogmatic (and often) binary oppositions. Emerson desires a philosophy of nature that is in accord with an ideal born *between* ideas and materiality. If we desire to overcome domination, then theory and practice must not be joined by what they "are," but by what they essentially "are not." That is, joined together in a tragic ontology of difference. This frees up space in which to think and to work in novel ways. To critique, to negate, to build. Theory and practice must also be social *and* personal. A philosophy of self-culture that ever finds the self already in a culture, as already having a set of relations, as already having, for better or worse, an inheritance.[160] Though building self-trust requires a type of solitude, we are never simply solitary souls or sovereign agents (even though Emerson gives us passages here and there and works like *Self-Reliance* that make this aspect of his thought difficult to glean). In any event, by the end of *Nature*, it seems clear that Emerson wants to measure human facts against human ideals and cultivate the power—power between thought and action, power between self and world, power decoupled from force—to create a new and strange identity out of a differentially repeating *nothingness*. Once again: "To be great is to be misunderstood" and "greatness appeals to the future."[161]

Emerson's ideal philosophy, with all of its doubts and adversities intact, seeks to open up human experience to the poetic, to the "untaught sallies of the spirit," to "continual self-recovery," to indefatigable mysteries revealing the "occult relation" between all beings and forms and activities.[162] *If* we see ourselves as "lords of creation" it is only true in as much as we are *servants* of the *not me* and friends to all *others* who proceed from the *not me*. *Fools* before force. Persisting up to the present through our biases and assumptions, enlightenment rationalism—while generating glorious systems of thought—remains uninterested in, or unable to seek, such sensuous relations and nonreducible spiritual affiliations with *otherness*. And any strictly material philosophy or empirical science, while producing precise and actionable knowledge, lacks the potential for full self-recovery as we find ourselves—along with everything else—reduced to a class or classification. *Not a name* or *silence before namelessness*. Always a numerical designation stripped of any novel identity (which is always *different*). Such philosophies do not possess and cannot offer the liberating and associating power that the occult unity of the idea of nature provides. While everything for any material philosophy, as it has been characterized here, ultimately becomes functional and understood, and it becomes so in as much as it has been rendered unpoetic and thin in advance of—and in preparation for—its violent subordination to an unyielding portrait. (Not the metaphysical problem of "perfect representation" pertaining to the horizon of our thought that Emerson lays at Shakespeare's feet, rather merely a "correct portrayal" of the world monstrously and efficiently "perfected.") Even if these theorists employ the language of a dialectical drama, the power distributed to the people is only vulgar and the insights provided fixed and reified. The end in such philosophies does not transform and dignify the means; it only unjustly justifies them. The "great revolution" only inverts or flirts with inverting what its authors want to destroy. In this act of the tragedy, in our present age, instead of finding reconciliation, we largely no longer honor, whether silently or performatively, the mad forces of Dionysus (as nonrational energies, ecstatic unities, irreducible differences). We rather, ill-advisedly, attempt to present the brilliant powers of Apollo in his stead (as rational forces, drive to classification, absolute equivalency). Those that approach the riddle of the world in this way seek to answer it with finality. "As if God were dead."[163] Subsequently, the tragic drama, the festival of the wise—in which the riddle might authentically and astonishingly arise—becomes a disaster of a satire satirizing the possibility of salvation that the riddle represents. It is a denial of our most basic and life-affirming powers to pause and question and see differently and anew.

And what does Emerson name this salvific power? "Infancy is the perpetual Messiah, which comes into the arms of fallen men, and pleads with them to return to paradise."[164] It is the radically foolish refusal and intuitively wise alternative to force and its instruments of power. It is the promise of life held in nature and within ourselves during the winter years of blind ideologies and the long nights of declining culture. This other power, though it is as native as it is foreign, must nevertheless always be won. We must ever rescue it from out of the world of force. This power is our own most possibility to retrieve ourselves from out of the un-reified *difference* (*no-thing-ness*) that holds in advance what—*who*—we can ultimately become prior to the unnecessary delimitations of any particular identity. This *differential nothingness*—the imaginative ground of all possibilities—both births ideas and receives *every-thing*. Force and its unredeemed manifestations and exercises of power make everyone into *every-thing* and drives it all into oblivion. Back into the *differential nothingness*. But this happens most often before we are able—or even desirous—to win ourselves from out of the imagined abyss of possibilities. Unthinkingly, unpoetically, bereft of soul, we are dominated and without recourse. Without the retrieve—the drama of self-recovery—we remain merely the *things* the world made us to be, destined to do what all things do: die. This old epic use of power, though ever seeming to appear in novel ways—especially in terms of verifiable explanations and technological innovations—in fact never allows what is strange and new to be strange and new. *Nothingness* signals only death to cruel and violent power; never difference, never possibility, never life. Thus, in the world of force, wherein identity is prior to difference, we can never truly be ourselves. For when it does not produce corpses outright, force, in whatever guise it appears, categorizes and controls the world by its laws of epistemological identification and its irresistible technics, both of which, in concert with a culture both mesmerized and tranquilized by endless consumption, ceaselessly work to render all phenomena into things. A world defined by allowances and exclusions set by no one in particular. No real projects. No real villains. No real responsibilities. Only momentarily satiation or unending outrage.

Emerson chooses another way: "Build therefore your own world."[165]

Still, a world of our own requires the foolish art of difference, a performed or dramatized repetition of that difference from which the engine of being is itself comprised. We must forget much of what we have learned if we wish to retrieve that art. The young messiah "come again"—miraculously—signals a refusal to participate in the epic of force and an abdication of those inhumane and incarcerating uses of power to which we have become habituated. The infant messiah indicates another power, an alternative capability and choice: *to play instead*.[166] For even those of us already old can choose to become like children who stare, for a moment, mouths agape, at wondrous spectacles. We can relearn silence, the philosophy of questions, sensitivity to poetry, to life, adopting humility before affliction. We can become compassionate. We can venerate what is *not me*. And we can refuse what is not foolish and build something *else*.

The answer to the riddle of the Sphinx, which is never final, has always been secretly housed within our own most existential and social architecture. That is, within and among *us*. But only when we can see and speak the truth as childlike fools who have recovered from our ruinous state. The state of conformity and subjection. *Nature* is Emerson's orphic manifesto calling us to return to this original and wondrous relationship with the tragic world and with the others that comprise it, and which it itself socially and ontologically is. This insight, this mystery, leads to the awakening of our most truly human powers to do *otherwise* than we are told, to liberate ourselves from all those who "think they know what is [our] duty better than [we] know it."[167] This mystery is the eternally returning power within nature—which takes possession of us as an idea and frees us as an ideal—which resurrects what force has killed. Fate can once again come to signify the determinative pattern of material relations within nature: the unwritten and yet unyielding laws of life.[168] And life can once again return as performance of the tragic drama celebrated as the festival of the wise, the wise who have learned just how unwise and loving they needed to become in order to find freedom.

Still, is freedom an end unto itself?

4

Wiles of Innocence

When Emerson published his second series of essays in 1844, he included an essay entitled, "Nature." Not the grand manifesto of 1836, this shorter work by the same name—though retaining his signature dialectical style of provocative proclamation and entreaty—appears a more tempered meditation. Emerson seems more aware of, and at home with, his limitations, as well as the need to perform philosophical and rhetorical strategies that both harness and work through those very limitations: "My work may be of none, but I must not think it of none, or I shall not do it with impunity."[1] He speaks of potential continually outrunning performance, of always living in a system of approximation, of every end being only prospective, temporary, deferred, and of finding "final success nowhere."[2] As with many of his later writings, we see a fatalistic sense of life ready to accept nature's cruelty and deference to evolutionary laws.[3] He writes of an "aboriginal push," an "impulse," a violent "shove," of an "electricity" within the universe that ever drives us. He speaks of "secrets," "fools," and "folly." While not Emerson's finest essay, it nevertheless offers the mature insights and lexicon of a fully realized tragic philosophy. Like Nietzsche after him, Emerson remains one who—*because* the world is tragic—affirms life, one who says "yes." And he says yes in a way that does not lessen the harsh realities of the world. Nature's savagery and the curse of being place an existential demand upon us to conjure up sentiments and practices empowering us to ride such monstrous movements upward (whether or not nature's arc actually elevates).[4] Why else go on? Why else ask any important questions or attempt answers? Why else endeavor to make any cultural contributions rather than surrender to the wisdom of Silenus? Emerson also makes explicit here what we already surmised from the earlier 1836 manifesto: though we take "nature" *as if* it is a grand object present for our contemplations and ascending uses (*natura naturata*), "it" remains a dynamic, untamed, and alien becoming (*natura naturans*).[5] We only pretend to make nature (*difference*) hold still for its portrait (*identity*).[6] This includes ourselves.

Through the faculties granted us to do so, we abstract active nature as laws or principles or theories that slow it down in order to "expose and cure the insanity of men."[7] To offer ritualistic redress for desires and events from which we cannot escape. And yet these desires and events continue to elude our offerings and strategies. Nothing is ultimately solved, only temporarily salved.

Aside. Offering redress, however, usually means laying the groundwork for future strains of insanity. Unless, through convivial institutions like poetry, friendship, and the commons, we, remarkably, enact laws retrieved from our utmost potentialities of being, such as love, beauty, and forgiveness, which mitigate against force and its mechanisms of repression and its instruments of domination. Unless we, perhaps even more remarkably, allow any particular instantiations of such convivially instituted laws the freedom to fail, to change, and, when their time has come, to die. This allowance subsequently sets the stage for them—in accord with the tragic life-death cycle itself—to return in novel ways. Otherwise, all non-convivial attempts to institutionalize our explanations and our ethics only corrupt that which they set out to preserve, only profanes that which we truly need and, often unconsciously, most desire.

This activity enables us to play a part in the creation, destruction, and revision of any historical world structure. When attuned to the task it permits us to participate in the undergirding possibility of the *ordo amoris*: the *erotic* liberated from non-convivial convention and free to organize itself.[8] We each can have our own say in what it all means when—*if*—we, as *fools*, approach it as a riddle to be provisionally solved. This recurrent counter drama—*the tragic festival of the wise*—serves as our humble conspiracy against force and all of its totalizing techniques. And yet each performance of the conspiracy is, as all performances, only ephemeral. While through refusal and play each generation prepares the way for the return of the infant messiah—who comes near only ever to withdraw again—we must remain ever mindful that "nature cannot be cheated,"[9] nor the world of force forever overcome. And to accomplish this active preparation, each of us, though assisted in community and by collaboration, must, as a naked soul alone, learn to pause and slowly approach nature as a strange and wondrous unity of active multiplicities. An idea of difference so astonishing that we can but abandon ourselves to it: "I am nothing … I am part or parcel of God."[10] We come before this idea delicately *and* dangerously due to the requirement that we be stripped, or preferably that we strip ourselves—through theatrical levels of initiation—of all illusions of being as identity that have been predicated upon any order of reality preserved by force, which gives us only illusions in service of domination.[11] *Delusions*. Yet, we do this not in order to attain an objectivated understanding of nature bereft of mystery or a timeless sense of truth divorced from history, rather to retrieve a more honest truth about how things *are*, a more surprising truth alerting us to that which we genuinely *are*: brief mortal instances of difference endowed with reason and imagination. Why? To free ourselves to ask why. To see and solve the riddle of the world. To adorn ourselves anew with different illusions—life-affirming beliefs and techniques of thought—to assist us toward these ends. If it seems circular, or infinitely recurring, that is because it is. For the game of life must still be played, the drama acted out. Roles and props and purposes are still required. Although now the whole affair becomes a free collaboration in which we find ourselves more authentically invested. We write ourselves differently. We attain a grain of tragic wisdom that spurs us to change the style of our lives and fatefully accept what seems beyond our art. We now adorn ourselves selectively, with refinement, and live by our own consent. These new illusions of ours are illusions of identity fashioned from un-reified difference. They are the virtual tools of belief and for behavior arising from any ideal philosophy that questions the way things have "always been" or how they "really are." Any theory of intuition that seeks new imperatives and new arts by which to ground those imperatives. Any philosophy of self-culture that rejects imposed conformity and the assumption of finality. These new illusions serve *eros* and beauty and subvert force and its reality. Unlike the old ones we shed, these new illusions are not born of habituated conformity before power (*delusional identities*) but are instead creations of our now rehabilitated reason (*lógos*) and liberated imagination (*Einbildungskraft*). These new illusions are novel retrievals from out of the differential potentiality stirring within the *nothingness* from which the tragic world and all of its players endlessly emerge, turn, and exit: "from the nothing of life to the nothing of death."[12] It is Theseus' "airy nothing," Cordelia and the Fool's provocative and useful "nothing," Prospero's "baseless fabric," from which we construct not simply our own personal life-affirming illusions but every transhistorical idea and imaginary world structure relied upon to bear beautiful truths. Truths for which we ever remain personally responsible, yet truth for which we collectively conspire to enact aesthetically and ethically to challenge our reality. Personal and collaborative efforts that even occasionally, if only temporarily, allow reality to become something *else*: "The cloud-capp'd towers, the gorgeous palaces, / The solemn temples, the great globe itself."[13] Moreover, under these freely self-given illusions—named laws or principles or theories or beliefs—we invite necessity, forever a hallmark of a tragic world, to shed its callousness and become beautiful:

> There is nothing so wonderful in any particular landscape as the necessity of being beautiful under which every landscape lies. Nature cannot be surprised in undress. Beauty breaks in everywhere.[14]

And for Emerson no poet of the tragic frontier ever invites necessity to become beautiful quite so irresistibly as Shakespeare. The poet gives us such perfect representation that both the cruelty of the curse of being and the transforming miracle of art become one. A freedom born of reconciliation, of an art that forgives. He invites us to wonder if rather than nothing, *something*—something remarkable—"will come from nothing." That indeed it should.

―――

Vision and Suffering. In the opening scene, after Cordelia chooses silence—which draws out her father's true "darker purpose" and provokes him to reveal, without realizing it, the conditions for restoration, which, by tragic necessity, will be met and still fail in the end—Kent, in his own rough fashion, pleads with Lear to "Reverse thy doom" and "check / This hideous rashness."[15] A few lines later he issues the well-known imperative: "See better, Lear." Taken with the parallel tragedy of Gloucester and the gouging out of his eyes—as well as Goneril, Regan, and Edmund falsely appearing as faithful children, Edgar's disguise as Tom o' Bedlam, Kent's as Caius, the Fool as foolish, the probable double casting of Cordelia and the Fool, and of course Lear's lack of sufficient introspection and discernment—the motifs of sight and blindness recur throughout the play to reveal how *vision*, in a thematic and imaginative sense, relates to freedom and truth and its absence to captivity and delusions. How? More so than reason, in as much as it is force that vindicates reason through its instrumental use, it is an unguarded openness before the sensuous impulse for full (rather than restricted) gratification and the pious desire for necessity to become beautiful (the highest art) that author our best actions. We participate in the creation of truths or accept imaginary laws for self-overcoming. Laws and truths first *envisioned*, seen only in secret orders within nature, which we can then *foolishly* enact (even, if not especially, through radical passivity). Until we see truly and freely, we, due to force and all of its non-convivial expressions of power, always find the various injustices and impositions of reality we encounter on life's way highlighted by what *appear* to be inevitable erotic antagonisms and conflicts over wealth. *King Lear* demonstrates this with the eventual showdown between Lear and his eldest daughters, in which Lear, by his own admission, acknowledges the difference between the true and false needs and enlightened and base superfluidity:

> REGAN   What need one?
> LEAR   O, reason not the need! Our basest beggars
>   Are in the poorest thing superfluous.
>   Allow not nature more than nature needs,
>   Man's life's as cheap as beast's. Thou art a lady;
>   If only to go warm were gorgeous,
>   Why, nature needs not what thou gorgeous wear'st,
>   Which scarcely keeps thee warm. But, for true need—
>   You heaven's give me that patience, patience I need![16]

The heavens will, of course, answer his prayers in the timeless fashion of tragic irony. Lear will learn patience when that virtue, along with any other virtue, principle, law, or truth, is no longer of any restorative use to him personally.[17] And what might only seem an angry observation about the merits of privileged luxuries—Lear's knightly retinue and Regan's fine clothes—actually alludes to an aesthetic dimension of life that finds validation beyond mere reason or rationally determined necessity: there is more to life than degrees of bare necessity, the accumulation of wealth, and the exercising of political power.[18] For with *King Lear* Shakespeare arguably perfects the tragic retrieve begun with *Hamlet* in which an indifferent and indefinite world populated with imperfect characters takes center stage over any particular character.[19] So now, like Oedipus, like all genuinely tragic protagonists, Lear's culpability lies not with any list of identifiable causes that we might locate within his character—however insightful and instructive any item appears—rather with the curse of being at all.[20] Fate and destiny work against him and one another. The hero of tragedy is also its victim. Lear's chief culpability comes from being born at all. Yet this does not so much exempt Lear or anyone else from the responsibility of refusal and revision in accord with life's undergirding possibilities—the secret orders and laws of being that must always be discovered and created—as much as it presents a more complex and accurate representation of the imagined imperative (ever elective) that we see and render ourselves differently and transform (actual) necessity into something (potentially) beautiful. This development in Shakespeare—wherein the tragic world itself haunts us more so than any given character or deed—signals, consciously or not, a retrieve of "the tragic" that emphasizes ecstatic unity over existential individuation.

Aside. This retrieve also involves a less restrictive understanding of originality. Many, including Emerson, have noted that Shakespeare is not "original" in the sense we usually use that term.[21] Emerson tells us that originality consists in "weaving" together the materials and sources at our disposal. Most serious readers of and commentators on Shakespeare approach his plays through some aspect of his biography, various social and political tensions, or some event or aspect of the material and cultural conditions in which he lived. Like any great artist he becomes a conduit for social energies and his work a lens through which to see his world. Any given scholarly writing on *King Lear*, for example, might explore the decline of feudalism, fears of monarchical succession, national identity, the use of Holinshed or the anonymously authored *The True Chronicle History of King Leir and His Three Daughters*, the gunpowder plot, the plague, ecological crises, puritanism, scientific rationalism, an analysis of Renaissance gender and sexuality, or madness and the treatment of the insane. These investigations, whatever else they bear out, tend to demonstrate a most remarkably counterintuitive feature of poetic genius: "no great men are original" because they are "the most indebted."[22] Indebted to their situation, to the social problems and political possibilities surrounding them, to the ideological convictions and institutional practices that came before them, to certain events appearing on the horizon. Indebted to the tendencies in their language and the concreteness of their cultural iconography (and the sense of restraint and liberty they feel toward their tongue and tokens). The diversity of Shakespeare scholarship over four centuries after the fact testifies to his poetic power to represent perfectly the richness and uncertainty of his own world through his theatrically performed portraits in which we, age after age, continue to locate the richness and uncertainty of our own.

In this ancient and haunting world, however advanced or post-modern or decadent we find it, those tragic figures who most clearly bring the conflict between fate (natural or social) and destiny (personal and relational) into relief are those from whom force and power will strip all. Almost always privileged figures who forget, if they were ever able to recognize, that they only "have force on loan from fate" and that their reliance on force will blind them to the consequence that they will be destroyed by it.[23] And even admirable and principled figures like Antigone and Cordelia find themselves conspicuously caught up within this terrible system: not because tragedy is the result of individual sins or the consequence of greatness, however often those seem to lubricate and justify the tragic machinery, but because their very existence—our very existence—is a crime paid for with that very same existence: we will suffer and we will die.[24] Even those who do not have force on loan (in the form of authority, strength, gifts, wealth, etc.) and instead practice principles (virtues in the vein of charity, forgiveness, patience, compassion, etc.) that mitigate against power's pollutive influence must still live human lives shaped by finitude and mortality, contingency and circumstance. The origin and end are the same for all: a return to *nothing*. The Shakespearean and Emersonian retrieval of the original sense of the tragic embraces the *nothing* for purposes of art and the art of life, which in both cases results in an ecstatic unity of *what is as it really is* (the me dissolving into the *not me*) and *how it could be otherwise* (making life beautiful by elective participation in the *ordo amoris*). And while we can learn strategies (such as philosophy) and adopt ways of seeing differently (as with art) so that we might live joyfully and with some measure of peace, we must do so only without denying the harsh realities of life (whatever the state or stage of civilization) and the perpetual insecurities of our creaturely condition (however wise or advanced we believe we have become). This means that how we read the world and what lies hidden within it—regardless of where we begin or the roles fate has allotted to us—should also enact strategies concurrently "realistic" and "foolish": tragic heroes cannot deny their pathetic destiny or evade their dark fate. A crossroads always awaits. Tragic heroes can, as we all can, however, slowly habituate themselves to a way of life that accepts unforeseen and inevitable circumstances—and the differential potentialities they hold—as granting them the possibility to refuse to speak when speaking does more harm than good, to deny violence when (un-rehabilitated) reason or right justifies it.[25] *Possibilities otherwise*. This also means that blind belief in any ideology that purports to have a handle on fate and the use of any instruments pretending to direct force will never really serve love or bring genuine joy. Only the tragic art of life can accomplish such, though no guarantee exists that it will. We can only create illusions (strategies *as if*) to bear the weight of this world and choose to see it strangely (with honest and creative vision) and act foolishly (lovingly) in order to beautifully make or revise it.

Through Lear and his daughters and Gloucester and his sons Shakespeare invites us to reconsider our assumptions about taking our reality and relations for granted. The tensions he presents between fate (i.e., nature and the gods do not respond to our theories, beliefs, actions) and destiny (i.e., our actions, intentional or not, meaningfully shape us and our society) remain dialectically preserved and never adequately resolve outside of the expected tragic end. Beyond that end, however, who can say? Perhaps learning to "speak what we feel, not what we ought to say" is learning a new elective imperative.[26] In the play, Gloucester lamentingly defers to nature and the gods—"these late eclipses in the sun and moon portend no good to us"—while Edmund thinks blaming fate "the excellent foppery of the world."[27] A dramatic plot requires opposition. It creates the conditions by which different views and commitments come into conflict. And a complex and honest portrait of people and events rarely reduces to absolute judgments or certainties. But as we develop our interpretations and accounts afterward, the meaning of certain roles nevertheless tends to become more definitive. Even their ambiguities gain refinement. Upon reflection we have a better sense of things. As we discussed in Chapter 2, though no flat stereotype, Edmund is properly understood as primarily an opportunistic nihilist frustrated by social convention prior to seeing differently as a result of being wounded by his brother and facing his own death. His father first appears as a privileged fatalist before losing his eyes elicits a different sort of acquiescence to fate and his experience of the world: "I see it feelingly."[28] They execute their respective roles within the drama and are made to serve both the principal and the parallel plots.[29] They also both suffer and change, though—as with all tragedies—not in time to save themselves or alter the outcome. Similarly, at the end of *Oedipus Rex* we find the son of Laius changed by the sufferings demanded by the conflict between fate and destiny as well, but not for his deliverance or even the salvation of Thebes. He was cursed from the beginning. His life, like all uncanny riddle-solvers, became a living sacrifice so that whatever The Riddle of the Sphinx ever hides within itself might earn its temporary liberation from the tyranny of force and the forgetfulness of men: *truth arrives as the daughter of time and we measure that time by human suffering.*[30] Our apprenticeship to the truth, whatever shape the truth takes on or conclusions it carries, is then always tied to honest testimonies that attempt to recover what has been painfully taken by force and euphorically forgotten in time: we are not "things." By becoming what we are capable of recovering—through tragic transfiguration—we can remember that we are *good*. As Creon tells Oedipus near the end of *Oedipus the King*, "In season, all is good."[31] The tragic world—taken as nature, drama, history—will in time justify us and make us good. And truth appears as the testimony we live in response, silently or otherwise, to all of our suffering in this process of becoming. Vision born of a tragic imagination allows us to unearth laws that give us peace and joy while the cycle plays out before us. Life's sweetness returns in spite of all sufferings and teaches us, like Edgar, "to shift / Into madmen's rags."[32] To become fools.

Tragic figures, whether highlighted for the sake of a drama or not, will always become serviceable before *nothing*—that is, before the undergirding and recurring *difference* that houses the *ordo amoris* prior to any knowledge or belief—*because* their suffering and the suffering they bring down around them, intentionally or not, has run its course. In their brokenness they lose their privileged or functional use to the world of force. Their role is concluded. They have served whatever purpose force had for them and have become obsolete. The bit of force they had on loan has been defaulted on *or* it has been paid in full, either way those who "possessed" it are subsequently and mechanically disposed of. The joyous sense of tragedy—the Dionysian affirmation of the tragic life cycle—however, accepts suffering and death in a fashion that rather than serving force serves the undergirding potentiality of a future always undetermined. A future always open, except for the fact that the drama of difference will continue to recur. And all desirable outcomes, like those tragic crescendos wherein death is dealt out lavishly and all truths are revealed, will only ever be fleeting. That is, we, like the fictional characters bodied-forth in tragic drama or past personages of history, do not change the tragic nature of existence. Though these figures often neglect to do so themselves, or perhaps they try and fail, we nevertheless learn from them that we can and that we ought to discover the inner-possibility of being otherwise than the world of force would have us be: souls free to accept the world for what it is *and* desirous to make it beautiful where and when we can.

But our "view of the world," whatever it is, inhibits this retrieval of the joyous reception of the tragic. Prior to the rehabilitation of our reason (which we undertake due to its instrumental failure to see anything truly different) and the liberation of our imagination (which all great art conspires to do), the view of the world as "something that is viewed" necessitates that the world be a picture in the first place (which we should not confuse with a poetic portrait of nature like Shakespeare's that resists total enframement). This notion of "worldviews" whatsoever in fact profanes the world and distorts our understanding of it and ourselves.[33] It belittles what is at stake in interpretation. We should not confuse perspectivism with the meaningful interpretations of liberated subjects. Liberated subjects—authentic beings, self-cultured selves, *Übermenschen*—draw from a universal source. They lose themselves, become *nothing*, in order to do so. Then true *vision* comes. Vision as we find in the works of Shakespeare and Sophocles, Emerson and Nietzsche. Through the unity and perfection of its portrait—though it is not one—the world *becomes* a "metaphysical problem."

A riddle we feel drawn to solve. The portrait painted signals no mere perspective, the solution we pose no simple subjectivism. Rather, the drama rotates upon the axis of shared experiences, lexicons, values, myths, theories, histories: even if, and perhaps especially if, we hotly contest these common regions. Again, a dramatic plot requires opposition. Portraits of the world and of human interior life, ones which call attention to all of the recurring conflicts, come nearer to the truth of the way things are. A true vision of the world—a theory that will "explain all phenomena"—is no worldview as we normally use that term. We only attain true vision after dissolution into the *not me* and the subsequent drama of self-recovery. Further, the curse of being cannot be adequately acknowledged nor the subsequent imperative to see differently (vision) awakened when we receive the world simply as an object or thing "present" for us to experience. A cognitive resemblance that defers without alerting us to the fact that it is deferring. Under these conditions, no desire can be wrested from deep within and among us (personally and communally) to shed the illusory image of the world (to which society habituates us to confirm) and the delusive needs and truths it manufactures (and by which we order our lives). The parallel plots of Lear and his daughters and Gloucester and his sons show us that there is a dramatic reality that is being misread. They further show us that additional dissemblings—illusions—are required to strip Lear and Gloucester of their respective biases and views. They do not see the world or themselves for what they truly are and can be. Retrieving vision capable of seeing difference requires a unity without reduction or prior identity. Tragedy—which accomplishes a temporary disruption of the principle of individuation and a moment of ecstatic and occult unity—provides us this.

And without a tragic imagination? Without such vision *King Lear* would appear but an exquisitely terrible depiction of egocentrism in which frustrated desires to dominate the world only lead to the cursing of everything and everyone thought responsible for inhibiting those desires.[34] We would have but a couple of old, privileged, and unremarkable men who should have learned to "see better." Without the drama of self-recovery—souls won from out of the *nothing*—Lear himself would remain a kind of unliberated Narcissus whose actions reflect no consideration of the idealized possibilities of unrepressed *eros*.[35] Shakespeare's tragic retrieve, however, without denying the fate of force and its conflict with the drive of destiny, allows Lear and Gloucester and all around them to prepare the way for the return of the infant messiah—the possibility of life-affirming free play—indicating the brief respite before the enginery of tragedy once again begins its terrible down turn.

Love and Foolishness. We can trace the role of the fool in drama back to the *eirôn* of Greek comedy.[36] A genuine fool rarely comes across as entirely foolish or ineffectually mad ("This is not altogether fool, my lord"). His humorous function as such notwithstanding, the fool puts things into perspective. She states the obvious truths that those in positions of power seem unwilling or unable to see. He humorously inverts, cleverly turns the tables, brazenly brings up what others cannot admit. She cuts to the quick as if "in the know" and everyone—almost everyone—laughs at her wit and audacity. With the fool things become "ironic." And not only in comedy (e.g., Bottom), but in history (e.g., Falstaff), romance (e.g., Autolycus), tragedy (e.g., the Fool). A tragic fool in particular serves the drama by helping the protagonist—and not simply playgoers and readers—to realize that he too is ultimately a fool ("I am old and foolish"). The Fool informed Lear early on in the play:

LEAR Dost thou call me fool, boy?
FOOL All thy other titles thou hast given away; that thou wast born with.[37]

That he is perhaps even less than a fool:

FOOL now thou art an O without a figure. I am better than thou are now; I am a fool, thou art nothing.[38]

The fool holds up a mirror reminding us that we are all fools (we are all caught in "Lear's shadow" and "This cold night will turn us all to fools and madmen").[39] Or will become so as we realize our own follies and limitations by the role(s) allotted to us within the life drama. That *nothingness* awaits us too and no divine power spares us that fate. We are all doomed to become *different* again, so who are we kidding? Normally we would not entertain such demeaning determinations or pessimistic proclamations, but the fool delivers her message—which cuts through all ideologies—in such a way that both we and the protagonist can receive it, even if the latter can only do so near the end when toleration bypasses acceptance— "einem Possenreisser gleich"[40]—to land upon resignation by default of dying. Through ironic foolishness that acknowledges what witnesses are thinking and feeling—as well as whatever knowledge or emotions the "tragic hero" represses or fights to suppress—we enjoy not only confirmation but brief respites from the terrible tension slowly building in the tragedy: we can laugh and breathe a little ("sometimes I am whipped for holding *my peace*"). And when the words are not ironic or double entendres or puns, but are instead, as with Cordelia, direct, sincere, and loving, our breathing becomes sad exhalations, which are nevertheless still means of relief for our breaking hearts ("No cause, no, cause"). Additionally, beyond acknowledgment and mirroring, the fool can function as an informal chorus who "educates" us about what is happening and, in honor of his Dionysian or tragic function—the ecstatic expression of the erotic energies revealing the occult unity of nature's life-death cycle—he does so without trying to teach us morally explicit "lessons" ("not to give it away to his daughters, and leave his horns without a case"). And though the fool often operates with less overt agency to directly alter events, he possesses more dramatic liberty to say what he wants—or refuse to speak when she feels silence more fitting—thus, the fool's testimony, whether nodding and winking (the Fool) or quiet (Cordelia), almost always touches on truths that transcend the confines of what occurs on stage: the fool has a foot in both the play world and in ours. Whatever the fool says—even if we at first do not recognize the fool as a fool—is capable of rising to another register. In tragedy, this is the levity of truth and the gravity of love. It is as though the fool enjoys the blessings of serendipity as a curse and the curse of being as a good joke. And though the fool might be a slave, a servant, a clown, or a madman, she might also be an innocent, a darling; perhaps a trusted advisor or an unnamed servant. Clearly, a fool can be a loving daughter. And more so than his jokes, what really sets the fool apart is his ability to speak truth to power and to us with little to no regard—or at least an ironic regard—for his own well-being: he knows how tragedies end.

These dramatic truth-telling feats that the fool performs, as either subordinate clown or devastated darling, indicate the cyclical reversal of the world order. Those instances in which an "innocent"—one "who [has] fallen into the lowest degree of humiliation"—speaks more wisely than any ruler or sage of the age serves as a repetition of the ancient counter wisdom: tragedy shows us how liberation comes through destruction and knowledge through madness. The fool bests everyone and yet still loses because the *true fool*—Dionysus or any genuine instance of irrational eroticism or free play—must always win in order that the cycle itself, which he represents, can always win. The fool, whether a clown, a buffoon, or a jester, does not only act foolishly, he makes a fool of everyone else. Even if not especially of kings and gods. Through the Fool, Lear, like Dionysus, becomes, or already ever was, the *true fool*. The tragic hero is always the real fool. The uncanny "idiot."[41] He cannot outrun or outwit or overthrow the world of force or the ontological engine. He can only play his part for as long as force (or the drama) allows. Of course, Lear and Dionysus as characters—as repetitions or "perfect representations"—are not "the same," rather only what lies behind them, drives them, and is shared by them—the erotic and alien *not me* of nature: *difference*—finds expression through the fool's fool-making and explicit revelation as the suffering they endure strips away each illusion of identity and delusion of agency. The fool unmasks them. Or her silence invites them to unmask themselves. The fool makes it possible for the differential foolishness of others to become conspicuous and acknowledgeable (though never absolutely cognizable). While originally Dionysus might have been all the characters, the world inverting—destructing, correcting, restoring—character of the fool most pronouncedly manifests the god's essential representation in the drama.[42] *Until* the protagonist, whether king or god or faithful daughter, has undergone sufficient preparation (*suffering*) to be revealed as the *true fool* par excellence. Then it is time for the trick, the exchange, the true wisdom. The tragic engine turns the card or throws the dice and uncanny cleverness becomes the wiles of innocence. The darling's innocence becomes agency.

Aside. Instead of taking Christ as true tragic fool whose suffering *is* an affirmation of human life, whose silences *are* subversive to nihilistic social and political practices, whose sayings *are* pronounced recognitions of the world of force, Nietzsche's thought—which is, it should be clear by now, never far from our considerations here—alternates between an insightful and nuanced assessment that is more critical of Christianity than Christ on the one hand, and (often) inconsistent polemics against weakness, pity, equality, misunderstanding, and *ressentiment* on the other.[43] At times he seems able to acknowledge what a historical person named Jesus appears to represent—"there has been only one Christian"[44] who gave us the "best bit of an ideal life"[45]—but for the most part he has no interest in developing the revaluative possibilities this ancient figure could represent: as Nietzsche had all manner of metaphysics to overturn, he could only spare Christ so much "humiliation." In his estimation, which seems largely correct when measured against the historic institution and its masses, Christianity corrupted nobility, strength, and beauty.[46] It demonized them. But only as the religion *about* Jesus, not the collective myths and teachings *of* Jesus (to whatever degree we can reconstruct them).[47] Mythically and symbolically speaking, what Nietzsche finds fascinating and affirming about Dionysus' being cut to pieces, his association with intoxication, and his disguised appearance, appears parallel with Christ's passion, wine miracle, and the messianic secret. Reading Jesus in this way allows his stories to contribute to—rather than inhibit or act as cause further necessitating—the overturning of metaphysics and the revaluation of all values. The true fool—as suffering tragic hero serving as scapegoat—undermines the economically and politically powerful, not because power itself is necessarily bad but because it is usually illusory or the powerful perennially fail to affirm life through their use of it. The powerful almost always seem to lack vision for the *ordo amoris* (which, if taken as meaningful structure for life, Gadamer argues, would be the transformative result of joyous play[48]). They embrace their pathetic reification. Instead of joining in the joyous tragedy of suffering, the powerful—whom Dionysus topples long before Christ makes fools of them—use force and power to suppress the ancient and recurring conspiracy to overthrow old values and rescue pre-sublimated *eros*.[49] "O, it is excellent / To have a giant's strength, but it is tyrannous / To use it like a giant."[50] Had he permitted himself to read Jesus as Christ O' Bedlam, a role that joins peace and destruction (personally and politically) and that calls for a true fool's wily performance of innocence, then Nietzsche might have seen how the mythic account of his life did indeed testify to a tragic world without end or final redress: the βασιλεία τοῦ Θεοῦ ἐντὸς ὑμῶν ἐστιν, "The kingdom of God is within and among you."[51] He might have then seen how any possibility of heroic "transcendence" for Christ is tied to his authentically tragic "down-going," and that the whole affair begins and ends only *here*. But "*Nur* Narr! *Nur* Dichter!"[52] Jesus, as Emerson tells us, was "ravished by beauty," and he taught an equality born not of weakness as such but of divine—rather than merely illusory—power agonistically won from out of a slumbering conformity.[53] But only for fools, only for poets.[54]

Whatever the dissemination of energies throughout the various roles within the drama—though most pronounced in the fool and the tragic hero (who becomes the *true fool*)—the Dionysian finds its most peculiar expression in the performance of possession, in a feigned and dissembling madness.[55] The possessed, dissembling fool—*Lear's* mad Tom O' Bedlam—whatever his ostensible original motivation, makes it possible for others to participate in their own salvation. The poet plays upon the usual assumptions and fears of possession as unwelcome destructive displacements, and inverts them as welcomed oracles of wisdom and assistance. While the character of the Fool makes fools of everyone else—Lear, the tragic hero, in particular—the arrival of Edgar as Poor Tom, as dissembling madman, temporarily transfers the Dionysian energies away from the fool and other agents within the play and brings them to bear on his own performance of madness and impoverishment, his own display of "clownish demonology."⁵⁶ The temporary transfer and focus of these energies by way of feigned possession serves as a special invitation for others to respond to these energies in a new way: electing into the *ordo amoris* becomes desirable.⁵⁷ While fate remains unalterable, electing into the erotic order lets characters change their destiny. The inevitable conflict occurring at the crossroads—where fate and destiny meet—now takes on an *ideal difference*. The outcome is unchanged but the approach is inverted, the significance revalued. Idiocy becomes prudence, poverty wealth, powerlessness power. Poor Tom becomes Lear's philosopher and Gloucester's eyes. Lear literally strips, Gloucester leaps to his "death." And yet Lear will eventually come to rest and acknowledge the inversion of the world ("We'll go to supper i' the morning") and Gloucester will be reborn ("Thy life's a miracle"). They will of course still be destroyed, but the storm, the hearth, the imagined court and cliffs, provides them with the opportunity to acknowledge (without fully understanding) their own foolishness—to be stripped of their illusions and become *nothing*. And to do so in order that they can retrieve their most essential selves and find themselves en route to rehabilitated instincts, in order that they can prepare to meet their end. They now willingly offer themselves to the tragic world ("You ever-gentle gods, take my breath from me"). Their *pathos* (destiny) has been exorcised and they find themselves free for their unalterable fate. And the fools and madmen that assisted them in this terrible adventure did so without ideological promotion or negation.[58] And what we come to see through imaginative indication and poetic representation—rather than religious teachings or mere moral lessons—is that beyond simply telling us how heroes fall, tragedies (and sometimes dark romances) reveal the necessity of sacrifice under the curse of being and for the realization of our shame within the world of force.[59] In *Lear* nearly all of the principal players will serve as scapegoats for the world to begin again.[60] Not to lift the curse but to be able to bear it again with justification. For a while. Shakespeare shows us a generation—typified through the "sculptural relief" of the tragic hero and all those near to him—become fit, and the generation subsequently finds itself pardoned by a foolish conspiracy.

We find this Dionysian counter wisdom—true foolishness befitting and seasonally redressing the tragic world—not only in ancient Greek drama but in St. Paul:

> But God hath chosen the foolish things of the world to confound the wise; and God hath chosen the weak things of the world to confound the things which are mighty / And base things of the world, and things which are despised, hath God chosen, *yea*, and things which are not, to bring to nought things that are.[61]

And

> but as it is written, Eye hath not seen, nor ear heard, neither have entered into the heart of man, the things which God hath prepared for them that love him.[62]

We can find this counter wisdom and upending of the world order whenever a fool appears, whatever the dramatic category. In the comedy, *A Midsummer Night's Dream*, Shakespeare appropriates the Pauline language above to craft Bottom's famous speech, which masterfully allows clownishness and wisdom to coalesce:

> I have had a most rare vision. I have had a dream—past the wit of man to say what dream it was. Man is but an ass if he go about to expound this dream. Methought I was—there is no man can tell what. Methought I was, and methought I had—but man is but a patched fool if he will offer to say what methought I had. The eye of man hath not heard, the ear of man hath not seen, man's hand is not able to taste, his tongue to conceive, nor his heart to report what my dream was. I will get Peter Quince to write a ballad of this dream. It shall be called "Bottom's Dream" because it hath no bottom.[63]

In *Lear* we find something similar, not simply with the Fool's many cutting and amorous jibes but with his Prophecy:

> When priests are more in word than matter;
> When brewers mar their malt with water;
> When nobles are their tailors' tutors;
> No heretics burned, but wenches' suitors;
> When every case in law is right;
> No squire in debt, nor no poor knight;
> When slanders do not live in tongues,
> Nor cutpurses come not to throngs;
> When usurers tell their gold i' the field,
> And bawds and whores do churches build;
> Then shall the realm of Albion
> Come to great confusion.[64]

Many textual commentators believe the Prophecy to be spurious, an "incongruous theatrical interpolation."[65] Some, however, set the textual issue aside and offer readings of it that open up some of the play's deeper themes and which show it accomplishing something improbable for any simple or second-rate interpolation.[66] If we go beyond the easy laugh and read its satirical criticisms seriously, we see a fundamental breakdown of societal order: *when* priests extol virtue but have none and brewers water down their beer but not their prices and nobles follow fashion more closely than their tailors and instead of heretics burning in flames we have Johns burning with venereal diseases and all court cases are "just" from the lawyers' point of view and knights who should be living faithfully and frugally are deep in debt and everyone is slandering everyone and pickpockets and thieves run rampant and financial opportunists count their ill-gotten gain openly and the church hypocritically accepts money for its buildings and budgets from the sex industry it castigates, well, *then* Albion, Britain, will surely fall. Of course, the Fool's prophecy has him speaking from within a drama set in Britain's ancient past, but he is addressing what was—and will ever be—the contemporary world. The Fool points out a variety of lamentable social practices that everyone knows to be true in their actual daily life in the early seventeenth century. And in the early twenty-first century. Though we might think of it in terms of a "warning of things to come" that can be avoided, we have to remember that as humorous as anything the Fools says usually is, it is nevertheless still a prophecy in a tragedy: they always come true. Or more accurately: *they are already true.* An ideal Albion never was and never will be because in the tragic world "the human condition is permanent."[67] Perhaps the Fool presenting this bitter pill helps it go down more smoothly. In any case, at the end of the Prophecy we have an additional element that confirms its timeless timeliness.

> Then comes the time, who lives to see't,
> That going shall be used with feet.
> This prophecy of Merlin shall make; for I live before my time.[68]

The Fool here clearly steps outside of the dramatic framework and addresses his contemporaries.[69] In this moment he transcends the stage and the time, and speaks of what is as if it is to come, including his own life. Shakespeare has endowed him with an awareness that while he is present in the age in which the drama is set, long before even the time of Merlin—and Merlin tellingly lives his own life in reverse: the future is his past, his past is his future—the Fool's actual present lies with his audience, far in the future. The importance of this being? Though particulars and degrees of intensity will change, nothing essential about the world of force ever changes. No ideal world or enlightened age awaits us. Only the wiles of innocence and the various performances that allow us to accept the world as it is and yet still join in the "secret church of a better world" that itself never succumbs to or attempts to overtake the world in which we find ourselves.[70] This secret church allows us, as those who must endure this life, the opportunity to love everyone else who must endure it also. To collaborate with them when we can. To refuse them when necessary. It allows us the opportunity to become fools for them when we must. If only for a while.

Nature and Nothing. The story of King Lear reaches out from Britain's deep pagan past. Geoffrey of Monmouth's *History of the Kings of Britain* from the twelfth-century CE places him in the eighth-century BCE and provides Shakespeare, either directly or indirectly through Holinshed or the anonymously authored *True Chronicle History of King Leir*, with a basic anatomy for his *Lear*. Some have attempted to locate Lear among the legends of the Tuatha de Danann, wherein he becomes a water spirit and the father of the famous magician Manannan Mac Lir, a god of the sea.[71] In the medieval Irish *Book of Fermoy* we find a tale in which the son of Lir, elevated to the role of a "father-god," presides over an assembly of the divine chiefs after they have been granted (or relegated to) the "underworld" or "other world" after their war with the invading Milesians. He divides and apportions the land between them, establishing their well-known hillside residences or "fairy mounds" (*sidhes*). The old pagan gods retire from war and descend into the earth. There, within their lovely hills and valleys, they give themselves over to music, feasting, and love.[72] Hidden and at peace in their collective "land of promise" they daily renew their immortality and invulnerability by feasting upon a magic pig provided by Manannan.[73] In time, these beings become "the fair folk," "the gentle folk," "the good neighbors." And, largely, with the exception of *Samhain*, the one night a year on which the veil between the waking world and the dreaming world thins and spirits roam free, these old warrior gods—possibly the evolvements of heroes long buried under barrows—remain within their subterranean demesnes, celebrating their former glory in perpetuity while the mortal world tends to itself. Their work finished and their deeds poetically preserved. One intriguing detail, however, remains: the magic swine that the son of Lir supplies, which is resurrected daily so that the old gods might feast upon it and sustain their immortality, can only be cooked and served if four "true tales" are told. The son of Lir claims to come from a land where there is nothing but truth.[74] Lies, consequently, prohibit the feast from commencing and thus threaten the immortality of the gods. Without truth they would fade from myth and memory.

Aside. Of course, no reading should place too much weight upon the speculative connection between King Lear and the Lir who sired Manannan Mac Lir. Even if we could parse fact from fiction and establish a reliable historic portrait—which we cannot—strictly speaking, as a matter of interpretation, while interesting, it is for our purposes here only of mild consequence whether or not Geoffrey of Monmouth's account of the pseudohistorical king itself descended largely or solely from mythic tales (tales that were likely the work of earlier medieval scribes). Moreover, nothing guarantees that mining the old myths and folktales, however we find or reconstruct them, allows us to unearth insights otherwise inaccessible from Shakespeare's play itself. What then does an association with myth accomplish? Observing elements and connections from any known or prospective source—histories, mythologies, folktales, demonologies, classical texts, the Bible, contemporaneous events, legal documents, and so on—can indeed facilitate (*or* misdirect) an investigation, but they can never open up interpretive possibilities altogether absent without them. Interpretations begin with, and are delimited by, the text itself. Our self-transparency, research rigor, and imagination can only activate (*or* fail to activate) what the texts already possesses. Even glaring omissions must be omissions that properly belong to the text. The efficacy of the practice here—retrieving this small fragment of the mythic and folkloric tapestry related to Lear—ultimately rests with honoring tragedy's indebtedness to myth and the thematic elements it highlights. Clearly, not all of Shakespeare's tragic dramas draw upon mythology or medieval lore, rather the tragic frontier itself—the genuinely tragic world revealed *as hinterland* and *march*—signals an awareness that *certainty*, by any stripe other than our finite condition, is a delusion: a delusion to which myths have always testified. Myths contain an uncanny wisdom for all denizens of the tragic world, while tragedies, which draw directly or indirectly (even unconsciously) upon a cultural milieu of myths (or whatever passes for them), show us the *real value* of that wisdom: fate is unalterable, madness requires expression, everyone becomes fit for their end. Ritual and performance in concert with ideals, like love, justice, and beauty, mitigate such suffering without denying its necessity. In this way, myth and tragedy—and an idealism born from out of the world of force—work together to reveal humankind's oldest and most fundamental attempts to poetically "create an understandable place for itself in an indifferent universe."[75]

The gods gave up their rule of the land and entered into the earth, their days of war and worry behind them. In later centuries they would only meddle, menace, and assist on occasion in proportion to their new station. Sustained by "true tales" and culturally preserved in myth and custom, they are, on the one hand, buried and at peace, and, on the other, still present all about the countryside and in the memory of the living. Even in their departure the gods persist. But perhaps only because they willingly participated in their own *katábasis* and narratively continue to perform their daily eulogizing before the feast—which taken together might approximate their "funerary rites"—could they find immortality and peace in death. Perhaps their ritualistic return to the earth and to a generative nothingness allowed for their imagined recurrence in future cultural performances? Acts of storytelling and superstitious customs? The living who daydream among the mounds and feel watched in the forests? They are not forgotten. Subsequently, though capricious and proud, and with peculiar infractions notwithstanding, these spirits did not go about taking revenge upon the living while they withered away under the curse of resentment or madness.[76] Instead, at home and at peace in the earth, they became synonymous with the hills and the landscape. They went on to provide a rich and wonderfully unreliable narrative for the topographical surround and the cycles of nature, for the land's peace and sublimity, for the earth's terrors and mysteries. Whether the tales paint them mild and pranking, or cruel and peculiar, they endured as symbols for what appears both familiar and alien about nature.[77] And though Protestant Renaissance England would try to demonize them, these heroes who became gods who became the hidden folk of the hills would continue to find life in the ambiguous spaces provided them by superstition and poetry, as well as in nature and events of curious causation. With enviable ontological resilience within the imaginative realms they came to occupy, these beings resisted simple categorization as demoted angels or genus of demon.[78] They possessed such strange motives and demanded respect for such archaic customs that no final chapter can conclude the book of their being. Nevertheless, it must be made clear: *they are one with the land and part and parcel of Shakespeare's culture.*[79] They represent a vital part of the beliefs, habits, and natural surround of Renaissance England. And the mythic, folkloric, and religious imagery that a people inherent serve as frescoes adorning the interiors of their collective imagination. The cultural symbols that lay hold of us. Shakespeare's audience thus receives *King Lear*, in part, through an aggregate register of mystery plays, angels and demons, saints, churches, itinerant monks, *and* pagan festivals, hidden spirits, witches, ancient mounds, stone circles, and wandering madmen. A register well acquainted with the various realities of mortality and the very human need for some spiritual recourse.

Let us recall that Lear wishes for the benefits of kingship without the duties required of it. He wants to enter into his own *sidhe*, but without the necessary restrictions of movements and rights. Without dying. He still intends to come and go as he pleases, to consider any hearth his home. Without obligation. He desires to feast and sing and enjoy the glory of former days. Without sacrifice. And yet the logic of early abdication prior to debilitation or death aside: (1) instead of orchestrating a ritual of passage into the underworld (so as to become incorporated into an otherworld), (2) instead of placing the allotment of lands in the hands of another (whether an unbiased agent or a seer or based upon genuine merit or tradition), (3) instead of four repetitions of truthful speech (the number of a completed natural cycle), Lear initiates a funerary game that mocks the drama of descent. Part of the terrible power of *King Lear*—widely acknowledged as the most devastating of Shakespeare's plays—lies not only in the king's unconscious sabotaging of love but his profanation of tragedy itself as the human spectacle intended to venerate the curse of being. What he should accept he rejects, what he should honor he avoids.[80] Further, while heroes are doomed to demonstrate for us that the tragic engine, with terrible irony, uses their disavowals and avoidances to fulfil its purposes, Shakespeare perfects that doom with *King Lear* by writing it into the atmosphere for us to breathe.

―――

Aside. If tragedy already signals the particularization of a curse from which there is no escape, no avoiding the price of existence and the consequences of our actions—whether well intended or not, whether well considered or not— then *King Lear* extends the account beyond the tragic hero himself to encompass the whole of society. Put another way, Shakespeare retrieves the origins of tragic drama *as a social phenomenon*: Athenian tragic dramas from the fifth century were "public rites, performed at religious festivals … they were above all reflections of *group-experience*."[81] Whatever hides in our habits and institutions and metaphysical assumptions—in our myths and fables—is brought to light in tragic art. Moreover, genre itself seems to lose a distinctive step as tragedy's phenomenality touches everything. At the turn of the century, beginning with *Hamlet*, even Shakespeare's comedies unfold more darkly. We now find all of the plays, regardless of genre or plot, set in the tragic frontier. Cruel villains *and* loving fools begin to display greater fidelity to the audience's own growing anxiety and inner complexity. Audiences' nascent self-estrangement began to feel more familiar. Shakespeare's composite dramas drew out grave extremes in response to those underlying ambiguities. Subsequently, while still larger than life, all the protagonists after Hamlet—and Lear in particular—are no longer really the loci of the tragedy, only the most visible victims of society's crimes against itself presented in stark relief. The plots and performances of Shakespeare's fully realized tragedies, like those ancient Athenian dramatic venerations of the Dionysian, disclose the many ways in which we delude ourselves with self-importance and inevitably allow force to ruin, at least temporarily, what we should cherish. Put another way, these "high tragedies" reveal that what lays low a culture—and not simply rare individuals—is something to be found rooted in that culture's own spiritual structure[82]: societally specific desires more driven by fears of transition, or resistance to transition, than the convivially instantiated ideals derived in order to lessen the destructive tendencies found in those fearful desires. "Values" that assist us in holding off the temptation to let anxieties compel us to be certain about uncertain things, doubtful of reliable things, and confused about which is which. In any case—in every case—now the "tragic flaw" no longer resides exclusively within the moral psychology of the tragic hero as a lesson of character for us, but as an existential characteristic of the modern world in which we live. If only old spirits could still haunt the hills of this modern world and whisper alternative accounts, both natural and true. Tales old, different, and new.

―――

Lear, understandably, wants to benefit from death without dying or assuming death's limitations. And in place of burying a body or putting a scapegoat under the knife, his game sacrifices and inters truth.[83] He tries to orchestrate his own Faustian bargain *with himself*, treating his daughters as mere narcissistic proxies. Yet once he gives away the political power upon which the deal stands, and as Goneril and Regan move to reign him in, Lear realizes that he has no real remedy. His rage ascends as his sanity descends. All he has left are words that fail to persuade, curses writ upon tablets of fetid air:

> No, you unnatural hags,
> I will have such revenges on you both,
> That all the world shall—I will do such things—
> What they are, yet I know not; but they shall be
> The terrors of the earth![84]

What he needs is now impossible to acquire. He banished it at the outset along with the daughter who represented it:

> Thou hast her, France; let her be thine; for we
> Have no such daughter, nor shall ever see
> That face of hers again.[85]

Yet, as we know, Cordelia returns. She returns, however, as part of the formula of force, caught in dialectical conflict. No longer silent and loving witness to truth, she returns as "justice" to counter "injustice." It is, as it almost always is, utterly understandable. Her personal affection for her father and the offence she takes at his treatment by her sisters lures her out of her tragic idealism and into justifiable action. Justice is always betrayed by what can be justified. Rarely by actual injustice. And given his exquisite nihilistic rumblings and psychological descent—again, too late to matter—we are left wondering what is more maddening for Lear: his daughters perceived disloyalty or his self-imposed powerlessness? He does not yet hold the transcendental sense of proportion born of tragic idealism, so he does not see how his fate crosses his destiny by *necessity*. Clearly his elder daughters do not have his best interests at heart (and, really, *why* should they?). And whatever power Lear possesses post-abdication lingers only as fading prestige, which only moves those who value honor ("What is honor?"), and his allotment of knights was only ever force on loan, a loan his eldest daughters quickly refuse to underwrite.

Aside. We might wonder what would have happened had Cordelia capitulated in the opening scene. Or had her father desired truth rather than flattery? What if the topic had been justice? Or each daughter shared her favorite (true) story about their father? How different would the severity or timing of the tragedy been had Lear—or Cordelia—done something else? Had Goneril or Regan spoken truthfully? Being a tragic drama, a fall was forthcoming, but the particular brutality of it all emerges when a father and his daughters deviate extravagantly from the *love-truth* relation around which tragedy, one way or another, always entwines itself. Lovers, friendships, bonds of kinship, fidelity to the gods, love of virtue. Tragedy elicits expression of the relation, often spontaneously for dramatic effect, usually in acts or gestures responding in close proximity to death. Last words, passionate speeches, principled pronouncements, confessions. When we scorn the relation between love and truth, we call forth unseen furies to haunt and correct us. The *time-truth* relation, quite differently, proceeds without necessary erotic predicate or need for particular dialectical conditions (though love and conflict are always present). In a transhistorical sense, no biased party "possesses" truth, especially a monopoly on truth. Rather, in time, after much suffering, truth emerges from her imprisonment: *veritas filia temporis*.[86] "Time shall unfold what pleated cunning hides."[87] We find truth clothed in what has been preserved of the honest and courageous accounts given and witnessed in relation to love. This time-truth relation speaks to a violent and unhurried historical drama and a dark natural world we barely know. An alien providence for which we provide a scientific or religious explanation after the fact. The love-truth relation, however, rides upon a lesser necessity. It always comes down to decisions—acting upon moods or habituated hesitations—marked by fidelity (or infidelity) to *what is* as those who encounter it *feel it should be*. A matter of desire.[88] There is never a guarantee that truth—as it relates to love—will be spoken or silently attested to. The truth of time does not rely upon our caprice or earnestness. The imperative to speak the truth or silently witness it falls upon the powerless more often than not because they can see what is really going on. The innocent or (not so innocent) fool who sees the emperor's nakedness.

―――

Serving as fuel for the tragic engine, Lear's faults and failures guarantee that he will not partake in *nothing's* productive possibilities before "descending into the earth." He will not adequately face his death and retrieve the spiritual salve of imaginary ideals in time to own his destiny. No freedom, much less peace. He will not become a king under the hill who lives free in dreams of a better Albion, but a mad, impotent, and pathetic shadow. Homeless. Only poetic language, friendship, and the common heath allow him, even as madness sets in, to linger long enough for the engine of being to correct him. *By force.* Those convivial institutions—poetry, friendship, a free commons in which to work, wander, and wonder—often instruments of salvation, do not seem like blessings here. They provide no solace, create no secret church. They seem only retardants prolonging everyone's suffering. But tragedy, we must always remember, makes use of everything. Including what we rely on to endure it. *King Lear* shows us this. Not aristocratically as *Coriolanus* or seductively as *Antony and Cleopatra*, or as wickedly rewarding as *Macbeth*, but much more despairingly for its emphasis of the process' indifference. If forgiveness is what allows tragedies temporary deferment as tragicomic "romances," its lateness in *Lear* reverberates almost unbearably.

Further, Lear does not divide and allocate the land according to the will of the gods or an ancient tradition or an esteemed principle, nor does he follow any counsel on the matter. Shakespeare deviates from the anonymously authored *True Chronicle History* of 1605 on this point, wherein Leir listens to his counselors and engages in deliberation. The love test there speaks more to coercing Cordelia to marry for civic-minded reasons, rather than reflecting taboo energies or Lear's psychological inadequacies.[89] Dividing the kingdom might arguably stave off civil war (or perhaps provide more traction for it). Nevertheless, she refuses. But Shakespeare's *King Lear* omits such scenes and gives us a sovereign uninterested in calm deliberation or in seeking the will of the gods or in following traditions. He does not submit to anything; he rather requires that all submit to him. His actions arrive self-serving and, at best, as a caricature of concern for the land, its people, and his daughters. He no doubt loves Cordelia to the degree to which he is capable, but not freely and not ideally as a father ought to love a daughter. This explanation seems more in line with the mockery of ritualistic descent he performs and the implicit derision it demands of everyone else than in any genuine gesture of magnanimity or cunning statecraft. If freedom and peace were going to be possibilities for Lear, for his family, for his kingdom, then a real exchange—a meaningful sacrifice—needed to occur. Entering into an imagined "Land of Promise" as his mythic kin had done—as faithfully returned to the earth, as having overcome themselves through descent, as having achieved rest within the world (as it is otherwise)—requires submission to something greater than himself: a law, a tradition, a principle, an idea. *An ideal.* Even recognizing a truce or an honorable defeat. Perhaps *if* Shakespeare's Lear came to us as more of a "primal chief" among the ancient Celts rather than as an anachronistic "English monarch" historically interpolated, one with stronger affective ties to the land (rather than invoking nature to curse his children), one who sought and shared wisdom (rather than rejecting it as insubordination), one who lead through persuasion (rather than force)—which given the prestige, rhetorical facility, and poetic power that Shakespeare *has* bestowed upon him, gives these alternative capabilities a degree of plausibility—*then* we would have a very different tragedy.[90] When tragic protagonists do everything we could reasonably ask of them and a dark fate still imposes upon them, as with Oedipus and Hamlet, or they do everything we hope they do not do (or only secretly wish for them to do), as with Medea and Macbeth, or some variation within this ethical spectrum, we more easily dispense our character assassinations as analyses of their respective "tragic flaws" or "sins" (*hamartía*), which we deploy in order to explain why the tragedy happened and how it could have been avoided. However interesting or insightful, clearly such speculative analyses "miss the mark" in their lack of recognizing that *nothing* halts the tragic engine and alters the final doom of those so fated, which is precisely what every tragedy demonstrates whatever its particular plots and characterizations: we cannot deliberate or decide or act our way out of the tragedy. With Lear, though we catalogue his inadequacies, the anxiety and dread that the play educes ultimately lies not in the king's failure to be a sagacious chieftain rather than an impetuous monarch, or a loving father rather than a libidinally repressed or impotent old man, or an imprecator rather than a poet: the terrible feelings and uncomfortable responses arise as a result of the materiality of the age, the socio-psychological conditions of life, and the realities of mortality itself being perfectly captured and reflected back at the audience. From whatever time and from whatever world a genuine tragedy comes, it reminds us, like the fool's mirror does so explicitly for our own foolishness, that though we might refuse to face it, we live in a tragic world and we inexorably return from whence we came. And no politics, religion, economics, technology, or blissful ignorance will spare us.

Moreover, Lear's love contest in the opening scene not only ignores the repetitions of truth required of ritual descent—true songs, elegies, and stories—it instead requires repetitions of lies. It profanes both the *ordo amoris* (which underlies the *topos* of the speeches) and truth as testimony (silent or spoken witness of what is as it is and as it should be). Only Cordelia's foolish silence in that scene allowed for a moment of truth. Kent does indeed speak up in accord with his conscience, and the unnamed First Servant of Act 3 admirably attempts to stop his master, Cornwall, from gouging out Gloucester's remaining eye, but nothing ever draws-out injustice and political madness like loving silence. Such silence is utterly vulnerable, dangerous, foolish. The shame it generates has no equal in history or in works of imagination. Emerson understands the power of silence: "I like the silent church before the service begins, better than any preaching;" "Let us be silent,—so we may hear the whisper of the gods"; "Meantime within man is the soul of the whole; the wise silence; the universal beauty, to which every part and particle is equally related, the eternal ONE."[91] And though Emerson also advocates for speaking up when silence serves disenfranchising traditions or facilitates complicity in social injustices, it is more often the case, then as now, that what passes for truth or righteous judgment proceeds from ideological biases and dominating rationalities rather than from any freely won ideals. Social conflicts tend to show us how force, in one form or another, still reigns and determines all the roles: victim, victor, villain, and so on. Part of the reason Emerson restricts his social and political proclamations to select topics, and often manages to retain an element of ambiguity even then—except in the most execrable extremes, like slavery and women's rights—lies with how groups require conformity, place demands on individuals to surrender the integrity of their conscience, and enforce misrepresentations regarding the severity and clarity of any given issue. In general, we should think more and speak less. Emerson exhorts us not to be so quickly inclined to identify ourselves with any exclusionary association (even in the name of inclusion). Now a new issue arises every day by which society expects us to divide ourselves and take up positions that prohibit quiet contemplation, that disallow time, consideration, equivocality, and careful responses and nuanced articulations. As with our habituated needs to be immediately affirmed, amused, and respected, every event now requires immediate attention and "just" redress. No mysteries, no secret spaces, no private lives.[92] This results in a view of vulnerability that demands acceptance (if not admiration), thereby ensuring that nothing about it actually remains perilous. Outside of maintaining certain institutions and securing the viability of select social relations, socially enforced reciprocity regarding our own most possibilities to be ourselves—with our own strange plans and daring convictions—only delegitimizes shame's authentic role within society.[93] Reason here remains instrumental and *eros* remains repressed and society subsequently distorts even further. If any offense, irrespective of its actual social intensity, can become rhetorically framed in terms of social injustice—when the basic commitments and conventions of an oppressive ideology condition our very subjectivity and sociality—then, ipso facto, no offense will find genuine redress in the justice provided by society. The formula for the frame fails. "But let the frame of things disjoint, both the worlds suffer." Injustices within society, subsequently, become more deeply submerged within the non-convivial institutional mechanisms that enforce them and which invisibly promote their practice. And not unlike other mad tyrants found in Shakespeare—Richard, Macbeth, Leontes[94]—Lear foreruns this socio-psychological fever pitch of modernity in which we demand noise in place of silence, and chatter takes the place of genuine discourse.[95] This development has been radicalized by a modern technological infrastructure that makes information and communication direct and instantaneous, granting a false sense of agency and bolstering the illusion of force's retreat into history. And except for cynics, this explains why everyone expresses such surprise when power and force reveal themselves openly. When all of the unresolved matters come to light. As when a father curses his children as they reveal who they really are. As when racists march openly, torches in hand, through the town square. As when our politicians curse us and we respond in kind.

We must remember here, once again, that neither Lear or Cordelia or anyone else possesses the power to pause or correct the tragedy. It is fated. And our roles as readers and attendees rests with recognizing the various truths the playwright has poetically indicated about the world and human existence. As we speculate about what Lear "could have done" or "should have done" we do so only to understand better the implications of what he actually did. To understand better the many ways in which force works against *us*. Tirelessly, invisibly, plainly. And, if we are fortunate, we succumb to the desire to retrieve strategies from the Stoics, Spinoza, Emerson, Nietzsche, Marcuse, Deleuze and anyone else able to assist us in developing our own tragic idealism (even if the source appears loath to celebrate tragedy or laments the lexicon of idealism).

Where does this leave us? The full realization of the tragic world that Shakespeare accomplishes with *Lear* warrants its well-known thematization of nature and nothing. Spirits and old gods populate the hills and forests of this ancient world. Nature herself is a goddess (and invoked as such by Lear and Edmund).[96] In that mythic Britain, "natural" indicates alignment with divine purposes present in and as nature itself. "Unnatural," conversely, signifies that someone or something is set against those purposes, reminding us that the corruption of the best is that which becomes the worst (*corruptio optimi quae est pessima*).[97] When Lear addresses the elements and rages against his daughters, he implores the gods to take vengeance on his "two pernicious daughters."[98] Due to their unnatural acts against him, they have become nature's "enemies."[99] Enemies to the gods. The old powers within the earth "that keep this dreadful pother o' er our heads" ought to awaken and take vengeance on those who have violated the laws of nature. Should they fail do so, we will fulfill that role and destroy each other. As Albany will go on to say to Goneril:

> If that the heavens do not their visible spirits
> Send quickly down to tame these vile offenses,
> It will come,
> Humanity must perforce prey on itself,
> Like monsters of the deep.[100]

If the gods do nothing then we ourselves must, by necessity, become the agents of divine retribution. And our justice is monstrous. In cursing his daughters Lear continues to curse himself for his own violations against nature, against veneration of the tragic engine in his descent. Additionally, outside of the ancient world of the play, in Shakespeare's own time, the wheels of Renaissance humanism and early scientific method had begun to turn and the sense of what was natural and unnatural slowly began shedding its medieval structure and certainty in favor of a burgeoning skepticism and Baconian empiricism (with Cartesian rationalism not far behind). A new mechanistic model of the universe was taking hold as Europe's communal world and the explanatory and moral powers of its myths waned. The full exchange of the old world for a modern one would require time, but the anxieties born of these tensions easily found fertile ground. And exploration and expansion on all fronts provided only delusory balms for the existential uncertainty whereby the order of things could no longer be taken for granted. We can now retroactively read the growing (irrational) passion for novelty as anticipation of what would become fully realized with the capitalist ethos of excessive consumption. A way of life without satiety, without seasonality. New worlds, new peoples, new resources, new economics, new governments, new theories. Revolutions upon revolutions. The novel and the exotic highlighted not only a shift in passion but in what constituted a "need."[101] In any case, Shakespeare's natural and social world lost definition more quickly than the emerging one gained it, and an increasing number of things began appearing "unnatural." Simultaneously the unthinkable became more thinkable. The unnatural began to find its place in the world and was well on its way to being not so unnatural after all. A new world of illusions inverting means and ends.[102] Lear's actions, as well as Edmund's, Goneril, and Regan's, make this perfectly clear. And recall that Lear and his Fool famously go back and forth about "nothing." For those in power or who aspire to power "nothing" is nothing desirable. It is lack, nonexistence, nihilation, a cypher, insignificance. While the Fool deftly dances around the topic to make a fool of Lear, it is Cordelia at the outset who demonstrates an awareness that nothing *can* mean more than a mere negation or absence. And Edgar comes along later and helps us to realize this more productive sense and use of nothing—"Edgar I nothing am"—in order to transform into mad Tom O' Bedlam and perform acts of healing, if not deliverance. As Lear continues his descent into madness, Shakespeare, ironically, has him retrieve Cordelia's earlier counter wisdom even though he has not yet suffered enough to truly embrace it: "No, I will be the pattern of all patience; I will say nothing."[103] As we well know he will indeed suffer sufficiently before the end—"and these same crosses spoil me"[104]— as will so many others. Perhaps more so than any other play, *King Lear* reminds us that Emerson's exhortation from *Nature* to "vanish" and become "nothing" arises precisely in response to the tragic conditions of life whereby we find ourselves alone, unknown to ourselves, and estranged from the world.[105]

It is then with acute poetic sorrow that near the end, captured and in a Dionysian delirium, Lear recalls for Cordelia the very dream his actions prohibited:

> So we'll live,
> And pray, and sing, and tell old tales, and laugh
> At gilded butterflies.[106]

His dream of wild freedom, unwavering love, a cosmopolitan hearth, of ceaseless feasting and singing, of a seamless transition into an entitled retirement—to join the old kings under the hills and become one with the earth without attending to the ritual of descent, without sacrifice, without truthful repetitions—is finally realized as a delusion born of his descent into madness. What he was unwilling or unable to do for himself force did to him. What Emerson's tragic philosophy accomplishes—that is, the sensuous material outlay of nature as that into which we imaginatively sacrifice ourselves, then the working up through nature's four uses (our "tales" of commodity, beauty, language, discipline), in order to arrive at the theory of the ideal (which grounds the initial imaginative act in reason) upon which we intelligibly feast, enabling us, with rehabilitated instincts (or childlikeness) to overcome our alienation and spiritually return to nature with new possibilities of purpose and power—*King Lear* accomplishes as a perverse inversion. A series of avoidances, denials, betrayals, grotesque revelations, monstrous becomings. He does not elect to become an erotic fool sensitive to silence and shame, rather a remnant of a king who force stripped down to but a memory of a great soul now fit to die. Emerson's tragic art of ascension into wonder becomes, in *Lear*, a drama of forced descent into extravagant cruelty. And after much suffering and foolishness, Lear arrives—transformed—at the entry to his *sidhe*, finally able, in madness, to offer himself as a sacrifice to the gods: "Upon such sacrifices, my Cordelia, / The gods themselves throw incense."[107] He may now join the tragic festival of the wise, but only as a haunting portrait preserved in our cultural memory and dramatic performances. Through this preservation and enactment of his tragic descent, we, as active readers and witnesses, prepare for the ascending return of the infant messiah, of unrepressed *eros*. Of the tragic imagination's recovery of rational ideals for life and the future. In the mysterious way that only the most beautifully terrible of tales seems able to do, *Lear* helps us to liberate the tragic from mere fear and pity, and to restore its secret admonishments to become graceful and joyful, to rediscover the instinct to play.[108]

"Sorrow," Emerson tells us, "makes us all children again."[109]

5

A Fool Speaks

Review. We began with a reading of the first scene of *King Lear*, essaying toward silence's secret possibility to lure force and power out into the open. Silence accomplishes this by simply providing space for them to occupy. The living instruments of force—ever driven, ever busy—can resist no opportunities to territorialize. *Nothing* can remain unrealized. Cordelia arises as our heroine. Our sublime fool. She refuses her father's contest, responding instead with love and silence. A most rare act. The energies that direct the king, when opposed by nothing but loving silence, cannot hide behind his disingenuous, nor genuinely playful, rhetoric or ancient cultural traditions or state institutions. His defense mechanisms fail. No more repression, displacement, sublimation. Force (whatever turns a person into a thing) and power (whatever means exists at force's disposal) then shed any pretense of sanity or play. The intoxicating madness they induce in their deputies and the destruction they inflict upon their victims can no longer wear the illusory justifications of any theory. Lear, his family, his kingdom, come to suffer in the grand fashion of a tragic relief, which highlights the terrible contrasts and inevitabilities comprising the human condition. The tragic portrait is a "relief" because the hero stands out from, while still being fundamentally connected to, a shared world. Attentively reading or witnessing *King Lear*, or any truly great tragedy, allows us to become absorbed into its muted background. We find a deemphasized, depersonalized place—though a place nonetheless—along with everyone and everything else. The whole affair rings strangely festive. Like other communal activities inviting contemplation, for a little while our solitary lives fade away as we become one with the world and with others. Yet, beyond the scope of most other contemplative activities, whether private or social, our individuated sufferings and triumphs, our projects and horizons, all the aspects and dimensions of our existence, are—in performance of the tragic—for a moment, all drawn into an undeniable unity. A unity usually unnoticed in the ebb and flow of ordinary life. As it concludes, we slowly awaken from the ecstatic unity of the tragic world (as art or performance) having gained that elusive (and still temporary) sense of proportion toward which philosophy ever endeavors. Whether we experience a genuine catharsis or not, the usual reductions to optimism or pessimism lose purchase, all our attempts to escape or reframe the curse of being cease, and—for only a spell and as if under a spell—we are free to accept the shame of our existence.[1] Not merely guilt as a private psychological phenomenon—though much remains there to be won—but shame as a pious humility and awe at being engendered by a social existence, a shared ethos, a sense of being with and among other beings who make up our lifeworld.[2] A shame at being at all. Only those who have become alienated (*Entfremdung*) or idiots (*idiótēs*) default to feelings of interior guilt (*Schuld*) instead of open shame (*aidōs*). And by design, tragedy—not epic or melodrama or horror—beckons us to return to our public existence and bear the shame of our being. This has little, perhaps nothing, to do with tragedy *pleasing* us as art. For all of the charm of certain lines and all of the exquisiteness of distinct performances, tragedy saws slowly on the heart, preparing us for what it leaves behind: *a sense for the beautiful*. Not the object or performance itself but what it awakens or indicates. The shame we feel in response to the "tragic festival" comes upon us because we discover—when we attend it circumspectly in advance or have become receptive to the unexpected—we can no longer deny the necessity of sacrifice, of myriad sacrifices, in order not only to live but to live free enough to experience beauty.[3] A genuine, transformative sense of beauty. The deep ache of which, beyond all practical reciprocities, awakens us to the underlying dynamic structure that serves as the basis of all meaningful social bonds and common undertakings: *love*.[4] The spiritual *ordo amoris*. Nature sacrifices itself to itself for its many wonders to flourish, and we too render life to life to make it livable and fine, if only fleetingly. To affirm that, despite so much to the contrary, despite its utter recurring monstrousness, the world we inhabit is always beautiful. Lear's journey into madness and the mad world he helps inaugurate—whether contextualized by the *collapse of feudalism* or conditioned by a collapse *back into* feudalism[5]—provides us, in the fashion reserved for tragic form, with ascending revelations only accessible on the way down.[6] Other heroes fall or come to see the way things truly are, but only tragic protagonists, in flagrant relief of our shared social and existential condition, learn they were always the criminal, the victim, the riddle-solver, the fool, the walking dead.[7] That their choices—maddeningly—fulfilled the fate from which they ran. And with this Dionysian revelation, what is there left to do but shake off the gloom and find joy?

Emerson enters here to tell us that silence shames discourse (any dialogical reasoning toward identifications) and that he prefers the silent church to sermons. He knows that much of what is said between us, to us, and for us, does not serve us. Emerson arrives best known for reminding us time and again—challenging us—not to listen to voices demanding conformity, to those who would have us heed their word over our own intuition, adopt their views instead of discover our own. In one formulation or another, his advice has become so well-known we often forget its origins and implications, which, if received without danger, neuters its life-altering possibilities. Trusting yourself has devolved to a fond cultural exhortation to "follow your heart" because "you only live once," but prior to any liberated subjectivity or prolonged introspection or social revolution, all such activities merely reflect the conforming practices and ideological biases of the world in which we find ourselves. True self-trust and self-culture come at great risk and offer us the opportunity to become "fools."

We then turned toward laying the groundwork for our reading of *Nature* as a major work of tragic idealism (or a version of idealism emerging within and in response to the tragic). We briefly survey the biographical, the quite personal experiences of loss provoking Emerson's grand attempt to theorize nature. If these events remained consigned to private experience, they would mean little. They must be read back into a larger account. Thus, when Emerson writes of becoming nothing—becoming quiet and still—it is in order that he (as *not me*) might "see all." This disciplined act of imagination (arguably the most powerful use of a creative thinker's negative capability) allows him to temporarily see (or know) by feeling—spiritually inhabiting—the occult unity of all things. This bestows the thinker with a better sense of proportion. Put another way, we find in Emerson that silence is a key ingredient in turning inward to answer the *Riddle of the Sphinx* (or a theory of the world that approached as an enigma), for returning to childlikeness and play, for attaining the prospect of being able to speak again, to speak anew. Turning inward refers to a comportment that allows for nature to once again become mysterious, to be experienced as the spiritual surround of being. It is a sensuous-imaginative act leading to rational determinations. Here we find the heart of Emersonianism, his variation of a perennial idealism. Not conventionally opposed to empiricism or materialism, but a philosophical approach that begins with the edges of embodied existence—defined by loss and limits—that, in response to life, endeavors to elevate to ideas (unities of thought) that provisionally make sense of existence. An approach that brings all life and all events into view. That, should we allow them, can take possession of us as *ideals* by which not only to endure this life but to see and participate in its beauty. All without denying the curse of being, the tragic enginery, the realities of force, or the illusions of power.

We move here to explicating *Nature* chapter by chapter. We began by emphasizing the role *eros* plays in the "Introduction." How *eros*, beyond the merely sexual, sensuously draws us toward the *not* of the *not me*—to difference and otherness stirring in the muted background, veiled by stark and shining reliefs—which permits the reframing of our existence in terms other than a priori identities that determine all beings, relations, and events in advance. Surrendering to the erotic lure of nature—a solitary stroll through the woods that arrests the senses, the simple pleasure taken from birdsong, terror at sea, awe before the scope of the landscape, that longing awakened from the evanescent colors of twilight—not only allows the beauty of the world to be experienced but reconnects us to the world through the very idea of nature. To be part and parcel of it. We discover that we have a role to play which—essentially—cannot be understood apart from the whole. With this insight we take up "Nothing," both theoretically and as the untitled first section of *Nature*. As a reader might assume of an introduction, Emerson lays out some central concepts of the overall project (solitude, sentiment, nature, nothing, beauty, etc.) and introduces the importance of our erotic-imaginative immersion into nature by becoming "nothing" and thus transparent, resulting in the revelation—not to be quickly dismissed—that there is an occult unity between all things. We get a glimpse of what Emerson will work toward: achieving harmony with nature through a type of theorizing that does not set the material world against an ideal world, nor abides the metaphysical fictions and certainties that strictly separate subject and object, nature and spirit, thought and action. He will attempt this primarily by examining nature's "uses," beginning with commodity.

Emerson spends the least amount of time with commodity as a use of nature, and his observations and assertions seem roundly laudatory. The commodification of the world has led to the glories of civilization. New techniques and technologies, the scope and scale of cities, the pace and privileges of life. Yet, through a romantic lens, he also sees that the benefits that result from this use are temporary, mediate, not ultimate, pale in comparison to what nature freely offers us, provide little profit to the soul, and that these boons are mercenary. Commodified uses of nature *ideally* ought only to enhance life materially without retarding our spiritual progression toward harmony with nature in accord with our intuition (as rehabilitated reason). Consequently, when we notice that the lowest use has become the highest use, we have sufficient reason to suspect the bankruptcy of our criteria determining profitability. Today, it, like much else, carries within it few lessons from past sages.[8] Then, as if in gracious redress, beauty enters as Emerson's next use of nature. He presents it in three modes: beauty as a basic aesthetic experience resulting in delight, beauty as cultivation of and synonymous with virtue, and beauty as proper object of and for intellection (understanding and reason working together within a unified system of ideation). Our gayest moments, our most excellent deeds, and our grandest constructions (including tragic drama) are all in some way expressions of nature's beauty. Nevertheless, the last modality of beauty is the most important, serving as the herald for spirit—that which animates the universe—which Emerson takes up in the penultimate chapter. The next use of nature he takes up, language, also arrives in three aspects: words are natural facts indicating our original material relation to the world, particular natural facts as symbols of particular spiritual facts, and nature itself as the symbol of spirit. The first point understands language as arising from embodied material existence; all original connotations refer to some naturalistic experience or observation. The second aspect takes us from natural experience to spiritual meaning. That is, though they begin as signs for the world around us, the words elevate to grander conceptions and nuanced meanings. Language becomes weightier, more humanly significant, theoretically abstract. Symbolic. This paves the way for language in its final and finest use to unlock dimensions of our mental life previously inaccessible. We gain entry into the impenetrable mysteries and inner workings of the human mind. While this claim has implications for the evolution of language in a broad historical sense, it is primarily—like other dramas perennially played out upon the stage of private psychological life[9]—an insight into language that all thinkers must win for themselves. Language, if so won, regains its poetic capability to restore us to an original relationship with nature. And it can do so without having to discard the various conceptions, nuanced meanings, and specialized knowledges it has made possible on the way. Wisdom and play can coexist in this use of language. Here discipline, the last of the four uses, enters as Emerson works through the relationship between understanding and reason. The former bespeaks the faculty by which we organize our experiences of phenomena into various schemes of knowledge, attempting to explain those phenomena in relation to each other (and to ourselves), while the latter, after rehabilitation through the refusal of convention and habituated modes of thought, signifies an intuitive-receptive capacity for universals (*pure knowledge*) that transcend individuated experience. Divisions of philosophical method, both ancient and modern, often hinge on privileging one faculty over another. Emerson, however, believes both must be actively engaged to attain a unified system—developed in *Nature's* next chapter,

"Idealism"—which results in attaining both "pure" and "practical" knowledge. Discipline, in this sense, means bringing rehabilitated reason into contrapuntal harmony with our cultivated understanding. Our knowledge of the world can then become something else. It can become *spiritual*. Spiritual in this sense means that our knowledge of the world moves to the center of our being, to the meaningful intersection of our various disciplinary and social concerns. And this unity of multiplicitous areas, Emerson suggests, recovers *difference* as divine, and by so doing transcends the lower senses of divided and commodified uses, allowing for a new and redeemed sense of means that overcomes itself. A means for the end that redefines everything: the *ideal*.

We progress toward the ideal by participating in the drama of understanding. We set up problems for ourselves. We wrestle with the various issues arising from the chasm of incommensurability and conflict between the world we live in and our beliefs and theories that try to explain it. To the chagrin of systematic thinkers, Emerson demonstrates that we can mitigate such problems and tensions by reinterpreting their role within the drama, or we can simply evade them if necessary. We can learn from Descartes without adopting his dualism, read Kant without accepting his noumenal realm, reflect on Schmitt without endorsing his politics. It is the "apocalypse of the mind," the *durance vile*, the *katábasis* we undergo en route to the idea of nature that matters. After the down-going the hero emerges victorious, after serving the sentence the prisoner is freed, after Armageddon a new world begins. Attainment of the idea (unity of thought) through the play of imagination (creative immersion into nature as that which is *not me*) and pure reason (apprehension of principles prior to our synthetic constructions) does not signal the end but the pivotal transition to being enchanted by the idea become the ideal. Then only *nothing* separates "the way things are" from "the way things should be." This honest idealism—this complimentary competition of faculties that dialectically elevate without leaving the ground—empowers Emerson to move on from or absorb philosophy's unresolved tensions and illusory problems so as to represent the world as whole and divine. The prospect of an underlying order of love, which beauty earlier heralded, now remerges as the divine basis of a new spiritual reality—unfixed, unfinished, cruel, and yet meaningful, ordered, beautiful—in which there are no enemies of the soul, only those people and events and circumstances providing us with opportunities to refine our theories and practices of implementing the ideal that has come to capture us.

Emerson then offers a repetition of transcendentalism, but with an emphasis on spirit. We find that the escalatory winding and selective repetition of uses toward ends that work to unify all parts and regions of experience and thought are, in the highest and final sense, derived from reason and discovered within "God" or the "Over-Soul" or that which is "NOT ME," which are all particular ways of inscribing spirit. For Emerson, spirit—behind which lies only *nothing*—denominates the *anima mundi*. It is the principle of life in general, bound only to the task of expressing and organizing itself through the manifold dimensions and processes of nature, which we particularize as world, individualize as self, and realize as *self-culture*. Failure to realize ourselves or heed the spirit's herald, beauty—which teaches us to love and worship nature in relation to the repetition of its origin toward its end—results in spirit's irresistible animating force becoming the *epic of force*. Emerson's tragic philosophy of idealism endeavors to resist this. The classical ideals we all know so well—justice, beauty, truth, goodness—testify to any manner of strange resistance to spirit's fall into subordinating classification devoid of life-affirming ends. Much work and suffering, however, lie ahead. Many "problems" remain to be solved, absorbed, and evaded. Artfully so. As we work our way through the prisons of metaphysical problems—as stages of *apocalyptic gnōsis*—we journey back to a place of vision and significance awakening an unconventional sense of responsibility for the world. A free imperative accompanied by prospects, chief of which is the answer to the riddle of the Sphinx.

Emerson tells us that the answer to the riddle of the Sphinx has always been housed *within* and *among us*. Yet it is not readily accessible to us. Beauty must awaken a longing for it, to the point of it becoming and necessary. We have to search for it, work toward it, return to it. We have to find it and, in the end, accept it. We have to become childlike fools who stop solving all of our manufactured problems—though we had to invent them and attempt to solve them—and we learn to remain silent and see differently. *Nature* is an orphic manifesto calling each of us to return to this original and wondrous relationship with the tragic world of difference, a world comprising others. It exhorts us to discover our most truly human powers to do *otherwise* than we are told. The riddle is a mystery of eternally returning power within nature—which takes possession of us as an idea and frees us as an ideal—which resurrects what force ever kills. Fate then becomes what it always was: a game. But not a game bereft of love. Life becomes a performance of the tragic drama celebrated as the festival of the wise who have learned how unwise they needed to become in order to be free. In order to play. This is the hope laid at the feet of the perpetually returning messiah, the next generation, the new idea.

At this point we turned to *King Lear* and offered a reading of it inspired, in large part, by the concepts and themes mined from *Nature*. We begin by attempting to anatomize further the tragic imagination by exploring the drama of self-recovery as performed by Lear. We find that without this performance he—that any genuine tragic hero—would remain a kind of unliberated Narcissus whose actions could never reflect the idealized possibilities of unrepressed *eros*. An authentic retrieval of the tragic, however, can only occur by the poet affirming the conflict between the fate of force and our own drive of destiny. No unilateral reductions. The eternal conflict and the suffering it engenders affectively prepares the world of the hero (and ours) for the return of the infant messiah—the perpetual possibility of life-affirming free play—indicating the brief respite (and only a respite) before the enginery of tragedy once again enfolds the world (and us) within its terrible down turn. We then once again emphasize the importance of fools and their ability to offer penetrating insights though jests and counter wisdom. We noted how fools best everyone and yet still lose as the *true fool*—Dionysus or any genuine instance of pre-rational eroticism or free play—must always win because the cycle itself that the god represents always wins. The true fool makes fools of everyone else, especially those who actively resist the irresistible, who try to deny the undeniable. The foolishness of the fool or the darling becomes a devastating critique of culture, a type of counter wisdom to the wisdom of the age. It becomes the wiles of innocence.

From foolishness we took up the mythic and folkloric world in which *King Lear* arises. Lear wishes for the benefits of kingship without the duties required of it; he wants to enter into his own *sidhe*, but without the necessary forfeiture of rights or sacrifice of life. We considered how instead of orchestrating a legitimate ritual of transition to a diminutive legal or social status, instead of handing off the work of allotment to an unbiased party or process, instead of inviting truth and repetitions of truth, Lear instead mocks the drama of descent and its associated aspects. A large part of *Lear's* terrible power lies not only in the king's unconscious sabotaging of love but this profanation of tragedy as ritual performance and festival of descent, as spectacle venerating the curse of being. Going beyond the irresistible developments consistent with the genre, the play seems unique as a "tragic tragedy." The doom of the tragic hero has been written into the very atmosphere of the play.

Cordelia then returns to our consideration. She has become part of the formula of force. No longer the silent and loving witness to truth, she returns as "justice" to counter "injustice." Given what has happened since she left, it is utterly understandable. Easily justified. Justice is always betrayed by what can be justified. And, of course, neither Lear or Cordelia (or anyone else) possesses the power to pause the tragedy itself, much less correct it. It is fated. Our agency lies elsewhere, within us (an ontological paradox, as what is nearest is also furthest away). Still, when we speculate about what a tragic hero "could have done" or "should have done," we do so only to understand better the implications of what he actually did or did not do. To understand better the many ways in which force works against *us*. Tirelessly, invisibly, plainly. To realize and ultimately affirm our situation. The full realization—as perfect representation—of the tragic world through Shakespeare's *Lear* occurs with its well-known thematization of nature and nothing. In that mythic Britain "natural" indicates alignment with divine purposes present in and as nature itself. "Unnatural," conversely, signifies that someone or something is set against those purposes. If the gods do not take timely vengeance upon those who have become unnatural then we ourselves must become the agents of divine retribution. Our justice is monstrous. It exacerbates the curse of being. Shakespeare's own natural and social world of the early seventeenth century lost definition more quickly than the emerging one gained it and as a result an increasing number of social phenomena began appearing "unnatural." Simultaneously the unthinkable became more thinkable and the unnatural began to make a place for itself in the world and would slowly seem not so unnatural after all. A new world of illusions inverting means and ends. *Nothing* then loses its contemplative meaning as a counter measure to force, and comes instead to signal lack, nonexistence, nihilation, insignificance. But we see how with the Fool and Edgar as mad Tom O' Bedlam that retrieving the critical and restorative capabilities of *nothing* (again, contemplatively considered) remains possible whatever the state of things.

We wind down the reading by asserting that what Emerson's tragic philosophy accomplishes *King Lear* also accomplishes but through perverse inversion. A series of avoidances, denials, betrayals, grotesque revelations, monstrous becomings. Lear does not elect to become an erotic fool sensitive to silence and shame (as Emersonianism encourages), rather a remnant of a king whom force strips down to a mere memory of his former self. Emerson's tragic art of elevation into awe in *Lear* becomes a drama of forced descent into cruelty. After much suffering and foolishness, Lear finally arrives—through compulsory transformation—at the entry to his *sidhe*, finally able, in madness, to offer himself as a sacrifice. What Emerson advocates through election, Shakespeare demonstrates through subjugation: we are all fated to become fit for our end. Lear is then able to join the tragic festival of the wise, but only as a haunting portrait of himself, one preserved in our cultural memory and dramatic performances. Through this preservation and enactment of his tragic descent, we, as active readers and attentive theatergoers, prepare for the ascending return of the infant messiah, of unrepressed *eros*, of the ancient arriving as new. In the mysterious way that only the most beautifully terrible of tales seems able to do, *Lear* helps us to liberate the tragic from mere fear and pity, and to restore its secret admonishments to become graceful and joyful, to rediscover the instinct to play.[10] It shows us through sorrow and beauty why we must become children again.

Festivity and Sacrifice. We have used the term "festival" throughout this work both in reference to dramatic tragedy and the practice of philosophy as conditioned by the tragic. We have occasionally used the phrase, "the tragic festival of the wise," primarily in reference to the latter, but also with respect to the weighty protagonists of the former. The recurring reminder of festivity in relation to tragedy and the philosophical drama has been, of course, intentional. Not only was tragedy originally an aspect of The Great Dionysia, it was central to that major festival. And though scholars, and even the ancient Greeks themselves, have offered compelling reasons why tragedy occupied this place of centrality among the dramatic festivals, it nevertheless remains largely within the realm of speculation. We prefaced our investigation, in part, with the claim that dramatic tragedy acts out the truth of the human situation, particularly in terms considered difficult to confront. It wrestles with natural forces, divine powers, irrational drives, social energies, historical events, and political instruments—all beyond our control.[11] An acknowledgment of the uncertainty accompanying existence whatsoever, which is especially heightened in times of sociopolitical transition.[12] Leaning into the psychological, we can approach tragedy as an expression of our subconscious suspicion that our confidence in the economic and political environments in which we find ourselves rests primarily on little else than habit. If we consider it all at length, honestly, the most conspicuous aspects of our endeavors and commitments appear quite hollow. Although we work to acquire the fine illusions of security and deflections of amusement, deep down we know a fall awaits us and that by sheer virtue of our various styles of living—by our very existence—we deserve the coming catastrophe. Degrees and intensities of explicit guilt with which we can sympathize notwithstanding, with tragedy we find ourselves drawn into a dramatic world wherein we watch tragic heroes become fit for their end. As we will be. We will round out this cypher called life in dust and oblivion. Only the scope of the events and the depth of outrageous sadness between now and then remain unknown to us. And yet, of all that the art of tragedy reveals to us about the world and ourselves, its kindest gift, wrapped in misery, is the prospect of hesitation: it calls out to us to reclaim within ourselves—however assaulted, contracted, devitalized that kingdom of creativity and conscience has become—the ancient privilege of humbly and momentarily pausing the graceless and dehumanizing effects of force and power. The travesty besetting tragedy today is that it arrives as merely a theatrical "genre." A cultural relic preserved for consumption. A signifier of sophistication. Our considerations here, however, have turned upon recalling that tragedy was not only culturally important for the Greeks and unequivocally devastating in its portrayal of humanity in stark relief, but it was, strangely, a time of feasting and celebration: "Cruelty is one of the oldest festive joys of mankind."[13] It was a sacred time of competition. Our hope has been that it can become so once again. Not in anachronistic imitation of the Greeks, but in novel repetitions of tragic possibilities. In reading and attending Shakespeare, in "dramatized" readings of Emerson.

Aside. The aim of our project to read *King Lear* (perfect representation of the tragic) and *Nature* (ideal philosophy's performative response to the tragic) closely and together, and with prefatory and concluding notes on Greek tragedy, lies with retrieving and rehabilitating the *tragic imagination* as a poetic dimension of thought capable of becoming attuned and receptive to the truth and possibilities of reality. We require a cultivated tragic imagination in order to honestly confront our mortal condition, deconstruct the deceptive ideologies that blind us, resist the subordinating structural and institutional procedures that enslave us, refuse to participate in the nihilistic social practices and discrete behaviors that ruin us. We can, beyond seeing the world for what it really is, elect to take up the perilous adventure of discovering *ideals* with which to meet force. We can fashion free inner lives, learn to question, to listen, to be thankful. We can, in the course of things to come, do otherwise than what is merely justified or understandable. We can reclaim an inner possibility of joyous contemplation and a shared possibility of communal festivity.

Now, we should note, that while we cannot cleanly separate the "political" from the "religious" when it comes to the ancients, it nevertheless remains basically correct to say that tragedy derived from religious practices and did not originally have any direct political aims or implications.[14] This is important because it is precisely its religious inception and festive occasion that gave tragedy its political voice. Plays certainly offered commentary on current events and criticism of political figures, but they did so predominantly elliptically through their proper subject: myth. Through tragedy the mythic past spoke portents to the present, providing poetic ("divine") wisdom for attendees to reflect upon. We know propaganda and ideology nevertheless made their way onto and near the stage as unavoidable political preambles praising Athenian wealth and power, but the art itself that was subsequently performed illuminated the cost of such state hubris and its recurrent mob madness. Tragedy's religious origin and artistic cultural station made this commentary and criticism possible in a way that outright political speech and action could not. How?

A common theory holds that tragedy traces back directly to mystic initiation rites into the cult of Dionysus, with the other game and festive elements being added to those rites as part of tragedy's organic elaboration into its final form.[15] If we take this theory seriously, then we can consider tragedy's content (its plot and themes) and form (its material and performative presentation) as retaining something of this mystical element. As theater attendees transformed into worshippers of Dionysus upon the image and procession of the god entering the theatrical space—temporarily redefining the space as sacred—they became witnesses to the hero's downfall as a necessary sacrifice for the survival of the state. The curse of being that tragedy acted out and venerated was *for* everyone in attendance: citizens, the wealthy, the poor, resident aliens, guests, slaves, prisoners.[16] A "universal lesson," so to speak, for something that could not be conventionally taught except through highly symbolic images and performances. And like the initiation into a mystery, wherein secrets are revealed through phases of descent corresponding to elevating stages of *gnōsis*, great truths otherwise unknowable or unteachable were theatrically acted out and piously observed. Much of tragedy's peculiar power came from publicly acting out certain secrets of the subconscious and mysteries of nature and the human condition explaining why the material always drew upon myth and not simply "history." And this art—this collective celebration of "going down" into the dangerous depths of being—spoke to the ancients in a way we can scarcely relate to now. And as we have extended this speculation of the meaning of Greek tragedy to our interpretation of *King Lear* and *Nature* wherein attendees and readers (can) allow themselves to become absorbed into the hero's descent and sacrifice in order that they themselves might emerge victorious.[17]

Plato encourages a similar absorption into his dramatic presentation of the descent of Socrates—prototype for the philosopher as "tragic hero"—with two significant developments: (1) turning from the common person's reliance upon external ritualization and artistic imitations toward the internalization and abstraction of the soul's heroic journey and (2) embracing the "pharmacological" advantages and complications of making the practice of philosophy primarily concerned with creating and interpreting written works.[18] Yet, Plato never really abandons the poetry and myth constituting the Greek world; he rather strategically deploys them in service to philosophy. He even generates a new mythology, with its own heroes (e.g., Socrates, philosophers), monsters (e.g., sophists, politicians), and themes (e.g., rationality, virtue). He gives us a hero who died for philosophy and becomes a sacrificial scapegoat (*pharmakós*) for the state's dissatisfaction with itself: an object of ritual violence for the diffusion of conflict, a final recourse for collective fears in times of political, ecological, and cyclical crisis.[19] And yet our hero goes without complaint, contented, victorious in defeat.

Reading tragedy and idealism together, at the outset, means accepting the invitation, as readers and attendees, to participate in the hero's sacrificial descent. It means joining in the festivity of dramatic and theoretical affirmation of the world, especially when to do so seems impossible: when it is most cruel, unusual, threatening, complex, destructive, even ordinary. As tragedy takes us down into the abyss, where it would leave us entombed with our failed loves and projects, stripping from us all delusions and false identities, we disinter ourselves through idealism—imaginative, intuitive, stoically disciplined—elevating to apprehend principles by which to see and love the world anew. We do not have to offer cups of blood and thigh bones wrapped in fat over flames, or noble heroes too great for the world. Though the tragic engine demands sacrifice for some specific sin or pollution—insisting on having its own feast to excuse us—our rites and performances today do not need these requisite crucifixions. Our imaginative absorption into their tragic portraits can suffice for our participation. The conflictual nature of the cosmos and our human failings, as well, will suffice to fulfill the curse and cost of being. We can now do otherwise. Pious enactment of those "laws invisible and eternal" might very well act as the catalyst of our demise, but our demise was underwritten the moment we arrived.[20] Enacting classical virtues—ever culturally correlated[21]—in truth makes us ourselves worthy "sacrifices." Emerson writes, "He who does a good deed is instantly ennobled"[22] and "All men have my blood and I all men's."[23] With no small amount of historical irony, these lines denote both a virtue ethic and a democratic shift. Tragedy always sacrificed heroes of noble or divine blood presumably due to it being more sumptuous and satisfying to the gods. It piously dramatized that satisfaction in hopes of (dissimulative) appeasement of those punitive appetites. Art's magical quality served as a currency for ontological exchange. It is, to some degree, what we speak of when we, following Benjamin, speak of its *aura*.[24] If we elected to offer ourselves freely as "living sacrifices" to the tragic engine of being, then it is we ourselves who assume the role of the uncanny noble hero.[25] We take on all the contradictions and doublings, including wearing wisdom and foolishness.[26] We can do this not in grotesque romanticization of martyrdom that fulfills some ideological delusion or metaphysical fiction but in response to our cultivated and principled desire to enact our own humble appeasement of those "demonic appetites" ever-working through force and power. We then have nothing to say *directly* to those instruments that render us nonhuman. Only silence. Or, perhaps, in rare moments, "I forgive you." *Indirectly*, however, through its refined duplicity—illogically more truthful than any logically true statement—the riddle of art indeed has much to say. As it should. Not as sanctioned propaganda or revolutionary counter-propaganda, rather only festively and of its own accord. And therein lies the source of tragedy's prophetic voice.

Emerson and Politics. In the spring of 1851, following the passage of the Fugitive Slave Law the previous year, Emerson abandoned his usual reticence to speak publicly and directly about social issues. "The last year has forced us all into politics."[27] His years of attempting to intellectually shepherd America through insightful and inspiring speeches and publications bore the hallmark of strategically evading conventionally structured philosophical arguments, clear positions on divisive social issues, and unequivocal institutional allegiances. Our pre-reading (Chapter 2) and reading (Chapter 3) of *Nature* attempts to demonstrate that Emerson did indeed develop a coherent transcendental (ideal) philosophy, one composed of discernable commitments, distinct operations, and identifiable aspirations—primarily for the individual but for society as well. We noted too that he had long been socially progressive and, albeit unofficially, stood in solidarity with various coalitions from time to time. Yet his principled commitment to self-culture remained. In tracing Emerson's role in the prehistory of American Pragmatism, Cornel West has claimed that the key to Emerson's success as a public figure lie in dual allegiance to both those in power and the powerless.[28] West sees no conservative or liberal or socialist or civic republican, rather a petit bourgeois with anarchistic tendencies and genuine, if limited, democratic sentiments.[29] We can easily trace this dual allegiance back to Emerson's original vocation. As a Unitarian minister it was incumbent upon him to appeal to as many members of his congregation as possible. His sermons could electrify, but only through moderated entreaty, restrained by intellectual refinement and the ecclesiastical context. By training and custom his sermons avoided novelty and brash antagonism, and instead took up what was, as much as possible, held in common. He tailored his homilies to his flock's interests and backgrounds, aiming for moral improvement, the presentation of "positive" views, and a general goal of inclusivity.[30] And Emerson had to follow these protocols knowing that no one liked to be preached at.[31] To some degree these constraints suited him and helped shape his early philosophical voice. Consequently, it would be more accurate to think of him not as having dual allegiances but of possessing multiple allegiances, all to which he wished to remain true. Or perhaps, even more accurately, he had only one allegiance: an underlying allegiance to the latent possibility housed within everyone to become more than social conventions and church doctrines would permit. True as well for the state.

We find this view in his essay, *Politics*, where Emerson critiques the state for its non-reliance on moral sentiment and its failure to cultivate wise citizens, opting instead for self-perpetuation through its political processes and governmental instruments of force.[32] (The end of that essay, we should note, pronouncedly derides force.) He believed that if the state did ever use its various institutions to facilitate the arrival of such citizens it would expire. An enlightened state comprising truly liberated and wise subjects would fulfill its mandate—whether implicit, explicit, or assumed—and its reason for being would cease; its powers ceded back to the citizens who (theoretically) granted them. Emerson reveals no real discernable optimism for this Kingdom of Ends, but it remains for him the ideal possibility, and thus guiding principle, of the state: the imaginary criteria for any political criticism. For while Emerson's second series of essays (1844) came to contain a degree of measured skepticism accompanying his transcendentalism, we can clearly identify his theory of an ideal state, grounded in the unrealized possibility of the *ordo amoris*: "The power of love, as the basis of a State, has never been tried."[33]

Eventually, however, Emerson could not hold his commitment to the ideal at a scholarly remove, nor honor likewise his allegiance to what was held in common if what was held in common were to remain anything worth honoring. For what he believed to be held in common—taken as a distinct ethos or as an assumed set of values and accompanying social institutions—had proven insufficient in morally guiding America away from the legislated preservation of slavery. All the talk of freedom and Christian principles could no longer shroud the symptoms of a sick nation. Emerson could no longer remain silent. It has been noted that his response to the Fugitive Slave Law had "the depth of a conversion experience."[34]

His subsequent passionate speeches tended not to address the federal government directly, but that which constituted it: individuals and individual states.[35] The scholar whose science had always required its own air and open aim came to see—diagnostically more clearly than anyone then or now[36]—what was, and would remain, at stake for a pluralistic democracy with extraordinary ambitions. Thus, no longer able or willing to evade, he preached resistance and civil disobedience.[37]

While it remains the task of philosophy to take up the riddle of the Sphinx, ever requiring a default to silence before force and power, there remain rare times of refusal, prophetic injunctions, poetic indictments, and actions *otherwise*. As Emerson discovered, circumstances can conspire against any personal liberty—spiritually or politically considered—which under "sane conditions" usually support the suspension of the subject above decisive or materially determinative deeds, thus allowing an operational distance between theory and practice (even if the theory *is* the practice). The stoic character of Emerson's philosophy would have had him treat circumstances with indifference, but that character is dispositional and ideal with regard to outcomes over which we have little to no influence. It does not, however, absolve us from humanity. The anachronistic and inhuman logic of slavery redirected Emerson's power to speak to the people—a power cultivated through rehabilitation and refinement—in order that what was, in part, legitimated through his fidelity to its indirect or elliptical free end, could directly address America's madness: "If our resistance to this law is not right, there is no right."[38]

Emerson claims in *Politics* that states are not aboriginal, nor superior to their citizens.[39] The state bears an illusory stability to the young who believe that "laws make the city."[40] The wise, however, know that "foolish legislation is a rope of sand," and that "law is only memorandum."[41] Further, when contrasted with its highest possibilities, "every actual state is corrupt."[42] Emerson in fact wonders if the state is not some trick we have played upon ourselves?[43] These suspicions, taken with his overarching aspirations for self-culture, make him an advocate for less government.[44] And if we allow ourselves to follow anthropologist Pierre Clastres in considering seriously societies without states, whose examples, however impractical or alien they seem, serve as historically assayable demonstrations of what has always been a collective possibility for humanity, then we can add to the texture of Emerson's eventual decision to speak where he had previously remained silent—not by categorizing that decision as simply a change of heart in the face of intensified conditions, but rather as fulfilling a fundamental social obligation.[45] Speech in such stateless societies indicates no legal right, nor does it signal some requisite activity. And yet, in a society septic with modern statehood, wherein force and power have become institutionally interwoven into almost every area of life, speech is also not a luxury.[46] All to say, when we consider Emerson's ideal theory of the state—which, like the "me" recovered from the "not me," is *no state at all*—and his romantic faith in the erotic possibilities of those subjects comprising society, it was his very *power* to speak that *obliged* him to speak. This power of obligatory speech concerning the well-being of society and its members (*parrēsía*), whether convivial or prophetic, when decoupled from political force and any compulsory mechanism, means no one was reciprocally obliged to listen.[47] If anyone ever *is* reciprocally obliged to listen—or obey—then the ideal imperative to speak rescinds itself. Under such conditions it becomes only another exercise of force. In those instances, silence and art remain our most authentic possibilities of protest and testimony.

Shakespeare and Politics. By any reading of *King Lear*, it should be clear that no outcome rested upon the shoulders of any one figure. Yes, we have a protagonist who, like the ancient tragic heroes before him, stands out in relief as the primary object of our considerations. Yet, the conundrum of tragedy remains: every action the hero takes either to avoid or to correct the situation ultimately serves to fulfill the tragic outcome. The hero becomes the true fool. No agent within the drama possesses the power to avert what is coming. It is the trick, the setup, the cruel device. This seems clear in Sophocles' *Oedipus the King*, perhaps less so in *Lear*—except when we recall that ostensibly Lear's division of the kingdom was arguably influenced, if not prompted, by a *desire* to stave off civil war, certainly not provoke it; his love contest was *intended* as a game to ease the gravity of the occasion, not as a catalyst to disinheritance and exile; his armed entourage was *meant* for comradery and to preserve his residual honors and prerogatives, not alarm or check his ambitious daughters. But these actions worked for rather than against the tragic conclusion. Any psychological or political analysis of the possible motives behind these actions would problematize their conspicuous efficacy to resolve themselves positively and offer penetrating speculations explaining how and why they sabotaged rather than accomplished their stated or implied intention. This includes Cordelia's choices, both her early silence and her later return as (sympathetic) agent of force. That all material actions, prima facie or ex post facto, end up working for the tragic conclusion—if only to wind up the engine and heighten the sorrow to come—might lead us to attribute all consequential developments to the paradoxical enigma of fate harnessed by the old poets in order to drive the narrative where it needed to go. Or perhaps wrapping ritualistically released violent energies and taboo violations in the folds of fate did indeed speak to a mythic sense of metaphysical necessity. Or perhaps, possibly, in moments of profound honesty, we might acknowledge that this tragic conception of fate speaks to the very real and numerous forces existing beyond the powers and talents of any hero. Beyond any institution or collective will. Beyond any reform, legislation, policies. The effect of this acknowledgment would be humiliating. Utterly shameful. It would even be felt more deeply and complexly when occurring at and as a festive occasion. It would—it should—leave the audience feeling as stripped of illusions as any down-going protagonist. But, to linger here a moment longer, if force appropriates all resistance and fate makes use of everything, then, outside of some moral admonition to guard against hubris and develop strategies against false (and forceful) agency, of what use is tragic art when it comes to political realities?

We have considered the pathological motives and defects of Lear himself, the astonishing merits and understandable failures of Cordelia, the cutting counter wisdom of the Fool, the dissembling and invitational interventions of Edgar as Tom O' Bedlam, and the villainous nihilism in the name of nature of Edmund. Goneril, Regan, Gloucester, Kent, Albany, Cornwall, Oswald, the unnamed Servant of Act 3—within this constellation of roles no one figure or scene or action or speech brings it all together for us in such a way as to believe that any of them bore sufficient agency to deny the tragic engine its crimson offering. While this theory of tragedy remains essentially unchanged in *Hamlet*, we nevertheless have no trouble seeing through Hamlet's traditional "inaction" to his masterful manipulations. As limited and misunderstood as the agency of tragic heroes most often is, we can still witness Hamlet playing with and against those around him. *King Lear*? Even granting that Cordelia's invasion and tender reconciliation with her father provided a brief moment of grace, the inevitability of the sacrifice of the entire royal family finds no effective misdirection in well-executed plans. So too with the parallel plot of Gloucester and his sons. As a consequence, only by projecting our own desires or assumptions about political agency into the world of *Lear*, would we ever locate sufficient corollaries to our contemporary situation and extract a prescriptive course of action. Which in no way means Shakespeare's art, like the art of the ancient tragedians, does not speak to contemporary events in his own time and channel the surrounding social energies. Rather, only by retrieving history, myth, and legend—imaginatively reworked and refined—in accordance with its own poetic laws, can tragic drama find its contemporaneous voice.[48] When it does, art speaks truth to its audience in a way that nature, philosophy, and political discourse cannot.[49] The tragic lives of fools and darlings, when rendered and received with cultivated sympathies, speaks similarly, even and especially when denied their voice. Propaganda and ideological appropriation, however, fail to honor what the theatrical cult of authentic tragedy offers: the temporary dissolution of the illusory distinction between divine violence and an innocent community.[50]

Again, whether we can still recognize it, it is shame we come to feel. Privately and collectively. Tragedy reveals the destructive futility of political rage, zeal, optimism, certainty. The engine eats everything the heroes throw at it. And when the violence ends, only ever momentarily, the community of witnesses are able to acknowledge the whole affair as divinely orchestrated through its dramatic presentation. By placing the necessity of terrible violence in the hands of divinity while simultaneously taking social responsibility for that violence by offering a surrogate sacrifice of those most innocent *and* most guilty—whether uncannily the same person or dispersed throughout the family—the tragic performance, *strangely*, humanizes the violence.[51] It transforms it from unnecessary human activity undermining the social order into a divinely orchestrated performance of the enrichment of the god who restores the social order. The real extent of human agency is surrendered as illusion to fate in order to be reclaimed as pious responsibility. This clearly has done little to prevent wars, but participating in the performance and becoming receptive to its revelations and transformative powers can certainly curtail our expectations of the outcome and cost of violence.

What is the *use* of tragic art to any given political reality? It teaches us that any utilitarian conception of use is too delimiting for art. Art gives to society what interiority gives to subjective experience.[52] It provides and reorganizes space for the contemplation of ideas, the formation of non-conforming identities, and an opportunity for healthy sublimation. Tragic art in particular ponders the violent elements of the riddle of the Sphinx. Vulnerability, loss, grief. It resolves to represent, through a creative retrieval of myth and history, the perineal epic of force, including the effects of the exercise of power, the madness of ambition, and the injustice of imposing justice.[53] With Shakespeare's retelling of the story of Lear and his three daughters, he was able to capture and speak to contemporary fears of succession, of a triple-crowned king ruling three sovereign states, of a divine cosmos seemingly ever more indifferent, of the hysteria of mass superstition, witches, and demonic activity, of divisions between royalists and parliamentarians and Catholics and protestants, of plots to topple the government, of plagues, of all manner of disenchantment and growing unease. Given low literacy rates, ecclesiastical agendas, and prohibitions against contemporaneous political and religious content, it was the conceit of English Renaissance theater that made elliptical commentary and critique possible. Most powerfully and particularly through tragedy, which honors the world and human history through honest—if wholly fabulous—representation, as well as, to the degree that it is genuinely tragic, the elicitation of shame. The intensity of the shame an audience is able to feel corresponds to how sensitive it is to the horror and the beauty that lingers in the trace of the tragedy they witnessed.

Our ability to correlate the events and figures of *King Lear* or any great tragic work to the events and figures in our own time does not determine the work's political relevance today so much as its ability to assault the illusory conventions concealing how violent and spiritually bereft we become in our attempts to fashion the world according to our own unliberated desires.

Epilogue. My hope has been to offer an anatomy of the tragic imagination— by offering a reading of Emerson's *Nature* with Shakespeare's *King Lear*— in order to rediscover an approach to freedom for subjects existing in a tragic world. A tragic world that has forgotten the truths of tragedy. As with any analysis carrying emancipatory aspirations, we will have failed if the criteria of success remains restricted to quantifications and matrixes solely or predominately determined by whatever particular repressive and hegemonic ideology and culturally conditioned worldview currently holds sway. We must allow philosophical attempts to answer the riddle of the Sphinx and artistic endeavors to represent that riddle their authentic possibilities to transcend their specific sociohistorical sphere.[54] They must be free to accord themselves to their own inner logics, their own laws. The forgoing exegetical exercises endeavored to retrieve and rehabilitate these philosophical and creative desires under the rubric of *Emersonianism* toward *tragic idealism*. If we can honestly and vulnerably collaborate—in reading, discourse, and creative performance— for the negation of the absolute commodification of art and the excessive professionalization of philosophy as elitist activities limited to practitioners of high culture or as anesthetizing pastimes for the psychological management of an unhappy and unfree workforce—if not serving as disingenuous intellectual embellishments—we will have taken a critical step in reclaiming philosophy and art's truly transformative capabilities. Until then, the de-distancing of art's mysterious aura and the contraction of thought by the intrusion of technological innovation and various contemporary aesthetic and theoretical tactics perfecting our self-entrapment will continue unimpeded.[55] A conspiracy born of the tragic imagination—a conspiracy both cultic and democratic, offering both interior and communal sanctuary against the repressive reality and its beguiling gifts—freely invites us to hesitate and to reflect: to refuse force's claim on our inner lives, the violent reactions it spurs, the dominating ambitions it propagates. This conspiracy refuses complicity in alienating practices, however convenient or expedient. It celebrates authentic liberatory contemplations and questions, the recovery of the underlying erotic order within and among us, and the truly human power to become someone else. It celebrates becoming graceful before terror and beautiful in times of sorrow. It celebrates the wisdom of the fool.

Exeunt, with joyous march.

Notes

Preface

1 Jan Kott, *Shakespeare Our Contemporary*, trans. Boleslaw Taborski (New York: W. W. Norton, 1974), 132. Kott writes that "the swindler is more just than the swindled, and the swindled wiser than the swindler." By our formulation, nature is the "just swindler," we are the "wise" who are swindled. Also, as René Girard points out, the object of ritual sacrifice—which we will connect to tragedy's protagonist—is intended "to 'trick' violence into spending itself on victims whose death will provide no reprisals." That is, the "swindle" or "trick" serves to preserve—by appeasing—the community against endless cycles of revenge and to restrict ritual purification to seasonal or calendrical sequences and times of extreme crisis. See René Girard, *Violence and the Sacred*, trans. Patrick Gregory (Baltimore: Johns Hopkins University Press, 1979), 36.
2 Regarding tragedy's treachery, we have in mind here the Greek *apátē*. See chapter 6 of Marcel Detienne's *The Masters of Truth in Archaic Greece*, trans. Janet Lloyd (New York: Zone Books, 1996), 107–34; as well as Simon Critchley's comments on Gorgias in *Tragedy, the Greeks, and Us* (New York: Pantheon Books, 2019), 21–4, 45.
3 Tragedy, from Greek *tragōidía*, literally means "goat song." Tragedy likely originated with the Dorians and began as lyrical or dithyrambic performances before moving to Athens where it developed its fuller and graver dramatic form. The meaning of tragedy as "goat song" is thought to derive from the fact that the actors wore goat-skins or that the prize for best tragedy was a goat. In the analysis to come, we will explore the sacrificial aspects of tragedy in light of the ritualistic importance of offering up "scapegoats" for the diffusion of conflict and as a final recourse for collective fears in times of political, ecological, and cyclical crisis.
4 Cf. George Steiner, *The Death of Tragedy* (New Haven: Yale University Press, 1996), 5–7; Peter Berger, *The Sacred Canopy: Elements of a Sociological Theory of Religion* (New York: Doubleday, 1969), 29–51.
5 See Martin Heidegger, "The Origin of the Work of Art," in *Poetry, Language, Art*, trans. Albert Hofstadter (New York: HarperCollins, 2001), 60–1.
6 Ibid., 61.
7 Paul Cartledge, "The Greek Religious Festivals," in *Greek Religion and Society*, ed. P. E. Easterling and J. V. Muir (Cambridge: Cambridge University Press, 1985), 123.

8 Richard Halpern, "Theater and Democratic Thought: Arendt to Ranciere," *Critical Inquiry* 37 (Spring 2011): 545.
9 Although a permanent festival fund (*theōriká*) did not appear until the fourth century BCE, it has been convincingly demonstrated that occasional disbursements from the state treasury to the people for festival attendance in the fifth century most certainly occurred. See David Kawalko Roselli, "*Theorika* in Fifth-Century Athens," *Greek, Roman, and Byzantine Studies* 49 (2009): 5–30.
10 We will to some degree address these various topics and questions at length in our fifth and final chapter, "A Fool Speaks." Though various primary and secondary sources will be considered, we will make particular use of René Girard's work on sacrifice.
11 Ralph Waldo Emerson, "The Tragic," in *The Works of Ralph Waldo Emerson*, 14 vols., ed. Edward W. Emerson (Cambridge: H. O. Houghton, 1883), XII, 262. This multivolume edition of *The Works of Ralph Waldo Emerson* will be used throughout. The title of the essay will be italicized followed by the volume in which it is found and page number.
12 Cf. Sophocles, *Sophocles I: Oedipus the King, Oedipus at Colonus, Antigone*, second edition, ed. and trans. David Greene and Richard Lattimore (Chicago: University of Chicago Press, 1991), 1140–5; see also Albert Henrichs, "Between City and Country: Cultic Dimensions of Dionysus in Athens and Attica," in *Cabinet of the Muses: Essays on Classical and Comparative Literature in Honor of Thomas G. Rosenmeyer*, ed. Mark Griffith and Donald J. Mastronarde (Atlanta: Scholars Press, 1990), 265–6. It should also be pointed out that Henrichs criticizes contemporary (non-classicist) readers of tragedy, George Steiner in particular, for tending to conflate a Sophoclean Dionysus, associated with death and the afterlife, with an Euripidean Dionysus, representing death and destruction (267–8). We note this as we too will rely upon a composite portrait of Dionysus taken from cult, myth, poetry, philological and historical monographs, and so on. If not already apparent, we should note the influence of Nietzsche—as well as other influential nineteenth- and twentieth-century writers and scholars like Walter Pater, Walter Otto, E. R. Dodds, and Károly Kerényi—upon our own reception and deployment of Dionysus and the Dionysian.
13 See Sophocles' Theban plays, *Sophocles I*.
14 See Aeschylus' *Aeschylus: Prometheus Bound, The Suppliants, Seven against Thebes, the Persians*, trans. Philip Vellacott (New York: Penguin Books, 1961).
15 From Homer to Thucydides, Anaximander to Sophocles, the Greeks give us a view of life as being predominately determined by suffering. The "curse of being" signals that *nemesis* is not reserved for special crimes but for everything that comes into being. The "public cursing of being" (*kataráomai*) refers to our collective

response to the tragic conditions of life, most explicitly—but not exclusively—with tragic drama.
16 Fritz Graf, *Magic in the Ancient World*, trans. Franklin Philip (Cambridge: Harvard University Press, 1999), 118–34.
17 Simone Weil, "The *Iliad* or the Poem of Force," in *Simone Weil: An Anthology*, ed. Sian Miles (New York: Grove Press, 2000), 191–2.
18 *Bia* is the Greek personification of violence and force. *Bia* (force) and *Kratos* (power) appear in Aeschylus' *Prometheus Bound* as Zeus' agents enacting his punishment against Prometheus. *Bia*, notably, is silent.
19 Critchley, *Tragedy, the Greeks, and Us*, 277.
20 Gilles Deleuze, *Nietzsche and Philosophy*, trans. Hugh Tomlinson (New York: Columbia University Press, 1983), 18.
21 Thomas Traherne, *Centuries of Meditation*, I, 85, ed. B. Dobell (London: P. J. and A. E. Dobell, 1927), 62. Emphasis added.
22 Emerson, *Nature*, I, 16.
23 Ibid., 21.
24 Stephen Booth, *King Lear, Macbeth, Indefinition, and Tragedy* (New Haven: Yale University Press, 1983), 85.
25 James Shapiro, *The Year of Lear: Shakespeare in 1606* (New York: Simon & Schuster, 2015), 63.
26 Cf. Plato in the *Sophist*: "Then since we are in perplexity, do you tell us plainly what you wish to designate when you say 'being.' For it is clear that you have known this all along, whereas we formerly thought we knew, but are now perplexed." As well as Leibniz during the Enlightenment: "Why is there something rather than nothing?" And, of course, Heidegger in the twentieth century: "What is the meaning of being?"
27 William Shakespeare, "*King Lear: A Conflated Text*," in *The Norton Shakespeare*, ed. Stephen Greenblatt (New York: W. W. Norton, 1997), 1.1.92. *The Norton Shakespeare* will be used throughout. I will list and italicize the title of the play, followed by the act, scene, and line numbers. Following Richard Halpern and others, use of the conflated text for critical interpretive reasons requires no justification.
28 Friedrich Nietzsche, *Twilight of the Idols*, trans. R. J. Hollingdale (New York: Penguin Books, 1990), 31.
29 Walter F. Otto, *Dionysus: Myth and Cult*, trans. Robert B. Palmer (Dallas: Spring Publications, 1981), 78.
30 Samuel Taylor Coleridge, *Biographia Literaria: or Biographical Sketches of My Literary Life and Opinions*, ed. George Watson (London: J. M. Dent, 1975), 167.
31 Cf. Louis Althusser, *On the Reproduction of Capitalism*, trans. G. M. Goshgarian (New York: Verso, 2014), 256–61.

32 See Peter Holbrook, *English Renaissance Tragedy* (New York: Bloomsbury, 2015), 15–37.
33 Friedrich Nietzsche, *The Gay Science*, trans. Walter Kaufmann (New York: Vintage Books, 1974), 273; aphorism 341.
34 Cf. Jonathan Dollimore, *Radical Tragedy* (Durham: Duke University Press, 1993), xvii–xx. Dollimore cites J. W. Lever—"In Jacobean tragedy it is not primarily the conduct of the individual, but of the society which assails him, that stands condemned"—to help demonstrate a shift in late twentieth century criticism away from reading tragedies as dramas of an *individual's* sin and suffering, predicated on some variation of "idealism," to a "materialist" interpretation of tragedy as predominately social and political in nature, serving as a theatrical indictment, however parallel or elliptical, of the state and its ideological *subjects*. This interpretive shift should also hold true for all genuine tragedies, if not especially the works of Aeschylus and Sophocles.
35 George J. Stack, *Nietzsche and Emerson: An Elective Affinity* (Athens: Ohio University Press, 1992), 6.
36 Cf. Weil, "The *Iliad* or the Poem of Force."
37 Cf. Meister Eckhart, "About Disinterest," in *The Essential Writings*, trans. Raymond D. Blakney (New York: HarperCollins, 2009).
38 Ivan Illich, *Tools for Conviviality* (London: Marion Boyars Publishers, 2009), 2, 46–7.
39 Max Horkheimer and Theodor W. Adorno, *Dialectic of Enlightenment: Philosophical Fragments*, ed. Mieke Bal and Hent de Vries (Stanford: Stanford University Press, 2002), 124.
40 As this project unfolds it should become clear that our use of the term "subject," "discrete subject," "genuine subject," or similar variations will alternate between subjectivity as, on the one hand, championed by existential philosophers and critical theorists and, on the other, as bearing the Levinasian proviso that a subject is one who is *subject to* and *for* the "other," which, for ethical reasons, inverts the usual connotation of enlightenment autonomy so often associated with the modern subject.
41 Cf. Martin Heidegger, *What Is Called Thinking?*, trans. J. Glenn Gray (New York: HarperCollins, 2004), 3–18.
42 Cf. Hannah Arendt, *The Human Condition* (Chicago: University of Chicago Press, 1974), 4–5, 179, 187–8.
43 Cf. Dollimore, *Radical Tragedy*, 202.
44 Iatrogenic usually refers to illnesses created by medical cures and procedures. Here the context is cultural and philosophical. That is, our solutions to our false needs are insidiously lethal both to our society and our subjectivity.

45 See Robert D. Putnam, *Bowling Alone: The Collapse and Revival of American Community* (New York: Simon & Schuster, 2020).
46 Nahum Tate's "adaptation" of *King Lear* (1681) entirely removes the fool, the king and army of France, Edmund's remorse, and the deaths of Cordelia, Lear, and Gloucester. Instead of the foreign army of France invading to reinstall Lear, there is an uprising among the British people. Moreover, the people win and Lear appoints Cordelia as queen. Edgar ends the play—tragicomically—with these words:

> Our drooping country now erects her head,
> Peace spreads her balmy wings, and plenty blooms.
> Divine Cordelia, all the gods can witness
> How much thy love to empire I prefer!
> Thy bright example shall convince the world
> (Whatever storms of fortune are decreed)
> That truth and virtue shall at last succeed.
>
> *Exeunt all.*

47 Ralph Waldo Emerson, *Emerson in His Journals*, ed. Joel Porte (Cambridge: Harvard University Press, 1982), 45.
48 We will discuss Emerson's method and style more fully in Chapter 2, "The Riddle Is an Elegy."
49 When we consider that the pre-Socratic fragments read like poetry, that Montaigne established the legitimacy of the essay form, that Kierkegaard worked under pseudonyms presenting different positions, that Nietzsche (and many others) authored aphorisms and highly stylized polemics, that various existentialists wrote novels and plays to articulate their philosophies, that Deleuze and Guattari's production of rhizomatic connections in order to avoid hierarchical, linear interpretations, to name but a few, we should pause before placing unsystematic and unconventional thinkers outside the tradition of philosophy based solely upon their manner of presentation—especially when that manner of presentation intentionally attempts to call into question the assumed efficacy of conventional philosophical presentation.
50 Robert D. Richardson Jr., *Emerson: The Mind on Fire* (Berkeley: University of California Press, 1995), 562–3.

1 A Silent Fool

1 Simone Weil, *Simone Weil: An Anthology*, ed. Sian Miles (New York: Grove Press, 2000), 1.
2 Ibid., 2.

3 We might compare the use of "fool" here to the *eirôn* (εἴρων), a stock character in classical Greek comedy, known for buffoonery, mock modesty, and for besting his braggadocios opponent, the *alazṓn*. Xanthias, the servant to Dionysus in Aristophanes' *Frogs*, is a prime example. In addition to comic theater, some consider the *eirôn* to have inspired Plato's depiction of Socrates and his many encounters with sophists, as well as the Gospel writers' portrait of Jesus, particularly in his confrontations with learned religious figures. In this sense, the "fool"—servant, slave, clown, madman—has a long history of exposing ignorance, challenging convention, and of speaking truth to power. Shakespeare continues the tradition with his fools. Our word "irony" derives from this theatrical term. Additionally, in Shakespeare's time, we find "fool" used in the sense of "darling" or "innocent," which adds context and complexity to the double casting of Cordelia and the Fool in *King Lear*: "And my poor fool is hanged!"
4 Weil, *The 'Iliad'*, 163. Emphasis in original.
5 See Stephen Greenblatt, *Shakespearean Negotiations* (Los Angeles: University of California Press, 1988), 65; also Alan Sinfield, "Shakespeare and Education," in *Political Shakespeare: Essays in Cultural Materialism*, 2nd edition, ed. Jonathan Dollimore and Alan Sinfield (Manchester: Manchester University Press, 2005), 178.
6 See Johan Huizinga, "Play and Contest as Civilizing Function" and "Play and Law," in *Homo Ludens: A Study of the Play-Element in Culture*, ed. Johan Huizinga (Boston: Beacon Press, 1955), 46–88.
7 Cf. Max Scheler, "Ordo Amoris," in *Selected Philosophical Essays*, ed. and trans. David R. Lachterman (Evanston: Northwestern University Press, 1973), 106–8.
8 See Booth, *King Lear*, 134–5; also Richard Abrams, "The Double Casting of Cordelia and Lear's Fool: A Theatrical View," *Texas Studies in Literature and Language* 27, no. 4 (Winter, 1985): 354–68.
9 Our fourth chapter, "Wiles of Innocence," will offer an Emersonian reading of *King Lear*, which, in part, pays special attention to Edgar's transformation into Tom O' Bedlam.
10 *King Lear*, 1.1.37–9.
11 Friedrich Nietzsche, *The Birth of Tragedy*, trans. Walter Kaufmann (New York: Vintage Books, 1967), 73. Some classicists and scholars of the Athenian theater, whether following Aristotle or not, would disagree with Nietzsche's reading. The assertion, however, besides having textual evidence, sees tragedy phenomenologically as an ontological state of affairs *and* a performative response venerating the god symbolizing that state of affairs. Tragedy, in this way, is more about the nature of being and the trials of existence than it is about the localized and individuated virtues and vices of a particular mortal character.
12 John Kerrigan, *Shakespeare's Originality* (Oxford: Oxford University Press, 2018), 74.

13 Ibid., 70.
14 *King Lear*, 1.1.123-4.
15 Ibid., 1.1.46-51.
16 Ibid., 1.1.53-9.
17 Ibid., 1.1.71-4.
18 Ibid., 1.1.60.
19 Ibid., 1.1.75-7.
20 Cf. Christina Luckyj, "'A Moving Rhetoricke': Women's Silences and Renaissance Texts," *Renaissance Drama* 24 (1993): 33-56.
21 *King Lear*, 1.1.86-103.
22 Albert Camus, *The Rebel: An Essay on Man in Revolt*, trans. Anthony Bower (New York: Vintage Books, 1991), 13.
23 Martin Heidegger, *Being and Time*, trans. Joan Stambaugh (New York: State University of New York Press, 1996), 154.
24 Ibid.
25 Ibid., 150-1. Emphasis in original.
26 Ibid., 154.
27 Virgil, *The Aeneid of Virgil*, trans. Rolfe Humphries (New York: Charles Scribner's, 1951), 145.
28 Ibid., emphasis added.
29 Cf. Peter Van Nuffelen, "Words of Truth: Mystical Silence as a Philosophical and Rhetorical Tool in Plutarch," *Hermathena*, no. 182 (2007): 9-39.
30 Herbert Marcuse, *Eros and Civilization: A Philosophical Inquiry into Freud* (Boston: Beacon Press, 1974), 116-17.
31 *King Lear*, 4.1.37-8.
32 Ibid., 1.4.161.
33 Friedrich Nietzsche, "On Truth and Lies in a Non-moral Sense," in *The Nietzsche Reader*, ed. Keith Ansell Pearson and Duncan Large (Malden: Blackwell Publishing, 2006), 117.
34 *King Lear*, 1.1.104-22.
35 Coppelia Kahn, "The Absent Mother in King Lear," in *Rewriting the Renaissance: The Discourses of Sexual Difference in Early Modern Europe*, ed. Margaret W. Ferguson, Maureen Quilligan, Nancy J. Vickers (Chicago: University of Chicago Press, 1992), 248.
36 Mark Taylor, *Shakespeare's Darker Purpose: A Question of Incest* (New York: AMS Press, 1982), x.
37 Diane Elizabeth Dreher, *Domination and Defiance: Fathers and Daughters in Shakespeare* (Lexington: University Press of Kentucky, 1986), 64.
38 Cf. Girard, *Violence and the Sacred*, 49.

39 Thorkild Jacobsen, *The Treasures of Darkness: A History of Mesopotamian Religion* (New Haven: Yale University Press, 1976), 57.
40 Phil. 2:5-8 King James Version.
41 Cf. William Rosen, *Shakespeare and the Craft of Tragedy* (Cambridge: Harvard University Press, 1964), 1–51.
42 Compare these passages from the opening scene of *Othello* with Iago's notorious lines at the end: "I know my price, I am worth no worse a place" (1.1.11); "In following him I follow but myself. / Heaven is my judge, not I for love and duty, / But seeming so for my peculiar end" (1.1.58–60); "Even now, now, very now, an old black ram / Is tupping your white ewe" (1.1.88–9); and at the end, "Demand me nothing. What you know, you know. / From this time forth I never will speak word" (5.2.309–10). Iago has already told and shown us everything we need to make informed determinations about his motivations.
43 *King Lear*, 3.2.68–9.
44 David Margolies, *Monsters of the Deep: Social Dissolution in Shakespeare's Tragedies* (New York: Manchester University Press, 1992), 6.
45 Arnold Van Gennep, *The Rites of Passage*, trans. Monika B. Vizedom and Gabrielle L. Caffee (Chicago: University of Chicago Press, 1960), 160–1. The full passage might be helpful here:

> Persons for whom funeral rites are not performed are condemned to a pitiable existence, since they are never able to enter the world of the dead or to become incorporated in the society established there. These are the most dangerous dead. They would like to be reincorporated into the world of the living, and since they cannot be, they behave like hostile strangers to it. They lack the means of subsistence which the other dead find in their own world and consequently must obtain them at the expense of the living. Furthermore, the dead without hearth or home sometimes have an intense desire for vengeance.

46 Cf. Scheler, *Ordo Amoris*, 119–20; and Weil, *The 'Iliad'*, 94.
47 Emerson, *Love*, II, 161, emphasis added.
48 Emerson, *Circles*, II, 290.
49 Emerson, *Self-Reliance*, II, 71.
50 Jean-Pierre Vernant and Pierre Vidal-Naquet, *Myth and Tragedy in Ancient Greece*, trans. Janet Lloyd (New York: Zone Books, 1988), 43.
51 Cf. Stanley Cavell, "The Avoidance of Love: A Reading of King Lear," in *Disowning Knowledge in Seven Plays of Shakespeare*, ed. Stanley Cavell, updated edition (New York: Cambridge University Press, 2003), 39–123.
52 Provisionally, "the world to come" here suggests what awaits those who discover a liberated subjectivity and an authentic sense of community in the tragic world. They free themselves from the "formula of force," refusing to be subordinated

to all powers that restrict or deny an active inner life, that dictate the terms of a meaningful material existence, and that atomize and alienate all manner of social life. And these free subjects discover a way of accomplishing this without succumbing to violence or revenge.

53 Cf. Nietzsche, *Twilight of the Idols*, 120.

2 The Riddle Is an Elegy

1 Emerson, *Quotations and Originality*, VIII, 170. Emerson goes on to consider and challenge the reverential—as referential—attitude and practice:

> The highest statement of new philosophy complacently caps itself with some prophetic maxim from the oldest learning. There is something mortifying in this perpetual circle. This extreme economy argues a very small capital of invention. The stream of affection flows broad and strong; the practical activity is a river of supply; but the dearth of design accuses the penury of intellect. How few thoughts! (171)

2 Cf. Giorgio Agamben, *The Man Without Content*, trans. Georgia Albert (Stanford: Stanford University Press, 1999), 104. In the last chapter, "The Melancholy Angel," Agamben reflects on Benjamin's consideration of quotations.

3 The *katábasis*, as "descent" or "down-going," is a common heroic motif or convention found in Greek and Latin epics. While it contains other connotations, most relevant for us is the act of descent into the underworld in fulfillment of a heroic quest or the retrieval of repressed memories in order to understand and restore the subject to wholeness. A necessary nadir on the way to victory and the return home.

4 Emerson, *Experience*, III, 53.
5 *King Lear*, 5.3.306–7.
6 This should be apparent throughout Emerson's oeuvre to attentive readers, but this sense of loss is undeniably highlighted in essays like *Circles* (1841), *Experience* (1844), *The Tragic* (1844), *Fate* (1860), and his poem *Threnody* (1846).
7 Emerson, *Self-Reliance*, II, 87.
8 Emerson, *Nature*, I, 39–40.
9 Friedrich Nietzsche, *Beyond Good and Evil: Prelude to a Philosophy of the Future*, trans. Walter Kaufmann (New York: Vintage, 1989), 9.
10 Emerson, *Nature*, I, 51.
11 Ralph Waldo Emerson, *The Letters of Ralph Waldo Emerson*, ed. Ralph L. Rusk, vols. 1–6, ed. Eleanor Tilton, vols. 7–8 (New York: Columbia University Press, 1939), 2:19, 20, 25.

12 Ralph Waldo Emerson, *The Journals and Miscellaneous Notebooks of Ralph Waldo Emerson*, ed. William H. Gilman et al., 16 vols. (Cambridge: Harvard University Press, 1960–82), 13:352.
13 Richardson, *Emerson*, 221.
14 Cf. Shakespeare's Sonnet 15:

> When I consider everything that grows
> Holds in perfection but a little moment,
> That this huge stage presenteth naught but shows
> Whereon the stars in secret influence comment;
> When I perceive that men as plants increase,
> Cheered and checked even by the selfsame sky;
> Vaunt in their youthful sap, at height decrease,
> And wear their brave state out of memory;
> Then the conceit of this inconstant stay
> Sets you most rich in youth before my sight,
> Where wasteful Time debateth with Decay
> To change your day of youth to sullied night;
> And all in war with Time for love of you,
> As he takes from you, I engraft you new.

15 Ralph L. Rusk, *The Life of Ralph Waldo Emerson* (New York: Charles Scribner's, 1949), 149.
16 Emerson, *Emerson in His Journals*, 75.
17 Richardson, *Emerson*, 110.
18 Emerson, *Journals and Miscellaneous Notebooks*, 3:227.
19 Ibid., 4:199–200.
20 Richardson, *Emerson*, 151.
21 Emerson, *An Address*, I, 143.
22 Emerson, *Transcendentalist*, I, 312.
23 John L. McDermott, *Streams of Experience: Reflections on the History and Philosophy of American Culture* (Amherst: University of Massachusetts Press, 1986), 131.
24 Friedrich Nietzsche, *Thus Spoke Zarathustra: A Book for Everyone and No One*, trans. R. J. Hollingdale (New York: Penguin Books, 2003), 336.
25 B. L. Packer, *Emerson's Fall: A New Interpretation of the Major Essays* (New York: Continuum, 1982), 30.
26 John Corrigan and Winthrop S. Hudson, *Religion in America: An Historical Account of the Development of American Religious Life* (New Jersey: Prentice-Hall, 2004), 196.
27 Emerson, *The Fugitive Slave Law*, XI, 205.
28 Richardson, *Emerson*, 239–40.

29 Emerson, *The Fugitive Slave Law*, XI, 224. Also, see G. W. F. Hegel's *The Elements of the Philosophy of Right*, ed. Allen W. Wood, trans. H. B. Nisbet (Cambridge: Cambridge University Press, 1991), 127–31; sections 101–3.
30 Robert D. Habich, Introduction to *Selected Writings of Ralph Waldo Emerson*, ed. Robert D. Habich (Peterborough: Broadview Press, 2018), 15.
31 Emerson, *Circles*, I, 281.
32 Nietzsche, *Thus Spoke Zarathustra*, 336.
33 Ibid., 288.
34 Emerson, *Illusions*, VI, 297.
35 While this characterization of the time period under consideration seems widely shared, the reader is encouraged to consult D. M. Palliser's *The Age of Elizabeth: England under the Later Tudors 1547–1603* (London: Longman Group, 1983) for a fuller account of England's social and economic conditions leading up to and contextualizing the year(s) in which Shakespeare wrote *King Lear*. While Palliser would no doubt take issue with some of our less nuanced claims about the age, his text would nevertheless leave the reader with many of the same impressions we have and will present in this work. For example, in his conclusion, he writes, "All ages are ages of transition, blends of continuity and change: the problem is to identify the relative proportions of each" (377). The population was not precisely aware that they were "leaving the medieval world" and "entering a modern one"; clean dates and descriptions, and connective and explanatory implications arise, as always, much later. And yet, Palliser concedes, "If what are sought in the later sixteenth century are signs of England's later rise to commercial and industrial predominance, they are certainly present" (378).
36 Cf. Theodor Adorno, *Aesthetic Theory*, trans. Robert Hullot-Kentor (London: University of Minnesota Press, 1997), 4–5; Northrop Frye, *The Great Code: The Bible and Literature* (New York: Harcourt Brace Jovanovich Publishers, 1982), 217.
37 See Margolies, *Monsters of the Deep*, 6.
38 Emerson, *Nature*, I, 9.
39 Richardson, *Emerson*, 226.
40 Emerson, *The American Scholar*, I, 90.
41 Emerson, *Emerson in His Journals*, 148.
42 Ibid.
43 Emerson, *The American Scholar*, I, 91.
44 Martin Heidegger, "The Question Concerning Technology," in *Basic Writings*, ed. David Farrell Krell (New York: HarperCollins, 1993), 341.
45 Emerson, *Nature*, I, 9–10.
46 Ibid., 15–6.

47 A hallmark of Emersonianism, perhaps idealism in general, is to treat or consider things—people, institutions, social practices, natural phenomena, and so on—in light of what those things could become or come to mean. This does not appear to be done in denial of any historical fact or current state of affairs, rather it is facilitated in hopes of realizing as yet fully determined apical possibilities. Such activity might occur through archaic retrievals, revolutionary practices, creative representations, or novel theorization. In this sense, the "as if" of idealism most fundamentally indicates a performance or dramatization.

48 Russel B. Goodman, following Stanley Cavell, correctly reads Emerson as an American Romantic philosopher. Our use of the term "Emersonianism" carries with it the particular texture of American Romanticism, usually designated as "American transcendentalism" or, simply, "idealism." See Russel B. Goodman's *American Philosophy and the Romantic Tradition* (Cambridge: Cambridge University Press, 1990), 1–57.

49 Cf. Cameron Thompson, "John Locke and New England Transcendentalism," *The New England Quarterly* 35, no. 4 (December, 1962): 435–57. The much remarked on phrase, "paltry empiricism," appears in Emerson's *Experience*, III, 85.

50 Coleridge, *Biographia Literaria*, 154; Stanley Cavell, "Emerson, Coleridge, Kant," in *Emerson's Transcendental Etudes* (Stanford: Stanford University Press, 2003), 59–82.

51 Coleridge, *Biographia Literaria*, 167.

52 Emerson, *The Over-Soul*, II, 262, 265, 276, emphasis added.

53 Goodman, *American Philosophy*, 41.

54 Cf. Emerson, *Circles*, II, 283: "Permanence is but a word of degrees"; *Experience*, III, 53–4: "Life is a train of moods like a string of beads, and as we pass through them they prove to be many-colored lenses which paint the world their own hue, and each shows only what lies in its focus." See also Stanley Cavell, *The Senses of Walden* (Chicago: University of Chicago Press, 1992), 125; John Lysaker, *Emerson and Self-Culture* (Bloomington: University of Indiana Press, 2008), 41–51.

55 Emerson, *Experience*, III, 52.

56 Emerson, *Circles*, II, 283.

57 To compare our use of illusions and imaginary relations here and in what follows with a more decidedly Marxist interpretation, see Althusser, *On the Reproduction of Capitalism*, 181–3.

58 Willard Farnham makes a similar argument but only addresses it to Shakespeare's last four tragedies—*Timon of Athens*, *Macbeth*, *Antony and Cleopatra*, *Coriolanus*—plays wherein the nobility of the protagonist arises from his ignobleness. His virtues emerge from his vices. This inner complexity and paradox indicates a shift in Shakespeare's understanding of tragic figures. And though these changes in the inner lives of the tragic heroes provide us with many intriguing insights, our assertion here rests with the presentation of the world itself changing—becoming

(or retrieving) an "evening world"—and the characters stand primarily as reflections or expressions of this development. See *Shakespeare's Tragic Frontier* (Berkeley: University of California Press, 1963).

59 Margolies, *Monsters of the Deep*, 78.
60 See Sarah Beckwith, *Shakespeare and the Grammar of Forgiveness* (New York: Cornell University Press, 2011), 34–56.
61 See Andy Amato, *The Ethical Imagination in Shakespeare and Heidegger* (New York: Bloomsbury Academic, 2019), 151–6.
62 *The Tempest*, 5.1.57, 278–9, 322, Epilogue 19–20.
63 Cf. Margolies, *Monsters of the Deep*.
64 Sophocles, "Antigone," 127.
65 *King Lear*, 1.2.1–22.
66 Nietzsche, *Thus Spoke Zarathustra*, 137.
67 Jonathan Dollimore offers an example of this when he contrasts Tamburlaine and Faustus's respective transgressions, the former's enactment of will to power leads to liberation, while the latter's ends in despair. And more directly to the point here, he offers a material analysis of Edmund wherein it is in fact "society's obsession with power, property, and inheritance," and its simultaneous rendering of Edmund as an illegitimate child excluded from any conventional attainment of those objectives—thus granting him deep, yet incomplete, insight into how society really works—that grants him revolutionary possibilities that fall short because those possibilities are, *tragically*, "folded back into a dominant ideology." See *Radical Tragedy*, 114, 201.
68 Emerson, *Self-Reliance*, II, 60.
69 Gilles Deleuze, *Difference and Repetition*, trans. Paul Patton (New York: Columbia University Press, 1994), 139.
70 Cf. Jerome S. Bruner, "Myth and Identity," in *Myth and Mythmaking*, ed. Henry A. Murray (New York: George Braziller, 1960), 276–87. The idea Bruner puts forward pertains to reading a work of art—principally drama—as "containing and cleansing" the terror of our inner impulses through the very act of exteriorizing them. Bringing them out into the open, as it were, and by that same process simultaneously creating laws and destinies—aesthetic determinations and possibilities—to which those terrors must conform. Myth and ritual as such represent the basic patterns that take shape culturally in response to the recurrent playing-out of these manifest exorcisms. He refers to an "internal cast of identities" representing the roles that correspond to particular community plights and struggles, but which, in time, travel too far from the original energies (and context) that birthed them, thus they lose the power (and relevance) required to continue to "contain and cleanse" those inner terrors. (It therefore remains remarkable that some works, like Shakespeare's major plays, seem to have attained a transcultural and transhistorical resonance.) The point of comparison here lies with how we are attempting to develop the idea

of nomadically fluid identities in relation to critical projects aimed at liberation and authenticity in conjunction with the rehabilitation of the tragic imagination.
71 Emerson, *Culture*, VI, 158–9.
72 *King Lear*, 1.2.22.
73 Cf. Stack, *Nietzsche and Emerson*, 8–9; Walter Kaufmann, Introduction to *The Gay Science*, 7–13; Cavell, *Emerson's Transcendental Etudes*, 213–14.
74 Emerson, *Nature*, I, 74.
75 Emerson, *Uses of Great Men*, IV, 20.
76 Emerson, *Nature*, I, 10–11. Rene Wellek points out that the *me – not me* distinction comes from Fichte, but that Emerson finds it in either Carlyle or Cousin's essay on Novalis. See "Emerson and German Philosophy," *The New England Quarterly* 16, no. 1 (March, 1943): 49.
77 John Lysaker, *Emerson and Self-Culture* (Bloomington: University of Indiana Press, 2008), 30.
78 Emerson, *The Over-Soul*, II, 253. We also have in mind here Levinas's subject-determining conception of the other, which couples subjectivity and responsibility. The subject is only a subject in so far as the other—before whom the subject *is subjected*—places a demand upon the subject to be asymmetrically and nonreciprocally responsible for the other.
79 Emerson, *Power*, VI, 55.
80 Emerson, *Experience*, III, 52–3.
81 Cf. Sharon Cameron, "Representing Grief: Emerson's 'Experience,'" *Representation*, no. 15 (Summer, 1986): 16.
82 Emerson, *Experience*, III, 53: "I take this evanescence and lubricity of all objects, which lets them slip through our fingers then when we clutch hardest, to be the most unhandsome part of our condition."
83 Emerson, *Nature*, I, 74.
84 Emerson, *Intellect*, II, 319: "Silence is a solvent that destroys personality, and gives us leave to be great and universal." It should also be noted here that our emphasis on alterity—difference, otherness, strangeness—in connection with Emerson's conceptualization and use of "nothing" and "not me" runs counter to Joseph Urbas's recent (and impressive) interpretation of Emerson. In contrast to certain post-structural trends, he highlights Emerson's understanding of "identity" in relation to "the same." Metaphysically considered, Urbas argues, Emerson finds an essential sameness and oneness underlying all things. Our path forward, however—paved by Nietzsche (overcoming nihilism), Marcuse (liberating eros), and Deleuze (being is difference)—challenges such interpretations of identity as largely a consequence of force. Difference is needed for liberatory projects. In any case, readers will ultimately have to decide for themselves how best to interpret Emerson's metaphysics and overall philosophy—a suggestion that Emerson himself

would surely support. See Joseph Urbas's *The Philosophy of Ralph Waldo Emerson* (New York: Routledge, 2021), 15–23. Also, for a materialist counterpoint to this interpretation—not directly of Emerson, but of the tragic dissolution into nothing *en route* to unity with being—see Dollimore, *Radical Tragedy*, 156–8.
85 Cf. Gilles Deleuze, *Pure Immanence: Essays on a Life*, trans. Anne Boyman (New York: Zone Books, 2005), 25–32.
86 Emerson, *Nature*, I, 16.
87 Emerson, *An Address*, I, 120.
88 Emerson, *Nature*, I, 16.
89 Emerson, *Self-Reliance*, II, 53. Emphasis in original.
90 Cf. James Woelfel, "The Beautiful Necessity: Emerson and the Stoic Tradition," *American Journal of Theology & Philosophy* 32, no. 2 (May 2011): 122–38. And in his own systematic treatment of idealism, Hegel also landed upon stoicism as indicative of freedom in thought but as yet realized in actual material life; see G. W. F. Hegel's *Phenomenology of Spirit*, trans. A. V. Miller (New York: Oxford University Press, 1977), §197–201, as well as Herbert Marcuse's insightful interpretation and elaboration in *Reason and Revolution: Hegel and the Rise of Social Theory* (London: Wool Haus, 2020), 88–9.
91 About twenty years later in *Illusions*, first published in *The Atlantic Monthly* (1857) and later collected in *The Conduct of Life* (1860), we find the mature expression of Emerson's thought regarding the identity of the subject or authentic self in relation to nonidentity. He cites the *Vishnu Purana*: "The notions, 'I am,' and 'This is mine,' which influences mankind, are but delusions of the mother of the world" (VI, 307).
92 Cf. Goodman, *American Philosophy*, 40.
93 Emerson, *Experience*, III, 53.
94 Packer, *Emerson's Fall*, 169.
95 Epictetus, *The Enchiridion*, trans. Nicholas P. White (Indianapolis: Hackett Publishing, 1983), 14; section 11.
96 Packer, *Emerson's Fall*, 24.
97 Ibid., 151.
98 Emerson, *Experience*, III, 85.
99 Richardson, *Emerson*, 359.
100 See Abrams, "The Double Casting of Cordelia and Lear's Fool," 354–68.
101 *King Lear*, 5.3.304–26.

3 The Perpetual Messiah

1 Emerson, *Nature*, I, 74.
2 Julie Ellison, *Emerson's Romantic Style* (Princeton: Princeton University Press, 1984), 96.

3 Packer, *Emerson's Fall*, 83.
4 A. M. Baumgartner, "'The Lyceum Is My Pulpit': Homiletics in Emerson's Early Lectures," *American Literature* 34, no. 4 (1963): 482.
5 Ibid., 483.
6 Cornel West, "The Emersonian Prehistory of American Pragmatism," in *Estimating Emerson: An Anthology of Criticism from Carlyle to Cavell*, ed. David LaRocca (New York: Bloomsbury Academic, 2013), 643.
7 Baumgartner, "The Lyceum Is My Pulpit," 485.
8 Ibid., 486.
9 Regarding the characterization of Emerson as a tragic thinker, see Stephen E. Whicher, "Emerson's Tragic Sense," in *Emerson: A Collection of Critical Essays*, ed. Milton Konvitz and Stephen Whicher (Englewood Cliffs: Prentice-Hall, 1962).
10 Packer, *Emerson's Fall*, 83.
11 Emerson, *The American Scholar*, I, 91.
12 Ibid.
13 David L. Smith, "'The Sphinx Must Solve Her Own Riddle': Emerson, Secrecy, and the Self-Reflexive Method," *Journal of the American Academy of Religion* 71, no. 4 (2003): 837.
14 As with many things, if not all things, we will see that the beginning holds and foretells the ending. In the first chapter of *Nature*, Emerson writes: "The lover of nature is he whose inward and outward senses are still truly adjusted to each other; who has retained the spirit of infancy even into the era of manhood. His intercourse with heaven and earth, becomes part of his daily food. In the presence of nature, a wild delight runs through the man, in spite of real sorrows" (I, 14–15).
15 Cf. Jacques and Raissa Maritain, *The Situation of Poetry* (New York: Philosophical Library, 1955); Harold Bloom, *The Anxiety of Influence* (New York: Oxford University Press, 1997); the reader could also explore the concept of "misreading" through the hermeneutical practices of Heidegger and Derrida.
16 Gilles Deleuze and Felix Guattari, *What Is Philosophy?*, trans. Hugh Tomlinson and Graham Burchell (New York: Columbia University Press, 1994), 82.
17 Given our topic here, the last few lines of Shakespeare's twelfth sonnet are worth noting:

> That thou among the wastes of time must go,
> Since sweets and beauties do themselves forsake
> And die as fast as they see others grow;
> > And nothing 'gainst time's scythe can make defence
> > Save breed, to brave him when he takes thee hence.

18 Emerson, *The Lord's Supper*, XI, 29.

19 See Marcuse, *Eros and Civilization*. While Marcuse's overall work speaks to this idea, the reader can find succinct statements in the "Political Preface 1966" and chapter 10, "The Transformation of Sexuality into Eros."
20 Erik Ingvar Thurin, *Emerson as Priest of Pan: A Study in the Metaphysics of Sex* (Lawrence: The Regents Press of Kansas, 1981), 222.
21 Cf. St. Augustine, *City of God*, XV.22; Scheler, *Ordo Amoris*. Our use here does not designate a fixed hierarchy of proper love objects, rather an underlying dynamic instinctual structure (*eros*) always novel in its authentic expression.
22 Emerson, *Self-Reliance*, II, 51.
23 Emerson, *Nature*, I, 9.
24 John Dewey, "Emerson," 295.
25 Emerson, *Nature*, I, 9.
26 Ibid., 10.
27 Emerson, *The Transcendentalist*, I, 311–12.
28 Emerson, *An Address*, I, 129.
29 Emerson, *Nature*, I, 10.
30 Ibid., 10–1.
31 Cf. Marcuse, *Reason and Revolution*, 74–8. Here, in the context of Hegel's critique of propositional truth statements, Marcuse analyzes the *negation* of epistemological certainty gained from (1) sense experience when we assume the essence and reality of objects lie within the objects themselves and (2) the individuated "I" (Emerson's *me*). It is rather the case that "universals" and the "essential reality" of objects lie in the conscious processes of the universal subject (the *not me*). Knowledge whatsoever is grounded in the activity of the universal subject—*dialectically retrieved from what it is not*—subsequently, when not adequately apprehended, it presents us with some of modernity's major (sophistic) anxieties: truth as subjective, knowledge as perspectival, and so on.
32 The use of "abyss" here in relation to ethics signals a radically humbling relational asymmetry of staggering imaginative depth. I have in mind the ethics of Emmanuel Levinas, wherein subjects are constituted by their very *being subject to and for* the other. Ethics subsequently takes precedence over ontology and metaphysics, which have conceptually or schematically totalized the other prior to any sense of responsibility for the other. "[Levinas's] ethical subjectivity is," as Thomas Carl Wall writes, "infinite vulnerability." See Wall, *Radical Passivity: Levinas, Blanchot, and Agamben* (New York: State University of New York Press, 1999), 40; regarding how this reversal of the constitution of subjectivity relates to freedom, see Levinas, *Humanism of the Other*, trans. Nidra Poller (Chicago: University of Illinois Press, 2003), 49–52.
33 Emerson, *Circles*, II, 282.

34 Plato, *Symposium*, trans. A. Nehamas and P. Woodruff (Indianapolis: Hackett Publishing, 1989), 203e.
35 See Katie Geneva Cannon, *Katie's Canon: Womanism and the Soul of the Black Community* (New York: Continuum Publishing Company, 2003), 33:

> In spite of every form of institutional constraint, Afro-American slaves were able to create another world, a counterculture within the White-defined world, complete with their own folklore, spirituals, and religious practices. These tales, songs, and prayers are the most distinctive cultural windows through which I was taught to see the nature and range of Black people's response to the dehumanizing pressures of slavery and plantation life. Even with cultural self-expression outlawed, my ancestors never surrendered their humanity or lost sight of a vision of freedom and justice they believed to be their due. There was a critical difference between what Whites tried to teach and what slaves actually learned. Against all odds, Afro-American slaves created a culture saturated with their own values and heavily laden with their dreams.

36 Emerson, *Nature*, I, 74.
37 Stanley Brodwin, "Emerson's Version of Plotinus: The Flight to Beauty," *Journal of the History of Ideas* 35, no. 3 (1974): 466.
38 Ibid., 14.
39 Ibid., 14–15.
40 Cf. Giorgio Agamben, *The Man Without Content*, trans. Georgia Albert (Stanford: Stanford University Press, 1999), 114–15.
41 To understand better the sense of "forgiven" here, consider the Greek word for "forgiveness," *apolýō* (ἀπολύω), which means "loosed," "released," "freed," as well as the German word, *vergeben*, signifying "already given," "assigned," "awarded." Older forms of *remit* and romance variations of *pardon* can also contribute to this sense of forgiven. Concisely stated, this transcendental operation of forgiveness joins us to nature in a way that seems original and restorative, and by being so joined and gaining the strange sense of retroactive union, we become free for our situation. Liberated for life itself.
42 Emerson, *The Poet*, III, 28: "But nature has a higher end, in the production of new individuals, than security, namely *ascension*, or the passage of the soul into higher forms." Emphasis in original.
43 Emerson, *Nature*, I, 20.
44 Ibid.
45 Ibid., 19–20.
46 Ibid., 20.
47 See beginning of Chapter 1, "A Silent Fool," as well as notes 1 and 3.
48 Emerson, *Wealth*, VI, 93.

49 Ibid., 96.
50 Ibid.
51 Ibid.
52 David La Rocca, "Emerson Recomposed: Nietzsche's Uses of His American 'Soul-Brother,'" *Nietzsche and the Philosophers*, ed. Mark T. Conrad (New York: Rutledge: 2017), 224.
53 Nietzsche, *The Gay Science*, 107; aphorism 40.
54 Emerson, *Nature*, I, 21. For a succinct explanation of *kósmos* see W. K. C. Guthrie, *The Greek Philosophers: From Thales to Aristotle* (New York: Harper Perennial, 1975), 37–9, 101, 107.
55 Ibid.
56 Ibid.
57 See Brodwin, "Emerson's Version of Plotinus," 482. Also, we are not attempting to use the term "intellection" in any highly technical or restricted sense, rather as a way of initially distinguishing the thinking that occurs in relation to objects of thought as such from thinking in relation to sense experience. But we might also use intellection here in an even broader manner to include both sensible phenomena and intelligible objects when taken together within a unified system of knowing in which all sensible phenomena and intelligible objects are thought in relation to one another in the "bright light" of reason alone (whereby they are stripped of their illusory qualities) and then later in the more subdued and sustainable light of reason's harmony with the understanding (whereby their illusory qualities are restored to them as necessary). On the one hand, intellection here indicates thinking in relation to intelligible objects, and, on the other, a way of thinking in general as it pertains to a system (or even style) of thought that generates concepts and arguments in order to give an account of the world, our experiences of the world, and our beliefs and habits about the world and our experiences of it. In this latter sense intellection is strongly associated with *ideation*, the creation or recognition of ideas meta-narrativizing our life as beings who think about the world and reflect upon our experiences of it.
58 Emerson, *Nature*, I, 22.
59 Ibid.
60 Ibid., 22–3, emphasis added.
61 See Emerson, *Shakespeare; Or, The Poet*, IV, 204.
62 Emerson, *Nature*, I, 24–5, emphasis added.
63 Ibid., 25.
64 Ibid., 26.
65 Ibid., 28.
66 If the "game" appears with a warped or indiscernible play instinct, then the "game of knowing" becomes the "politics of knowing" in which force alone determines

victory through the spiritual, if not bodily, nihilation of those caught in the equation.

67 Ibid., 29–30, emphasis added.
68 Ibid., 30.
69 Ibid., 31.
70 Stack, *Nietzsche and Emerson*, 13–6.
71 Emerson, *Nature*, I, 31–2. Emphasis in original.
72 Ibid., 32.
73 Ibid., 34.
74 Ibid., 33.
75 Ibid., 34–5. Regarding how we find the material and abstract senses of reality conditioned by the state of our affective or inner-life, see also Emerson, *Fate*, VI, 24–5:

> Whatever limits us, we call Fate. If we are brute and barbarous, the fate takes a brute and dreadful shape. As we refine, our checks become finer. If we rise to spiritual culture, the antagonism takes a spiritual form. In the Hindoo fables, Vishnu follows Maya through all her ascending changes, from insect and crawfish up to elephant; whatever form she took, he took the male form of that kind, until she became at last woman and goddess, and he a man and a god. The limitations refine as the soul purifies, but the ring of necessity is always perched at the top.

76 Emerson, *Nature*, I, 35.
77 Ibid., 35–6.
78 Ibid., 37.
79 Ibid., 38.
80 Ibid.
81 Friedrich Nietzsche, "On Truth," 114: "One might invent such a fable, and yet he still would not have adequately illustrated how miserable, how shadowy and transient, how aimless and arbitrary the human intellect looks within nature. There were eternities during which it did not exist. And when it is all over with the human intellect, nothing will have happened."
82 Samuel Beckett, "All Strange Away," in *The Complete Short Prose, 1929–1989*, ed. S. E. Gontarski (New York: Grove Press, 1995), 169.
83 See chapter one, "Religion and World-Construction" of Peter Berger's *The Sacred Canopy: Elements of a Sociological Theory of Religion* (New York: Anchor Books, 1990).
84 Emerson, *Nature*, I, 40–1. See also Paul Tillich, *Dynamics of Faith* (New York: Harper & Row, 1957), 42–3.

85 Cf. Hans-Georg Gadamer, *Truth and Method*, 2nd revised edition, trans. Joel Weinsheimer and Donald G. Marshall (New York: Continuum, 2004), 131–4.
86 Richardson, *Emerson*, 92–3.
87 Emerson, *Nature*, I, 43, emphasis added.
88 Ibid., 44.
89 Ibid., 45.
90 Arguing against the recent "antimetaphysical bias" in Emerson scholarship—which would superficially include our reading here—Joseph Urbas makes a compelling case that Emerson was not simply restricted by the conceptual language of his time but that he was indeed a thoroughly metaphysical philosopher. See chapter 1, "Metaphysics," of his book, *The Philosophy of Ralph Waldo Emerson* (New York: Routledge, 2021), 15–56.
91 Emerson, *The Transcendentalist*, I, 319.
92 Emerson, *Nature*, I, 42.
93 Ibid., 48–9.
94 Cf. Tillich, *Dynamics of Faith*, 1.
95 Emerson, *Nature*, I, 47.
96 Ibid., 52.
97 Cf. Giorgio Agamben, "The Time that Is Left," *Epoche* 7, no. 1 (Fall 2002): 1–14.
98 Richardson, *Emerson*, 232
99 Emerson, *Nature*, I, 53.
100 Packer, *Emerson's Fall*, 62.
101 Cf. Emerson, *Montaigne; Or, The Skeptic*, VI, 177: "Let a man learn to look for the permanent in the mutable and fleeting; let him learn to bear the disappearance of the things he has want to reverence, without losing his reverence."
102 Cf. Gilles Deleuze, *Difference and Repetition*, trans. Paul Patton (New York: Columbia University Press, 1994), 28–69.
103 Emerson, *Self-Reliance*, II, 58.
104 Emerson, *Montaigne; Or, The Skeptic*, IV, 150. See also Packer, *Emerson's Fall*, 201.
105 Cf. Dan Smith, "Desire: Deleuze and the Question of Desire: Toward an Immanent Theory of Ethics," in *Essays on Deleuze* (Edinburgh: Edinburgh University Press, 2012), 175–88.
106 Emerson, *Nature*, I, 55.
107 Ibid.
108 Ibid.
109 Martin Heidegger, "The Age of the World Picture," in *Off the Beaten Track*, ed. and trans. Julian Young and Kenneth Haynes (Cambridge: Cambridge University Press, 2002), 71. See also Jean Baudrillard's famous essay, *The Evil Demon of Images*, trans. P. Patton and P. Foss (Sydney: Power Institute of Fine Arts, 1984).
110 Emerson, *Nature*, I, 55.

111 Herbert Marcuse, *One-Dimensional Man: Studies in the Ideology of Advanced Industrial Society* (Boston: Beacon Press, 1991), 14; Peter Berger and Anton Zijderveld, *In Praise of Doubt: How to Have Convictions without Becoming a Fanatic* (New York: HarperOne, 2009), 18.
112 Emerson, *Circles*, II, 296–97.
113 Nietzsche, *The Gay Science*, 181; aphorism 125.
114 Emerson, *Nature*, I, 56.
115 Immanuel Kant, *Critique of Pure Reason*, trans. Werner S. Pluhar (Indianapolis: Hackett Publishing, 1996), B152.
116 Emerson, *Nature*, I, 56–7.
117 Emerson, *Self-Reliance*, II, 62.
118 Emerson, *Shakespeare; Or, The Poet*, IV, 204.
119 Emerson, *Nature*, I, 58.
120 Ibid., 59. Emphasis in original.
121 In *Radical Tragedy*, Jonathan Dollimore, referencing historian Christopher Hill, claims that the best histories of the seventeenth century were being written by literary critics (xlv). And I am suggesting here that the creative works themselves of this period, and perhaps of any period, serve as superior—though certainly not exclusive—artifacts with which to do history. An explicit example of this is M. I. Finley's *The World of Odysseus* (1954), in which the renowned historian sets out to reconstruct "a picture of a society based on a close reading of the Iliad and Odyssey."
122 Ibid.
123 Emerson, *Plato; Or, The Philosopher*, IV, 42.
124 Plato, "Phaedrus" in *Plato: Complete Works*, trans. A. Nehamas and P. Woodruff (Indianapolis: Hackett Publishing, 1997), 238d.
125 Emerson, *Nature*, I, 59.
126 Emerson, *Plato; Or, The Philosopher*, IV, 49.
127 In a well-known, if not notorious, passage from this section of *Nature* Emerson writes, "The problem of philosophy, according to Plato, is, for all that exists conditionally, to find a ground unconditioned and absolute." No such passage, however, can be found in Plato. It rather originates in Kant *Critique of Pure Reason*, though Emerson takes it directly from Coleridge's *Friend*, wherein Coleridge ascribes it to Plato rather than Kant. See Wellek, "Emerson and German Philosophy," 42.
128 Hegel, *Phenomenology of Spirit*, §20. Emphasis in original.
129 Emerson, *Circles*, II, 282.
130 Emerson, *Nature*, I, 60–1.
131 Ibid.

132 Ludwig Feuerbach, *The Essence of Christianity*, trans. George Eliot (Amherst: Prometheus Books, 1989), 40.
133 Prov. 8:23 King James Version; Emerson, *Nature*, I, 61.
134 Emerson, *Nature*, I, 61; See also *An Address*, I, 128.
135 Emerson, *Nature*, I, 61.
136 Ibid. Emphasis in original.
137 Ibid., 62.
138 Ibid., 63.
139 Ibid.
140 Marcuse, *Eros and Civilization*, 19.
141 Heraclitus fragment 52; Mt. 18:3 King James Version.
142 See Elizabeth Grosz, *The Incorporeal: Ontology, Ethics, and the Limits of Materialism* (New York: Columbia University Press, 2017). Grosz provides an account of the stoics, as well as on each of these thinkers mentioned here, convincingly demonstrating the explicit or implicit use of incorporeality in their respective philosophies, greatly problematizing any rigid claims to a reductive sense of materiality.
143 Emerson, *Nature*, I, 63.
144 Ibid., 64.
145 Cf. Marcuse, *Eros and Civilization*, 171.
146 Emerson, *Nature*, I, 64.
147 Ibid., 65.
148 Ibid.
149 Cf. Jean Paul Sartre, *Being and Nothingness: An Essay on Phenomenological Ontology*, trans. H. E. Barnes (London: Routledge, 1958), 8, 24–5.
150 Emerson, *Nature*, I, 66–7.
151 Ibid., 66.
152 Ibid., 68.
153 Ibid., 69.
154 Regarding the use of "uncanny," consider Sophocles' well-known use of *deinós*—marvelous, wonderful, monstrous, terrible, strange, dire, and so on—in *Antigone* at the start of the ode on humanity (lines 332–3). See also Amato, *Ethical Imagination*, 100–7.
155 Emerson, *Nature*, I, 74.
156 Cf. Mt. 16:25 and Lk. 17:33.
157 Cf. Hegel, *Phenomenology of Spirit*, §77.
158 In his essay, *Experience*, Emerson distinguishes between a purely theoretical form of dialectics, which he finds ineffectual, and dialectics as "muscular activity," which he believes is necessary and advantageous. He writes:

> Life is not dialectics. We, I think, in these times, have had enough of the futility of criticism. Our young people have thought and written much on labor and reform, and for all that they have written, neither the world not themselves have got on a step. Intellectual tasting of life will not supersede muscular activity. If a man should consider the nicety of the passage of bread down his throat, he would starve. (III, 61)

159 Emerson, *Nature*, I, 73.
160 Chapter 4 of Robert Zaretsky's recent intellectual biography of Simone Weil—*The Subversive Simone Weil: A Life in Five Ideas* (Chicago: University of Chicago Press, 2021)—entitled "Finding Roots," excellently parses out the complex entwinements of Weil's sense of cultural and national "roots." He reads her as retrieving an ancient Homeric sense of vulnerable horizontal "roots," distinct from our usual unyieldingly vertical conceptualization. Like Emerson toward the United States, she had many criticisms and admonishments for her native France, yet all countries—even those colonial European powers—provided unique cultural bonds of fraternity within a people, and thus between different peoples. Through their very fragility and imperfections, these vulnerable inheritances made a certain kind of compassionate beauty both possible and precious. While clearly more concerned with establishing an American ethos whatsoever, Emerson's social and political writings nevertheless seem to share this ambiguous, caveated endorsement of cultural inheritance.
161 Emerson, *Self-Reliance*, II, 59, 60.
162 Emerson, *Nature*, I, 70–1.
163 Emerson, *An Address*, I, 132.
164 Emerson, *Nature*, I, 74.
165 Ibid., 79.
166 Cf. Mark Mason and Michael O'Rourke, "Meillassoux's Messianicity," in *Speculation, Heresy, and Gnosis in Contemporary Philosophy of Religion*, ed. Joshua Ramey and Matthew S. Haar Farris (London: Rowman & Littlefield, 2016), 55.
167 Emerson, *Self-Reliance*, II, 55.
168 Sophocles, "Antigone," 178:
> "God's ordinances, unwritten and secure.
> They are not of today and yesterday;
> they live forever; none knows when first they were."

4 Wiles of Innocence

1 Emerson, *Nature*, III, 182.
2 Ibid.

3 Rusk, *Life of Ralph Waldo Emerson*, 300, 406.
4 Ibid., 407.
5 See Smith, "The Sphinx Must Solve Her Own Riddle," 846.
6 Cf. Emerson, *Shakespeare; Or, The Poet*, IV, 204.
7 Emerson, *Nature*, III, 187.
8 Cf. Marcuse, *Eros and Civilization*, 172–221.
9 Emerson, *Nature*, III, 187.
10 Emerson, *Nature*, I, 16.
11 See Emerson, *Illusions*, VI, 297, 306–7; also Marcuse, *Eros and Civilization*, part II.
12 Emerson, *Illusions*, VI, 305.
13 *The Tempest*, 4.1.152–3.
14 Emerson, *Nature*, III, 170.
15 *King Lear*, 1.1.149–51.
16 *King Lear*, 2.4.258–66.
17 Berel Lang, "Nothing Comes of All: Lear Dying," *New Literary History* 9, no. 3 (Spring 1978): 558–9.
18 Elizabeth D. Gruber, "Nature on the Verge," *Interdisciplinary Studies in Literature and Environment* 22, no. 1 (Winter, 2015): 99.
19 *Hamlet* does not complete this retrieval as the eponymous character and the world of the play are too bound up with one another. That is, despite the popular belief that he is inactive or ineffective, the character of Hamlet still drives and orchestrates all of the major events within the world, while the world itself has not, as with subsequent tragedies, fully absorbed him and taken center stage itself.
20 Kerrigan, *Shakespeare's Originality*, 74.
21 See Emerson, *Shakespeare; Or, The Poet*, IV, 181–3, 189–90; also Kerrigan's introduction to *Shakespeare's Originality*.
22 Emerson, *Shakespeare; Or, The Poet*, IV, 181.
23 Weil, *The 'Iliad' or the Poem of Force*, 174.
24 Cf. Anaximander fragment: "Whence things have their origin, there they must also pass away according to necessity; for they must pay penalty and be judged for their injustice, according to the ordinance of time" (trans. Nietzsche).
25 One of the hallmarks of tragedy is that tragic heroes *can* do as we have suggested, and yet, whether or not they do so, the drama's end remains the same: they will "cause" suffering, they will suffer, and (to some degree) they will be sacrificed. This does not diminish their agency, rather grounds it in reality. The difference primarily lies in whether or not world-affirming principles drive their action or perceived "inaction." If they do elect unprincipled action, then, for all their gifts and powers, the lesson of their being arrives *videtur quod non* instead of *videtur quod sic*. Of course, either way, we who witness the downfall have the opportunity to be

wounded by it, to identify with it, to recoil from it, and to do likewise or otherwise than they did (to the extent that "fate" has granted us the capacity and character to do so).
26 *King Lear*, 5.3.323.
27 *King Lear*, 1.2.96–7, 109.
28 *King Lear*, 4.6.145. There is a further confusion of the senses that the Fool's prophecy undertakes, which is common in religious teachings, indicating how in order to see the world rightly we have to see it differently, almost paradoxically or impossibly. Perhaps confounding the senses itself works as a riddle wherein we become tasked with recalibrating our assumptions about how it is that we perceive and receive the world.
29 For those unfamiliar with the play, King Lear and his daughters represent the primary plot, while Gloucester and his sons run secondary and parallel.
30 See Amato, *Ethical Imagination*, 197–209.
31 Sophocles, "Oedipus the King," 75.
32 *King Lear*, 5.3.185–6.
33 See Heidegger, *Age of the World Picture* (1938) and *The Question Concerning Technology* (1953).
34 Lang, "Nothing Comes of All," 555.
35 Cf. Marcuse, *Eros and Civilization*, 159–71.
36 See Note 3 of Chapter 1, "A Silent Fool."
37 *King Lear*, 1.4.129–30.
38 *King Lear*, 1.4.168–69.
39 See Alan R. Shickman, "The Fool's Mirror in *King Lear*," *English Literary Renaissance* 21, no. 1 (Winter 1991): 75–86; Kott, *Shakespeare Our Contemporary*, 164.
40 Friedrich Nietzsche, *Also sprach Zarathustra* (Stuttgart: Reclam, 2005), 17.
41 Cf. Dostoyevsky's ironic use of "idiot" for his novel *The Idiot* (1869).
42 Cf. Nietzsche, *Birth of Tragedy*, 73.
43 For the broad contours here see Nietzsche's *Genealogy of Moral* (1887) and *The Anti-Christ* (1888). Regarding the contrast between Dionysus and the Crucified, see Section 1052 of *The Will to Power*, trans. Walter Kaufmann and R. J. Hollingdale (New York: Random House, 1968).
44 Nietzsche, *Anti-Christ*, 161.
45 Karl Jaspers, *Nietzsche*, trans. C. Wallroff and F. Schmitz (Tucson: University of Arizona Press, 1965), 434.
46 Nietzsche *Anti-Christ*, 179, et passim.
47 Alistair Kee, *Nietzsche against the Crucified* (London: SCM Press, 1999), 147.
48 Gadamer, *Truth and Method*, 112–13.
49 Marcuse, *Eros and Civilization*, 69–71.
50 *Measure for Measure*, 2.2.109–11.

51 Luke 17:21; Nietzsche addresses this passage in sections 29 and 34 of *The Anti-Christ*, but largely only in criticism of Christianity's misunderstanding of it, on the one hand, and its exhortation to flee from reality, on the other.
52 Friedrich Nietzsche, "Only a Fool! Only a Poet!," in *Dithyrambs of Dionysus*, trans. R. J. Hollingdale (London: Anvil Press Poetry, 2001), 28–9.
53 Emerson, *An Address*, I, 128.
54 For more context surrounding this "aside," see René Girard, "Dionysus versus the Crucified," *MLN* 99, no. 4, French Issue (September, 1984): 816–35.
55 See Shapiro, *Year of Lear*, 65–88.
56 Kott, *Shakespeare Our Contemporary*, 160.
57 See Greenblatt, *Shakespearean Negotiations*, 128.
58 Kott, *Shakespeare Our Contemporary*, 166–7.
59 Critchley, *Tragedy*, 277.
60 It is worth recalling that our word "tragedy" comes from the Greek word *tragōidia*, which literally means "goat song." Many speculate that this derives from the practice of awarding goats as prizes in early dithyrambic contests, which were the precursors to tragic drama. That goats were also commonly sacrificed adds additional weight to the idea that tragic heroes can, and perhaps should, be read as "scapegoats."
61 1 Cor. 1:27-8 King James Version. Emphasis in original.
62 1 Cor. 2:9 King James Version.
63 *A Midsummer Night's Dream*, 4.1.199–209.
64 *King Lear*, 3.2.79–90.
65 Sheldon P. Zitner, "The Fool's Prophecy," *Shakespeare Quarterly* 18, no. 1 (Winter 1967): 76.
66 Ibid., 76–7.
67 Ibid., 79.
68 *King Lear*, 3.2.91–3.
69 Zitner, "Fool's Prophecy," 79–80.
70 The line, "secret church of a better world," comes from Novalis; see Tim Blanning, *The Romantic Revolution: A History* (New York: Modern Library, 2011), 39.
71 Edward Godfrey Cox, "King Lear in Celtic Tradition," *Modern Language Notes* 24, no. 1 (January 1909): 1–6.
72 David B. Spaan, "The Place of Manannan Mac Lir in Irish Mythology," *Folklore* 76, no. 3 (Autumn 1965): 185.
73 Ibid., 190–1.
74 Ibid.
75 Herbert Weinsinger, "Myth and Ritual Approach to Shakespeare," *Myth and Mythmaking*, ed. Henry A. Murray (New York: George Braziller 1960), 140.

76 There are plenty of stories to challenge this characterization. The point here is to try and reconstruct a general sense of how the Tuatha de Danann were preserved in the natural surround and collective imagination.
77 See Amato, *Ethical Imagination*, 29–35.
78 Piotr Spyra, "Shakespeare and the Demonization of Fairies," *Text Matters* 7, no. 7 (2017): 197.
79 Ibid., 211.
80 Cf. Cavell, *Disowning Knowledge*. In chapter 2, "The Avoidance of Love: A Reading of *King Lear*," Cavell explores at length how avoidance contributes to tragedy. Near the end of the chapter he distills this contribution: "The cause of tragedy is that we would rather murder the world than permit it to expose us to change" (122).
81 J. J. Pollitt, *Art and Experience in Classical Greece* (London: Cambridge University Press, 1972), 27, emphasis added.
82 Rosen, *Shakespeare*, 28.
83 Cf. Clifford Leech, *Tragedy* (London: Methuen, 1969), 54.
84 *King Lear*, 2.4.273–7.
85 *King Lear*, 1.1.263–5.
86 See Amato, *Ethical Imagination*, 198.
87 *King Lear*, 1.1.281.
88 Cf. Smith, "Desire: Deleuze and the Question of Desire: Toward an Immanent Theory of Ethics."
89 Rebecca Munson, "'The Marks of Sovereignty': The Division of the Kingdom and the Division of the Mind in King Lear," *Pacific Coast Philology* 46 (2011): 23–4.
90 Cf. Pierre Clastres, "Exchange and Power: Philosophy of the Indian Chieftainship," "The Duty to Speak," "Society against the State," in *Society against the State: Essays in Political Anthropology*, trans. Robert Hurley (New York: Zone Books, 1989).
91 Emerson, *Self-Reliance*, II, 71; *Friendship*, II, 202; *The Over-Soul*, II, 253.
92 Marcuse, *One Dimensional Man*, 10–12.
93 Cf. E. R. Dodds, *The Greeks and the Irrational* (Berkeley: University of California Press, 1951), 28–63; Bruce J. Malina, *The New Testament World: Insights from Cultural Anthropology* (Louisville: Westminster John Knox Press, 2001), 27–57; Frederick Turner, *Beauty: The Value of Values* (Charlottesville: University of Virginia Press, 1991), 17–32.
94 Cf. Greenblatt, *Tyrant*, 113–36.
95 Cf. Soren Kierkegaard, *The Present Age: On the Death of Rebellion*, trans. Alexander Dru (New York: Harper Perennial Modern Thought, 2010), 43–7; Heidegger, *Being and Time*, 164–8.
96 *King Lear*, 1.2.1–22 and 1.4.252–66.

97 This medieval Latin saying is usually translated as "the corruption of the best is that which becomes the worst." Perhaps originally a reference to Lucifer's fall from grace and subsequent transformation into the Devil, it generally refers to the principle that the best of virtues is capable of becoming the worst of vices.
98 *King Lear*, 3.2.1–56.
99 Ibid., 3.2.49.
100 Ibid., 4.2.47–51.
101 Marcuse, *One Dimensional Man*, 3–8.
102 Cf. Illich, *Tools for Conviviality*, 40.
103 *King Lear*, 3.2.36.
104 Ibid., 5.3.277.
105 Emerson, *Nature*, I, 15–16.
106 *King Lear*, 5.3.11–13.
107 *King Lear*, 5.3.20–1.
108 Cf. Deleuze, *Nietzsche and Philosophy*, 17–18.
109 Emerson wrote this on January 30, 1842, three days after his son, Waldo, died from scarlet fever. See Emerson, *Emerson's Journals*, ed. Bliss Perry (New York: Dover Publications, 1995), 173.

5 A Fool Speaks

1 Critchley, *Tragedy*, 276–7.
2 Cf. E. R. Dodds, *The Greeks and the Irrational* (Berkeley: University of California Press, 1973), 28–50.
3 Cf. Friedrich Nietzsche, "The Greek State," 88–94. Nietzsche makes the case that slavery, as a cruel form of social sacrifice, is necessary—in some form—in order for a higher culture to exist whatsoever. The "conceptual hallucinations" that life and work are inherently dignified allows modern laborers to perform the tasks of slaves "whilst anxiously avoiding the word 'slave.'"
4 See Emerson, *Love*, II, 161; also *Politics*, III, 209–11.
5 See Richard Halpern, *The Poetics of Primitive Acquisition: English Renaissance Culture and the Genealogy of Capital* (Ithaca: Cornell University Press, 1991), 215–69; also William Dodd, "Impossible Worlds: What Happens in King Lear, Act 1, Scene 1?," *Shakespeare Quarterly* 50, no. 4 (Winter, 1999): 477–507.
6 Cf. Heraclitus' fragment: "The way up and down is one and the same" (CII); Plato's use of the heroic *katabasis* in *The Republic*: "I went down to the Piraeus yesterday with Glaucon, the son of Ariston" (327a).
7 Cf. Nietzsche, *Birth of Tragedy*, 60. In chapter 7, Nietzsche writes:

> In this sense the Dionysian man resembles Hamlet: both have once looked truly into the essence of things, they have gained *knowledge*, and nausea inhibits action; for their action could not change anything in the eternal nature of things; they feel it to be ridiculous or humiliating that they should be asked to set right a world that is out of joint. (emphasis in original)

8 Of the many philosophers and sages that would be relevant to list here, Socrates "assisting" Thrasymachus in overturning the sophist's own argument on profitability in Book I of *The Republic* seems most appropriate:

> Therefore, a just person is happy, and an unjust one wretched.
> So be it.
> It profits no one to be wretched but to be happy.
> Of course.
> And so, Thrasymachus, injustice is never more profitable than justice. (354a)

9 Cf. Marcuse, *Eros and Civilization*, 21–54.
10 It could be argued that the instinct to play expresses itself in healthy competition, which might in fact be a way of reading Cordelia's reentry into the drama at the head of a French army. It seems incredibly difficult, however, to sustain a reading of war between states as a variation of healthy competition or an expression of the play instinct. Conflict as such goes hand in hand with games and competition, but war—the utter surrender of humanity to force in its most explicit form—ruins whatever it is that play as such wins for us from out of our own most being in the world and with others.
11 Gadamer states this plainly: "Indeed, [tragedy] is not even a specifically artistic phenomenon, inasmuch as it is found also in life." See Gadamer, *Truth and Method*, 129.
12 Girard, *Violence and the Sacred*, 42.
13 Friedrich Nietzsche, *Morgenröthe: Gedanken über die moralischen Vorurtheile* (Chemnitz: Verlag von Ernst Schmeitzner, 1881), aphorism 18.
14 Pickard-Cambridge, *Dramatic Festivals of Athens*, 56.
15 Ibid., 119.
16 Cf. Gadamer, *Truth and Method*, 128.
17 See Plato's *Symposium*, particularly when we read the speeches as elevating insights into the true nature of love, with the final revelation occurring through the comparison of Socrates' arguments to the Silenus statue opening to greater secrets of virtue and goodness (222); see also Morgan, *Platonic Piety*, 80–99; and the end of Book X of Plato's *The Republic*: "That way we'll be friends both to ourselves and the gods while we remain here on earth and afterwards—like victors in the games who go around collecting their prizes—we'll receive our rewards" (621d).

18 Regarding point (1) see *The Republic*, Book IV, 443d; point (2) see *Phaedrus*, the Myth of Theuth, 274c–279c.
19 The etymological connection between the *phármakon*, as simultaneously cure and poison within a magical and medicinal context, and *pharmakós*, as ritual victim and scapegoat, is not well established. Classicist Gilbert Murray believed the latter to be a foreign word with no original connection to the use (or user) of sorcerous potions and medicinal drugs. See Rene Girard, *Violence and the Sacred*, chapter 3, "Oedipus and the Surrogate Victim" (68–88). Nietzsche might also assist us here as he well understood the psychology of revenge arising out of dissatisfaction with oneself, which we might reasonably extend to a collective practice. In aphorism 290 of *The Gay Science*, he writes: "Whoever is dissatisfied with himself is constantly ready for revenge, and we others will be his victims" (232–3).
20 Sophocles, "Antigone," 178.
21 Cf. Tillich, *Systematic Theology*, volume 1 (Chicago: University of Chicago Press, 1973), 59–66.
22 Emerson, *An Address*, I, 122.
23 Emerson, *Self-Reliance*, II, 71.
24 See Walter Benjamin, "The Work of Art in the Age of Mechanical Representation," in *Illuminations*, trans. Harry Zohn (New York: Schocken Books, 2007), 221.
25 Cf. Nietzsche, *Morgenröthe*, aphorism 18; and Rom. 12:1.
26 Cf. Girard, *Violence and the Sacred*, 56–8, 61–3, 159–64.
27 Emerson, *Fugitive Slave Law* (1851), XI, 179.
28 West, "Emersonian Prehistory," 646.
29 Ibid., 647.
30 See Baumgartner, "The Lyceum Is My Pulpit," *American Literature* 34, no. 4 (1963): 477–86.
31 Ibid., 485–6.
32 Emerson, *Politics*, III, 209–11.
33 Ibid., 209–10.
34 Richardson, *Emerson*, 498.
35 Ibid., 496.
36 Lawrence Buell, *Emerson* (Cambridge: Belknap Press of Harvard University Press, 2003), 287.
37 Richardson, *Emerson*, 497.
38 Emerson, *Fugitive Slave Law* (1851), XI, 188.
39 Emerson, *Politics*, III, 191.
40 Ibid.
41 Ibid., 192.
42 Ibid., 199.
43 Ibid.

44 Ibid., 206.
45 Cf. Clastres, "Duty to Speak," 151–5.
46 Cf. Audre Lorde, "Poetry Is Not a Luxury" and "The Transformation of Silence into Language and Action," *Sister Outsider* (Berkeley: Crossing Press, 2007), 36–9; 40–4.
47 Cf. Saul Newman, *Political Theology: A Critical Introduction* (Cambridge: Polity, 2019), 123–4.
48 Cf. Herbert Marcuse, *The Aesthetic Dimension: Toward a Critique of Marxist Aesthetics* (Boston: Beacon Press, 1978), 6–7, 19–21, 52–3.
49 Adorno, *Aesthetic Theory*, 4–5.
50 Girard, *Violence and the Sacred*, 136.
51 Ibid., 134.
52 Adorno, *Aesthetic Theory*, 8.
53 Cf. Paulo Freire, *Pedagogy of the Oppressed* (New York: Bloomsbury, 2017), 44.
54 Marcuse, *Aesthetic Dimension*, 9.
55 Benjamin, "Work of Art," 220–3.

Bibliography

I have organized this bibliography according to four basic *topoi*: Shakespeare, Emerson, Greek tragedy, and continental philosophy. A few of the works listed here do not fit neatly under any of these headings, but I have nonetheless attempted to group them together with the topic for which I referenced or employed them, with the last set, principally dedicated to nineteenth- and twentieth-century continental philosophy, additionally serving as a catchall for various works of anthropology, sociology, religion, and literature.

Shakespeare, "King Lear," and English Renaissance Tragedy

Abrams, Richard. "The Double Casting of Cordelia and Lear's Fool: A Theatrical View." *Texas Studies in Literature and Language* 27, no. 4 (Winter 1985): 354–68.
Amato, Andy. *The Ethical Imagination in Shakespeare and Heidegger.* New York: Bloomsbury Academic, 2019.
Auden, W. H. *Lectures on Shakespeare.* Edited by Arthur Kirsch. Princeton: Princeton University Press, 2000.
Bates, Jennifer Ann, and Richard Wilson, eds. *Shakespeare and Continental Philosophy.* Edinburgh: Edinburgh University Press, 2014.
Beckwith, Sarah. *Shakespeare and the Grammar of Forgiveness.* New York: Cornell University Press, 2011.
Bevington, David. "King Lear in Cultural and Historical Context." In *Critical Insights: King Lear,* edited by Jay L. Halio, 31–44. Pasadena: Salem Press, 2011.
Bloom, Harold. *The Anxiety of Influence.* New York: Oxford University Press, 1997.
Bloom, Harold. *Shakespeare: The Invention of the Human.* New York: Riverhead Books, 1998.
Booth, Stephen. *King Lear, Macbeth, Indefinition, and Tragedy.* New Haven: Yale University Press, 1983.
Bradley, A. C. *Shakespearean Tragedy.* New York: Penguin Books, 1991.
Cavell, Stanley. "The Avoidance of Love: A Reading of King Lear." In Stanley Cavell, *Disowning Knowledge in Seven Plays of Shakespeare,* updated edition, 39–123. New York: Cambridge University Press, 2003.
Cox, Edward Godfrey. "King Lear in Celtic Tradition." *Modern Language Notes* 24, no. 1 (January 1909): 1–6.

Dodd, William. "Impossible Worlds: What Happens in King Lear, Act 1, Scene 1?" *Shakespeare Quarterly* 50, no. 4 (Winter 1999): 477–507.

Dollimore, Jonathan. *Radical Tragedy*. Durham: Duke University Press, 1993.

Dreher, Diane Elizabeth. *Domination and Defiance: Fathers and Daughters in Shakespeare*. Lexington: University Press of Kentucky, 1986.

Farnham, Willard. *Shakespeare's Tragic Frontier*. Berkeley: University of California Press, 1963.

Garber, Marjorie. *Shakespeare after All*. New York: Anchor Books, 2005.

Gibson, D. Blair. "Celtic Democracy: Appreciating the Role Played by Alliances and Elections in Celtic Political Systems." *Proceedings of the Harvard Celtic Colloquium* 28 (2008): 40–62.

Greenblatt, Stephen. *Shakespearean Negotiations*. Los Angeles: University of California Press, 1988.

Greenblatt, Stephen. *Will in the World: How Shakespeare Became Shakespeare*. New York: W. W. Norton, 2004.

Greenbelt, Stephen. *Tyrant: Shakespeare on Politics*. New York: W. W. Norton, 2018.

Gruber, Elizabeth D. "Nature on the Verge." *Interdisciplinary Studies in Literature and Environment* 22, no. 1 (Winter 2015): 98–114.

Hadfield, Andrew. "Shakespeare and Politics in the Time of the Gunpowder Plot." *The Review of Politics* 78, no. 4 (Fall 2016): 571–88.

Halpern, Richard. *The Poetics of Primitive Acquisition: English Renaissance Culture and the Genealogy of Capital*. Ithaca: Cornell University Press, 1991.

Halpern, Richard. *Eclipse of Action: Tragedy and Political Economy*. Chicago: University of Chicago Press, 2017.

Hadfield, Andrew. "Shakespeare and Politics in the Time of the Gunpowder Plot." *The Review of Politics* 78, no. 4 (Fall 2016): 571–88.

Holbrook, Peter. *English Renaissance Tragedy*. New York: Bloomsbury, 2015.

Ioppolo, Grace. "A Jointure More or Less": Re-measuring the True Chronicle History of King Leir and His Three Daughters." *Medieval & Renaissance Drama in England* 17 (2005): 165–79.

Kahn, Coppelia. "The Absent Mother in King Lear." In *Rewriting the Renaissance: The Discourses of Sexual Difference in Early Modern Europe*, edited by Margaret W. Ferguson, Maureen Quilligan, and J. Vickers, 239–62. Chicago: University of Chicago Press, 1992.

Kamps, Ivo, ed. *Shakespeare Left and Right*. New York: Routledge, 1991.

Kamps, Ivo, ed. *Materialist Shakespeare: A History*. New York: Verso, 1995.

Kerrigan, John. *Shakespeare's Originality*. Oxford: Oxford University Press, 2018.

Kott, Jan. *Shakespeare Our Contemporary*. Translated by Boleslaw Taborski. New York: W. W. Norton, 1974.

Kottman, Paul A., ed. *Philosophers on Shakespeare*. Stanford: Stanford University Press, 2009.

Lang, Berel. "Nothing Comes of All: Lear Dying." *New Literary History* 9, no. 3 (Spring 1978): 537–59.

Leech, Clifford. *Tragedy*. London: Methuen, 1969.

Luckyj, Christina. "'A Moving Rhetoricke': Women's Silences and Renaissance Texts." *Renaissance Drama* 24 (1993): 33–56.

Margolies, David. *Monsters of the Deep: Social Dissolution in Shakespeare's Tragedies*. New York: Manchester University Press, 1992.

Munson, Rebecca. "'The Marks of Sovereignty': The Division of the Kingdom and the Division of the Mind in King Lear." *Pacific Coast Philology* 46 (2011): 13–27.

O'Dair, Sharon. "'To Fright the Animals and to Kill Them Up': Shakespeare and Ecology." *Shakespeare Studies* 39 (2011): 74–83.

Orgel, Stephen. *The Illusion of Power: Political Theater in the English Renaissance*. Berkeley: University of California Press, 1991.

Palliser, D. M. *The Age of Elizabeth: England under the Later Tudors 1547–1603*. London: Longman Group, 1983.

Pertile, Giulio J. "'King Lear' and the Uses of Mortification." *Shakespeare Quarterly* 67, no. 3 (Fall 2016): 319–43.

Ribner, Irving. "The Gods Are Just: A Reading of 'King Lear.'" *The Tulane Drama Review* 2, no. 3 (May 1958): 34–54.

Rosen, William. *Shakespeare and the Craft of Tragedy*. Cambridge: Harvard University Press, 1964.

Shakespeare, William. *The Norton Shakespeare*. Edited by Stephen Greenblatt. New York: W. W. Norton, 1997.

Shakespeare, William. *William Shakespeare: The Complete Works*. Edited by Stephen Orgel and A. R. Braunmuller. New York: Penguin, 2002.

Shapiro, James. *The Year of Lear: Shakespeare in 1606*. New York: Simon & Schuster, 2015.

Shickman, Alan R. "The Fool's Mirror in *King Lear*." *English Literary Renaissance* 21, no. 1 (Winter 1991): 75–86.

Sierra, Horacio. "Bearing Witness and Taking Action: Audiences and Morality in Renaissance Tragedy and Activist Street Theater." *Comparative Drama* 48, no. 1/2 (2014): 39–57.

Sinfield, Alan. "Shakespeare and Education." In *Political Shakespeare: Essays in Cultural Materialism*, second edition, edited by Jonathan Dollimore and Alan Sinfield, 158–81. Manchester: Manchester University Press, 2005.

Spaan, David B. "The Place of Manannan Mac Lir in Irish Mythology." *Folklore* 76, no. 3 (Autumn 1965): 176–95.

Spyra, Piotr. "Shakespeare and the Demonization of Fairies." *Text Matters* 7, no. 7 (2017): 194–213.

Stroup, Thomas B. "Cordelia and the Fool." *Shakespeare Quarterly* 12, no. 2 (Spring 1961): 127–32.

Taylor, Mark. *Shakespeare's Darker Purpose: A Question of Incest*. New York: AMS Press, 1982.

Van Doren, Mark. *Shakespeare*. New York: New York Review Books, 2005.

Weinsinger, Herbert. "An Examination of the Myth and Ritual Approach to Shakespeare." In *Myth and Mythmaking*, edited by Henry A. Murray, 132–40. New York: George Braziller, 1960.

Zipes, Jack. "Speaking the Truth with Folk and Fairy Tales: The Power of the Powerless." *The Journal of American Folklore* 132, no. 525 (Summer 2019): 243–59.

Zitner, Sheldon, P. "The Fool's Prophecy." *Shakespeare Quarterly* 18, no. 1 (Winter 1967): 76–80.

Emerson, Romanticim, and American Transcendentalism

Allen, Gay Wilson. *Waldo Emerson*. New York: Penguin, 1982.

Arvin, Newton. "The House of Pain." In *Emerson: A Collection of Critical Essays*, edited by Milton Konvitz and Stephen Whicher, 46–59. Englewood Cliffs: Prentice-Hall, 1962.

Barish, Evelyn. *Emerson: The Roots of Prophecy*. New Jersey: Princeton University Press, 1989.

Baumgartner, A. M. "'The Lyceum Is My Pulpit': Homiletics in Emerson's Early Lectures." *American Literature* 34, no. 4 (1963): 477–86.

Bense, James. "At Odds with 'De-Transcendentalizing Emerson': The Case of William James." *The New England Quarterly* 79, no. 3 (September 2006): 355–86.

Blanning, Tim. *The Romantic Revolution: A History*. New York: Modern Library, 2011.

Brodwin, Stanley. "Emerson's Version of Plotinus: The Flight to Beauty." *Journal of the History of Ideas* 35, no. 3 (1974): 465–83.

Buell, Lawrence. *Emerson*. Cambridge: Belknap Press of Harvard University Press, 2003.

Cameron, Sharon. "Representing Grief: Emerson's 'Experience.'" *Representation*, no. 15 (Summer 1986): 15–41.

Cavell, Stanley. *The Senses of Walden*. Chicago: University of Chicago Press, 1992.

Cavell, Stanley. *Emerson's Transcendental Etudes*. Stanford: Stanford University Press, 2003.

Chapman, Mary. "The Economics of Loss: Emerson's 'Threnody.'" *American Transcendental Quarterly; Kingston* 16, no. 2 (June 2002): 73–87.

Dewey, John. "Emerson—The Philosopher of Democracy." In *Estimating Emerson: An Anthology of Criticism from Carlyle to Cavell*, edited by David LaRocca, 291–6. New York: Bloomsbury Academic, 2013.

Dunston, Susan. "Philosophy and Personal Loss." *Journal of Speculative Philosophy* 24, no. 2 (2010): 158–70.

Ellison, Julie. *Emerson's Romantic Style*. Princeton: Princeton University Press, 1984.

Emerson, Ralph Waldo. *The Works of Ralph Waldo Emerson*. 14 vols. Edited by Edward W. Emerson. Cambridge: H. O. Houghton, 1883.

Emerson, Ralph Waldo. *The Letters of Ralph Waldo Emerson*. 8 vols. Edited by Ralph L. Rusk and Eleanor Tilton. New York: Columbia University Press, 1939.

Emerson, Ralph Waldo. *Selections from Ralph Waldo Emerson*. Edited by Stephen E. Whicher. Boston: Houghton Mifflin, 1960.

Emerson, Ralph Walso. *The Journals and Miscellaneous Notebooks of Ralph Waldo Emerson*. 16 vols. Edited by William H. Gilman, et al. Cambridge: Harvard University Press, 1960–82.

Emerson, Ralph Waldo. *Emerson in His Journals*. Edited by Joel Porte. Cambridge: Harvard University Press, 1982.

Emerson, Ralph Waldo. *Emerson's Journals*. Edited by Bliss Perry. New York: Dover Publications, 1995.

Flynn, Erin E. "The Intellectual Intuition in Emerson and the Early German Romantics." *The Philosophical Forum* 40, no. 3 (2009): 367–89.

Follett, Danielle. "The Tension between Immanence and Dualism in Coleridge and Emerson." In *Romanticism and Philosophy: Thinking with Literature*, edited by Sophie Laniel-Musitelli and Thomas Constantinesco, 209–21. New York: Routledge, 2015.

Goodman, Russel B. *American Philosophy and the Romantic Tradition*. Cambridge: Cambridge University Press, 1990.

Gura, Philip F. *American Transcendentalism: A History*. New York: Hill and Wang, 2007.

Habich, Robert D. Introduction to *Selected Writings of Ralph Waldo Emerson*, edited by Robert D. Habich, 11–36. Peterborough: Broadview Press, 2018.

Harvey, Samantha C. *Transatlantic Transcendentalism: Coleridge, Emerson and Nature*. Edinburgh: Edinburgh University Press, 2013.

Konvitz, Milton, and Stephen E Whicher, eds. *Emerson: A Collection of Critical Essays*. Englewood Cliffs: Prentice-Hall, 1962.

LaRocca, David, ed. *Estimating Emerson: An Anthology of Criticism from Carlyle to Cavell*. New York: Bloomsbury Academic, 2013.

LaRocca, David. "Emerson Recomposed: Nietzsche's Uses of His American 'Soul-Brother.'" In *Nietzsche and the Philosophers*, edited by Mark T. Conard, 211–30. New York: Routledge, 2017.

Leypoldt, Günter. "The Poet as Orphic Singer: Ralph Waldo Emerson." In Günter Leypoldt, *Cultural Authority in the Age of Whitman: A Transatlantic Perspective*, 73–100. Edinburgh: Edinburgh University Press, 2009.

Lysaker, John. *Emerson and Self-Culture*. Bloomington: University of Indiana Press, 2008.

Lysaker, John. *After Emerson*. Bloomington: University of Indiana Press, 2017.

Menand, Louis. *The Metaphysical Club: A Story of Ideas in America*. New York: Farrar, Straus and Giroux, 2001.

Packer, Barabara L. *Emerson's Fall: A New Interpretation of the Major Essays*. New York: Continuum, 1982.

Packer, Barabara L. *The Transcendentalists*. Athens: University of Georgia Press, 2007.

Richardson, Robert D., Jr. *Emerson: The Mind on Fire*. Berkeley: University of California Press, 1995.

Riepe, Dale. "Emerson and Indian Philosophy." *Journal of the History of Ideas* 28, no. 1 (1967): 115–22.

Smith, David L. "'The Sphinx Must Solve Her Own Riddle': Emerson, Secrecy, and the Self-Reflexive Method." *Journal of the American Academy of Religion* 71, no. 4 (2003): 835–61.

Stack, George J. *Nietzsche and Emerson: An Elective Affinity*. Athens: Ohio University Press, 1992.

Thompson, Cameron. "John Locke and New England Transcendentalism." *The New England Quarterly* 35, no. 4 (December 1962): 435–57.

Thurin, Erik Ingvar. *Emerson as Priest of Pan: A Study in the Metaphysics of Sex*. Lawrence: Regents Press of Kansas, 1981.

Urbas, Joseph. *The Philosophy of Ralph Waldo Emerson*. New York: Routledge, 2021.

Wellek, Rene. "Emerson and German Philosophy." *The New England Quarterly* 16, no. 1 (March 1943): 41–62.

West, Cornel. "The Emersonian Prehistory of American Pragmatism." In *Estimating Emerson: An Anthology of Criticism from Carlyle to Cavell*, edited by David LaRocca, 618–54. New York: Bloomsbury Academic, 2013.

Whicher, Stephen E. "Emerson's Tragic Sense." In *Emerson: A Collection of Critical Essays*, edited by Milton Konvitz and Stephen Whicher, 39–45. Englewood Cliffs: Prentice-Hall, 1962.

White, Ryan. "Neither Here nor There: On Grief and Absence in Emerson's 'Experience.'" *Journal of Speculative Philosophy* 23, no. 4 (2009): 285–306.

Woelfel, James. "The Beautiful Necessity: Emerson and the Stoic Tradition." *American Journal of Theology & Philosophy* 32, no. 2 (May 2011): 122–38.

Greek Tragedy, Ancient Philosophy, and Classical Antiquity

Aeschylus. *Aeschylus: Prometheus Bound, The Suppliants, Seven against Thebes, the Persians*. Translated by Philip Vellacott. New York: Penguin Books, 1961.

Aeschylus. *Aeschylus I: Oresteia: Agamemnon, the Libation Bearers, the Eumenides*. Edited by David Grene and Richard Lattimore. Translated by Richard Lattimore. Chicago: University of Chicago Press, 1953.

Cartledge, Paul. "The Greek Religious Festivals." In *Greek Religion and Society*, edited by P. E. Easterling and J. V. Muir, 98–127. Cambridge: Cambridge University Press, 1985.

Cornford, F. M. *From Religion to Philosophy: A Study in the Origins of Western Speculation*. New York: Harper Torchbooks, 1957.
Critchley, Simon. *Tragedy, the Greeks, and Us*. New York: Pantheon Books, 2019.
Detienne, Marcel. *The Masters of Truth in Archaic Greece*. Translated by Janet Lloyd. New York: Zone Books, 1996.
Dodds, E. R. *The Greeks and the Irrational*. Berkeley: University of California Press, 1951.
Dover, K. J., E. L. Bowie, Jasper Griffin, and M. L. West, eds. *Ancient Greek Literature*. Oxford: Oxford University Press, 1980.
Easterling, P. E. "Greek Poetry and Greek Religion." In *Greek Religion and Society*, edited by P. E. Easterling and J. V. Muir, 34–49. Cambridge: Cambridge University Press, 1985.
Edwards, Mark W. "The Expression of Stoic Ideas in the 'Aeneid.'" *Phoenix* 14, no. 3 (Autumn 1960): 151–65.
Epictetus. *The Enchiridion*. Translated by Nicholas P. White. Indianapolis: Hackett Publishing, 1983.
Euripides. *Euripides: Medea, Hippolytus, Alcestis, the Bacchae*. Edited by Robert W. Corrigan. New York: Dell Publishing, 1965.
Finley, M. I. *The Ancient Economy*. Berkeley: University of California Press, 1973.
Finley, M. I. *The World of Odysseus*. New York: Penguin Books, 1979.
Finley, M. I. *Economy and Society in Ancient Greece*. Edited by Brent D. Shaw and Richard P. Saller. New York: Viking Press, 1982.
Finley, M. I. *Democracy Ancient and Modern*, second edition. London: Hogarth Press, 1985.
Girard, René. *Violence and the Sacred*. Translated by Patrick Gregory. Baltimore: Johns Hopkins University Press, 1979.
Girard, Rene. "Dionysus versus the Crucified." *MLN* 99, no. 4, French Issue (September 1984): 816–35.
Gould, John. "On Making Sense of Greek Religion." In *Greek Religion and Society*, edited by P. E. Easterling and J. V. Muir, 1–33. Cambridge: Cambridge University Press, 1985.
Graf, Fritz. *Magic in the Ancient World*. Translated by Franklin Philip. Cambridge: Harvard University Press, 1999.
Guthrie, W. K. C. *The Greek Philosophers: From Thales to Aristotle*. New York: Harper Perennial, 1975.
Henrichs, Albert. "Between City and Country: Cultic Dimensions of Dionysus in Athens and Attica." In *Cabinet of the Muses: Essays on Classical and Comparative Literature in Honor of Thomas G. Rosenmeyer*, edited by Mark Griffith and Donald J. Mastronarde, 257–77. Atlanta: Scholars Press, 1990.
Jacobsen, Thorkild. *The Treasures of Darkness: A History of Mesopotamian Religion*. New Haven: Yale University Press, 1976.

Malina, Bruce L. *The New Testament World: Insights from Cultural Anthropology.* Louisville: Westminster John Knox Press, 2001.

Morgan, Michael L. *Platonic Piety: Philosophy and Ritual in Fourth-Century Athens.* New Haven: Yale University Press, 1990.

Murray, Gilbert. *Five Stages of Greek Religion.* New York: Doubleday Anchor Books, 1955.

Nietzsche, Friedrich. *The Birth of Tragedy.* Translated by Walter Kaufmann. New York: Vintage Books, 1967.

Nilsson, Martin P. *Greek Folk Religion.* Philadelphia: University of Pennsylvania Press, 1972.

Otto, Walter F. *Dionysus: Myth and Cult.* Translated by Robert B. Palmer. Dallas: Spring Publications, 1981.

Pater, Walter. *Greek Studies: A Series of Lectures.* New York: Chelsea House, 1983.

Pickard-Cambridge, Arthur. *The Dramatic Festivals of Athens.* London: Oxford University Press, 1953.

Plato. *Plato: Complete Works.* Translated by A. Nehamas and P. Woodruff. Indianapolis: Hackett Publishing, 1997.

Pollitt, J. J. *Art and Experience in Classical Greece.* London: Cambridge University Press, 1972.

Sophocles. *Sophocles I: Oedipus the King, Oedipus at Colonus, Antigone,* second edition. Edited and translated by David Greene and Richard Lattimore. Chicago: University of Chicago Press, 1991.

Taplin, Oliver. *Greek Tragedy in Action.* London: Routledge, 1985.

Van Nuffelen, Peter. "Words of Truth: Mystical Silence as a Philosophical and Rhetorical Tool in Plutarch." *Hermathena,* no. 182 (2007): 9–39.

Vernant, Jean-Pierre, and Pierre Vidal-Naquet. *Myth and Tragedy in Ancient Greece.* Translated by Janet Lloyd. New York: Zone Books, 1988.

Virgil. *The Aeneid of Virgil.* Translated by Rolfe Humphries. New York: Charles Scribner's, 1951.

Weil, Simone. "The *Iliad* or the Poem of Force." In *Simone Weil: An Anthology,* edited Sian Miles, 162–95. New York: Grove Press, 2000.

Weil, Simone. *Simone Weil's The Iliad or the Poem of Force: A Critical Edition.* Edited and translated by James P. Holoka. New York: Peter Lang, 2008.

Continental Philosophy and Other Works

Adorno, Theodor. *Aesthetic Theory.* Translated by Robert Hullot-Kentor. London: University of Minnesota Press, 1997.

Agamben, Giorgio. *The Man without Content.* Translated by Georgia Albert. Stanford: Stanford University Press, 1999.

Bibliography

Agamben, Giorgio. "The Time That Is Left." *Epoche* 7, no. 1 (Fall 2002): 1–14.

Althusser, Louis. *On the Reproduction of Capitalism: Ideology and Ideological State Apparatuses*. Translated by G. M. Goshgarian. New York: Verso, 2014.

Arendt, Hannah. *The Human Condition*. Chicago: University of Chicago Press, 1974.

Augustine. *City of God*. Translated by John K. Ryan. New York: Image Books, 1960.

Baudrillard, Jean. *The Evil Demon of Images*. Translated by P. Patton and P. Foss. Sydney: Power Institute of Fine Arts, 1987.

Beckett, Samuel. *The Complete Short Prose, 1929–1989*. Edited by S. E. Gontarski. New York: Grove Press, 1995.

Benjamin, Walter. *Illuminations*. Translated by Harry Zohn. New York: Schocken Books, 2007.

Berger, Peter. *The Sacred Canopy: Elements of a Sociological Theory of Religion*. New York: Doubleday, 1969.

Berger, Peter, and Anton Zijderveld. *In Praise of Doubt: How to Have Convictions without Becoming a Fanatic*. New York: HarperOne, 2009.

Bruner, Jerome S. "Myth and Identity." In *Myth and Mythmaking*, edited by Henry A. Murray, 276–87. New York: George Braziller Inc., 1960.

Camus, Albert. *The Rebel: An Essay on Man in Revolt*. Translated by Anthony Bower. New York: Vintage Books, 1991.

Cannon, Katie Geneva. *Katie's Canon: Womanism and the Soul of the Black Community*. New York: Continuum Publishing, 2003.

Clastres, Pierre. *Society against the State: Essays in Political Anthropology*. Translated by Robert Hurley. New York: Zone Books, 1989.

Coleridge, Samuel Taylor. *Biographia Literaria: Or Biographical Sketches of My Literary Life and Opinions*. Edited by George Watson. London: J. M. Dent, 1975.

Corrigan, John, and Winthrop S. Hudson. *Religion in America: An Historical Account of the Development of American Religious Life*. New Jersey: Prentice-Hall, 2004.

Deleuze, Gilles. *Nietzsche and Philosophy*. Translated by Hugh Tomlinson. New York: Columbia University Press, 1983.

Deleuze, Gilles. *Difference and Repetition*. Translated by Paul Patton. New York: Columbia University Press, 1994.

Deleuze, Gilles. *Pure Immanence: Essays on a Life*. Translated by Anne Boyman. New York: Zone Books, 2005.

Deleuze, Gilles, and Felix Guattari, *What Is Philosophy?* Translated by Hugh Tomlinson and Graham Burchell. New York: Columbia University Press, 1994.

Eckhart, Meister. *Meister Eckhart: The Essential Writings*. Translated by Raymond B. Blakney. New York: HarperCollins, 2009.

Feuerbach, Ludwig. *The Essence of Christianity*. Translated by George Eliot. Amherst: Prometheus Books, 1989.

Foucault, Michel. *Discipline and Punish: The Birth of the Prison*. Translated by Alan Sheridan. New York: Vintage Books, 1995.

Fraser, Nancy, and Rahel Jaeggi. *Capitalism: A Conversation in Critical Theory*. Edited by Brian Milstein. Cambridge: Polity, 2018.

Freire, Paulo. *Pedagogy of the Oppressed*. New York: Bloomsbury, 2017.

Frye, Northrop. *The Great Code: The Bible and Literature*. New York: Harcourt Brace Jovanovich Publishers, 1982.

Gadamer, Hans-Georg. *Truth and Method*, second revised edition. Translated by Joel Weinsheimer and Donald G. Marshall. New York: Continuum, 2004.

Grosz, Elizabeth. *The Incorporeal: Ontology, Ethics, and the Limits of Materialism*. New York: Columbia University Press, 2017.

Hegel, G. W. F. *Phenomenology of Spirit*. Translated by A. V. Miller. New York: Oxford University Press, 1977.

Hegel, G. W. F. *The Elements of the Philosophy of Right*. Edited by Allen W. Wood. Translated by H. B. Nisbet. New York: Cambridge University Press, 1991.

Heidegger, Martin. *Basic Writings*. Edited by David Farrell Krell. New York: HarperCollins, 1993.

Heidegger, Martin. *Being and Time*. Translated by Joan Stambaugh. New York: State University of New York Press, 1996.

Heidegger, Martin. *Poetry, Language, Art*. Translated by Albert Hofstadter. New York: HarperCollins, 2001.

Heidegger, Martin. "The Age of the World Picture." In *Off the Beaten Track*, edited and translated by Julian Young and Kenneth Haynes, 57–85. Cambridge: Cambridge University Press, 2002.

Heidegger, Martin. *What Is Called Thinking?* Translated by J. Glenn Gray. New York: HarperCollins, 2004.

Horkheimer, Max, and Theodor W. Adorno. *Dialectic of Enlightenment: Philosophical Fragments*, edited by Gunzelin Schmid Noerr and translated by Edmund Jephcott. Stanford: Stanford University Press, 2002.

Huizinga, Johan. *Homo Ludens: A Study of the Play-Element in Culture*. Boston: Beacon Press, 1955.

Illich, Ivan. *Tools for Conviviality*. London: Marion Boyars Publishers, 2009.

Jaspers, Karl. *Nietzsche*. Translated by C. Wallroff and F. Schmitz. Tucson: University of Arizona Press, 1965.

Kant, Immanuel. *Critique of Pure Reason*. Translated by Werner S. Pluhar. Indianapolis: Hackett Publishing, 1996.

Kee, Alistair. *Nietzsche against the Crucified*. London: SCM Press, 1999.

Kierkegaard, Soren. *The Present Age: On the Death of Rebellion*. Translated by Alexander Dru. New York: Harper Perennial Modern Thought, 2010.

Lasch, Christopher. *The Culture of Narcissism: American Life in an Age of Diminishing Expectation*. New York: W. W. Norton, 1991.

Levinas, Emmanuel. *Totality and Infinity*. Translated by Alphonso Lingis. Pittsburgh: Duquesne University Press, 1969.

Levinas, Emmanuel. *Humanism of the Other*. Translated by Nidra Poller. Chicago: University of Illinois Press, 2003.

Lorde, Audre. *Sister Outsider*. Berkeley: Crossing Press, 2007.

Lukács, Georg. *History and Class Consciousness: Studies in Marxist Dialectics*. Translated by Rodney Livingston. Cambridge: MIT Press, 1972.

McCumber, John. *Time and Philosophy: A History of Continental Thought*. Montreal: McGill-Queen's University Press, 2011.

Marcuse, Herbert. *Eros and Civilization: A Philosophical Inquiry into Freud*. Boston: Beacon Press, 1974.

Marcuse, Herbert. *The Aesthetic Dimension: Toward a Critique of Marxist Aesthetics*. Boston: Beacon Press, 1978.

Marcuse, Herbert. *One Dimensional Man: Studies in the Ideology of Advanced Industrial Society*. Boston: Beacon Press, 1991.

Marcuse, Herbert. *Reason and Revolution: Hegel and the Rise of Social Theory*. London: Wool Haus, 2020.

Maritain, Jacques, and Raissa Maritain. *The Situation of Poetry*. New York: Philosophical Library, 1955.

Marx, Karl, and Friedrich Engels. *The Marx-Engels Reader*, second edition. Edited by Robert C. Tucker. New York: W. W. Norton, 1978.

Mason, Mark, and Michael O'Rourke. "Meillassoux's Messianicity." In *Speculation, Heresy, and Gnosis in Contemporary Philosophy of Religion*, edited by Joshua Ramey and Matthew S. Haar Farris, 45–59. London: Rowman & Littlefield, 2016.

McDermott, John L. *Streams of Experience: Reflections on the History and Philosophy of American Culture*. Amherst: University of Massachusetts Press, 1986.

Newman, Saul. *Political Theology: A Critical Introduction*. Cambridge: Polity, 2019.

Nietzsche, Fredrich. *Morgenröthe: Gedanken über die moralischen Vorurtheile*. Chemnitz: Verlag von Ernst Schmeitzner, 1881.

Nietzsche, Fredrich. *Also sprach Zarathustra: Ein Buch für Alle und Keinen*. Leipzig: C. G. Naumann, 1899.

Nietzsche, Fredrich. *The Gay Science*. Translated by Walter Kaufmann. New York: Vintage Books, 1974.

Nietzsche, Fredrich. *Beyond Good and Evil: Prelude to a Philosophy of the Future*. Translated by Walter Kaufmann. New York: Vintage, 1989.

Nietzsche, Fredrich. *Twilight of the Idols* and *The Anti-Christ*. Translated by R. J. Hollingdale. New York: Penguin Books, 1990.

Nietzsche, Fredrich. *Untimely Meditations*. Edited by Daniel Breazeale. Translated by R. J. Hollingdale. New York: Cambridge University Press, 1997.

Nietzsche, Fredrich. *Dithyrambs of Dionysus*. Translated by R. J. Hollingdale. London: Anvil Press Poetry, 2001.

Nietzsche, Fredrich. *Thus Spoke Zarathustra: A Book for Everyone and No One*. Translated by R. J. Hollingdale. New York: Penguin Books, 2003.

Nietzsche, Fredrich. *The Nietzsche Reader*. Edited by Keith Ansell Pearson and Duncan Large. Malden: Blackwell Publishing, 2006.

Nietzsche, Fredrich. *The Will to Power*. Translated by Walter Kaufmann and R. J. Hollingdale. New York: Random House, 1968.

Putnam, Robert D. *Bowling Alone: The Collapse and Revival of American Community*. New York: Simon & Schuster, 2020.

Sartre, Jean Paul. *Being and Nothingness: An Essay on Phenomenological Ontology*. Translated by H. E. Barnes. London: Routledge, 1958.

Scheler, Max. "Ordo Amoris." In *Selected Philosophical Essays*. Edited and translated by David R. Lachterman, 98–135. Evanston: Northwestern University Press, 1973.

Smith, Dan. *Essays on Deleuze*. Edinburgh: Edinburgh University Press, 2012.

Steiner, George. *The Death of Tragedy*. New Haven: Yale University Press, 1996.

Tillich, Paul. *Dynamics of Faith*. New York: Harper & Row, 1957.

Tillich, Paul. *Systematic Theology*, volume 1. Chicago: University of Chicago Press, 1973.

Traherne, Thomas. *Centuries of Meditation*. Edited by B. Dobell. London: P. J. and A. E. Dobell, 1927.

Turner, Frederick. *Beauty: The Value of Values*. Charlottesville: University of Virginia Press, 1991.

Van Gennep, Arnold. *The Rites of Passage*. Translated by Monika B. Vizedom and Gabrielle L. Caffee. Chicago: University of Chicago Press, 1960.

Wall, Thomas Carl. *Radical Passivity: Levinas, Blanchot, and Agamben*. New York: State University of New York Press, 1999.

Weil, Simone. *On the Abolition of All Political Parties*. Translated by Simon Leys. New York: New York Review Books, 2013.

Wiggershaus, Rolf. *The Frankfurt School: Its History, Theories, and Political Significance*. Translated by Michael Robertson. Cambridge: Polity Press, 1995.

Zaretsky, Robert. *The Subversive Simone Weil: A Life in Five Ideas*. Chicago: University of Chicago Press, 2021.

Index

Note: Endnotes are indicated by the page number followed by "n" and the endnote number e.g., 20 n.1 refers to endnote 1 on page 20

Aeneid (Virgil) 7
Aeschylus 147 n.18, 148 n.34
aesthetic silence 6–8
afterlife
　mysteries of 7
　religion and 23
alienated (*Entfremdung*) 124
America 23
　cultural influence of Europe 24
American ecology 24
American transcendentalism 58, 85,
　　156 n.48
Anaximander 146 n.15, 169 n.24
Antigone (Sophocles) 21, 34
"antimetaphysical bias" 165 n.90
Antony and Cleopatra (Shakespeare) 116,
　　156 n.58
Aquinas'
　intellectus 73
　ratio 69
Aristotle 150 n.11
　epistēmē 69
　nous 73
art 22, 27, 62, 78, 91, 99, 134, 136
Athenian ideology vii, 113–14, 134
authentic silence 7

beauty 59, 65, 68, 122, 129
　in actions 63
　for delight 61–2
　envoys of 57
　for intellection 61–2
　of intelligible objects 63
　tragic element of 63
　of tragic world 23
　and truth 80
　for virtue 61–2
de Beauvoir, Simone 72

Being and Time (Heidegger) 50
being 52, 101, 147 n.26
　curse of ix–x, 102, 131, 146 n.15
　tragic engine of 13, 52–3
　unity of 53
Benjamin, Walter 135
Beuys, Joseph 51
Bía (force) 147 n.18
Blake, William 51
Buber, Martin 72

Camus, Albert 72
capitalism xv, 24
Carlyle, Thomas 22
Catholics 141
Celan, Paul 51
childlikeness 83, 122, 125
Christ, Jesus 105
Circles (Emerson) 23, 29, 153 n.6
Clastres, Pierre 138
　philosophical anthropology xix
"clownish demonology" 106
Coleridge, Samuel Taylor 22, 31, 70
　dualistic idealism 74
　romanticism 67
collapse of feudalism 124
commodity 59, 65, 68, 122
common sense 69
community 24, 94, 141
　identity 2
　of values 14
The Conduct of Life (Emerson) 60
Coriolanus (Shakespeare) 116, 156 n.58
cosmos, *see* world
Critique of Pure Reason (Kant) 50,
　　166 n.127
curse 3, 11, 14, 17, 41–2, 43, 93, 102, 107,
　　120, 124, 130, 131

death 9, 40, 94, 107, 114
   and life 13, 34, 53
   and love 14
   and nothingness 12
   shadow of 43
   see also life
Deleuze, Gilles x, 50, 51, 70, 83, 120, 149 n.49, 158 n.84
post-structuralism xix
   differential repetitions 75
   reading difference 51
   transcendental empiricism 30
delusions 50, 77, 95
Derrida 51
Descartes 32, 72, 128
desire 2, 9, 21, 61, 116, 120, 136, 139, 142
   animalistic vs. enlightened 68
destiny 2-3, 14, 26, 30, 40, 88, 99, 100, 107, 115, 130
didáskaloi vii
Difference and Repetition (Deleuze) 50
difference 36, 39, 52-3, 70, 90, 101, 105, 128
differential nothingness 90
Dionysian affirmation 101
Dionysus vi, xi, xiv, 3, 104-5, 130, 134
discipline 55, 59, 65, 68-71, 73, 79, 122, 127
discourse 6-7, 8, 16, 32, 50, 119, 142
discrete subject 148 n.40
distrust 25
Dollimore, Jonathan 157 n.67, 166 n.121
drama 14, 83, 109, 132
   Athenian 114
   historical 116
   of self-recovery 90, 102
   structure of 13
   of understanding 49, 55-6, 128
   see also tragic drama

Electra (Sophocles) 21
elegy 20-3
   Emerson 19
   Shakespeare 19
Emerson, Ralph Waldo 19, 36, 47, 49, 51, 93, 101, 146 n.11, *see also* specific work
   beauty 61-5
   on capitalism 60-1
   commodity 59-61
   death of his beloved 22-3, 25, 38
   discipline 68-71
   enlightenment 24
   as Greek tutor 21
   ideal philosophy 89
   idealism 73
   language 65-8
   misfortune in childhood 21-2
   on love and tragedy 15, 20-1
   philosophy 26
   poetic intuition 49
   and Politics 136-9
   prospects 87-91
   reading nature 51
   resigns his pastorate 53
   romantic language 41
   spirit 64-5, 84-7
   transcendentalism 86
   as transcendentalist 25
Emersonianism 30, 142, 156 n.47
Enchiridion (Epictetus) 42
England 3, 80, 112
enlightenment 24, 53, 71, 88, 89
epic of force 85, 129
Epictetus 42
equanimity (*apatheia*) 20
eros 54, 55, 82, 95, 102, 106, 119, 122, 126, 130, 132
eroticism 54, 104, 130
existential silence xix, 6-7
"existentialists" 72
Experience (Emerson) 23, 37-8, 43, 153 n.6, 167 n.158

Fanon 72
Farnham, Willard 156 n.58
Fate (Emerson) 2-3, 23, 79, 153 n.6
fate 15, 68, 129
   and destiny 14, 26
   force of 2, 30, 10
   spirit 64-5
festival 63, 90, 91, 132-3
feudalism 98, 124
Feuerbach, Ludwig 82
   contemplative materialism 30
Fichte 36
Finley, M. I. 166 n.121
fools 1-10, 16, 60, 89, 91, 93, 103, 107, 109-10, 125, 130
   as tools for subversion 2

force 1–2, 15, 53, 90, 95, 99, 106, 118
  and power 10, 16, 123
forced silence 2
"forgiveness" 34, 43, 94, 99, 116, 162 n.41
Foucault, Michel 51
freedom xiii, 25, 34, 43, 52, 56, 94, 116–17, 122, 137, 142
Friend (Coleridge) 166 n.127
Fugitive Slave Law 137
Fuller, Margaret 24–5, 43

game to power 2, 4, 14, 44, 64, 88, 114, 129, 163 n.66
The Gay Science (Nietzsche) 77
genuine subject 148 n.40
Geoffrey of Monmouth 110, 111
German Idealism 22, 30, 74
Girdard, René xix
god(s) 3, 7, 12–13, 28, 30, 84–5, 129
  and nature 34
Goethe 60
good reading 51
goodness 32, 85, 129
Greek tragedy, divine in 25–6, 133–4
Greenblatt 51
  reading Shakespeare's life 51
guilt (*Schuld*) 124

Hamlet (Shakespeare) 32–3, 97, 113, 140, 169 n.19, 174 n.7
Hegel, G.W.F. 32, 50, 81
Heidegger, Martin 6, 29, 50, 51, 72, 77, 145 n.5
  das rechnende Denken 69
  das besinnliche Denken 73
  phenomenology xix
  reading being 51
  on speech and silence 6–7
Heraclitus 70, 83
hesitation 21, 60, 76, 116
Hill, Christopher 166 n.121
History of the Kings of Britain (Geoffrey of Monmouth) 110
Homer 51, 62, 146 n.15, 168 n.160
hope 22, 44, 53, 87, 133, 142
human drama 52
hypokritēs viii

ideal difference 107
idealism 55, 67, 73–9, 82, 115, 128, 135
  and materialism 30
idiots (*idiǒtēs*) 104, 124
Illich, Ivan
  reading schools 51
illusions 40, 42, 73, 95, 99, 102, 121
imagination 30, 67, 78, 82, 86, 95, 101, 102, 118, 125
  intuition and 52
  primary xii
  secondary xii
impropriety 69
incestuous feelings 12
indirect directness 48
injustice 24, 48, 88, 98, 115, 129, 130
innocence 93, 105, 106
instrumental rationality 71
"intellection" 62, 67, 87, 127, 163 n.57
intellectual freedom
  by solitude 25

justice 32, 78, 82, 85, 88, 111, 115, 129, 130

Kant, Immanuel 32, 36, 50, 66, 72, 78
  Idealism 67
  transcendental idealism 31
katábasis 19, 112, 153 n.3
kenōsis (self-emptying) 12
khrḗsimos 14
Kierkegaard, Soren 48, 51, 72, 149 n.49
  reading Christendom 51
King Lear (Shakespeare) 44–5, 49–52, 96–7, 110, 117, 123, 133, 142
  division of kingdom 3–4
  fool 1–2
  hidden solution 52
  love contest 4–5, 10–11
  nihilism present in 27
  review 123
  Tate's "adaptation" of 149 n.46
knowledge 31, 68, 72–3, 103, 127, 161 n.31
  "pure" and "practical" 128
  spiritual 128
Kratos (power) 147 n.18

language 59, 65–8, 122, 127
  abstract 66
  conceptual 71
  and devices 32

Emerson 30–1
  illusions and metaphors 39
  initial sense of 65
  poetic 76, 116
  Shakespeare poetic 19, 34
  understanding of 66
Levinas, Emmanuel 50
liberation 10, 16, 36, 53, 85, 100
  economic 56
  political 56
  social 56
life 3, 13, 91, 109, 125, 129
  affirming beliefs 95
  cycle 12, 13, 21
  and death cycle 104
  human 33
  imaginative 56
  inner and outer 61, 66
  intellectual 81
  mental 56, 66, 72, 127
  misfortunes and failures 22
  social 77
  spiritual 56, 39, 81
  taxonomic division of 58
  see also death
literature and philosophy 28
logic and systematic approaches 48
love 85, 94, 124, 129
  contest of 14, 139
  critical moments of 15
  and death 14
  for destruction
  Emerson about 15
  and foolishness 103
  order of 15
  and silence 5, 123
  test 4–6, 116–18
  and time 14
  and tragedy 20–1
  and truth relation 115
  and truth 115
  and worship 129
Lysaker, John 36

Macbeth (Shakespeare) 3, 28, 116, 117, 156 n.58
Marcuse, Herbert 120, 158 n.84
  critical theory xix
McDermott, John 23
me and *not me* 55–6, 58

meditative thinking 73
Mehretu 62
The Merchant of Venice (Shakespeare) 34
A Midsummer Night's Dream (Shakespeare) 108
Morrison 62
mystical silence 6–7, 8
myth and ritual 8, 23, 58, 77, 102, 105, 111, 134, 140, 157 n.70

narcissistic nihilism xv
"natural" 34, 36, 39, 120, 131
  sciences 21
  and unnatural 120, 121, 131
Nature (Emerson) 20, 28, 38, 43, 47–52, 93, 133
  beauty 61–5
  commodity 59–61
  complex tragic portrait 42
  discipline 68–71
  hidden solution 52
  idealism 73
  language 65–8
  and *nothing* 110
  Packer, Barbara on 42
  prospects 87–91
  spirit 64–5, 84–7
  summary 57–9
nature
  division of 58
  as goddess 36, 37
  uses of 59
Neoplatonic monism 74
Nietzsche, Friedrich 20, 28, 36, 48, 51, 61, 70, 72, 77, 83, 93, 101, 105, 149 n.49, 150 n.11, 158 n.84
  aphoristic tapestry 75
  reading the Greeks 51
not me (difference) 36, 42, 89, 91, 102, 105, 126
  me and 55–6, 58
nothing 52, 56, 57–8, 74, 131
  necessity of 53
nothingness 39–42, 44, 90–1, 103, *et passim*

Oedipus the King (Sophocles) 3, 100, 139
Ophelia xiv
ordo amoris (order of love) 14–15, 54, 83, 93, 94, 99, 101, 106, 118, 124, 137

Ortega y Gasset, José 72
Othello (Shakespeare) 13, 152 n.42

Packer, Barbara 42, 74
paltry empiricism 31
peace 10, 16, 99, 100
   and destruction 106, 112
peace 16, 20, 40, 99, 112
"perfect knowledge" 71
permanence 55, 81
pharmakós 135, 175 n.19
Phenomenology of Spirit (Hegel) 50
Plato 9, 31, 32, 51, 70, 72, 80, 134, 174 n.17
   reading reason 51
Plotinus 31
poiētḗs vii
power 2, 53, 66
   divine 103, 132
   and force 10, 16, 123, 136
   poetic 73, 117
   redeemed and refined 65, 87
   of silence 118
pragmatism xvi, 136
propriety 69
prospects 47, 87–91
protagonist 9, 33, 49, 97, 103, 132, 139
protestants 141
public cursing of being (*kataraomai*) 146 n.15

Radical Tragedy (Dollimore) 166 n.121
readings
   of Emerson 65, 133
   of Heraclitus 70
   influence of 51
   of Shakespeare xxi
reason 30, 63, 65, 69–70, 71, 72–3, 76, 84–5
riddle 20–1, 26
   of the Sphinx 37, 55, 91, 100, 125, 129, 138
Rilke 62

sacrifice 100, 107, 113, 114, 117, 122, 132–6
salvific power 90
Sartre, Jean Paul 72
Schmitt 128
Schopenhauerean 69
Scotland 3

self-culture 24–5, 28, 85, 95, 101, 125, 129, 136, 138
self-determination (*autárkeia*) 20
self-discipline (*askēsis*) 28
self-emptying (*kenōsis*) 12
self-overcoming (*Selbstuberwindung*) 20, 96
self-recovery 49, 89, 90, 102, 130
Self-Reliance (Emerson) 16, 89
self-trust 25, 29, 39, 71, 89, 125
Shakespeare 3, 32–3, 49, 51, 62, 79, 108,
   see also specific work
   and Emerson 19, 99
   and politics 139–43
   poetic language 19
   theatrical world 34
   tragic drama xiv
   tragic retrieve 102
   tragic world 43
   uncertainty 27–8
shame (*aidōs*) vii, x, 7–8, 16, 124
shared identity 2
silence 1–2, 16, 37, 39, 118, 123, 138
   three orders of 6–8
Silenus xiii, 36, 93, 174 n.17
Sisyphus xiii
slavery 25–6, 118, 137, 138
social projects 24
Socrates 36, 134, 150 n.3, 174 n.8
Sophocles viii, 101, 139, 146 n.15, 148 n.34, 167 n.154
soul 84–5
Spinoza 32, 83
Spinozan monism 30
spirit 65–6, 84–7
spiritual thinking 73
Stoicism 74, 83
Stoics 30, 41, 70, 83, 120
storytelling 112
subject 134, 148 n.40
suffering 14, 41, 48, 76, 96, 100–1
Swedenborgian mysticism 74
Symposium (Plato) 80, 174 n.17
Sze 62

Tate, Nahum 149 n.46
Taylor, Mark 11, 51
   reading capitalism 51
The Tempest (Shakespeare) 33, 34
theatrical tragedy 52

formula of 2–3
theory of intuition 95
Theseus' "airy nothing," 95
thinking 24, 30, 78
   calculative modes of 69
   and feeling 103
   meditative 73
Thrasymachus 174 n.8
Threnody (Emerson) 153 n.6
Thucydides 146 n.15
time 2, 9, 14, 23, 27, 42, 100, 120
   love and 14
   space and 78
   and time's effects 53
   and truth relation 115–16
Timon of Athens (Shakespeare) 156 n.58
Totality and Infinity (Levinas) 50
tragedy (*tragōidía*) vi, xi, 21, 145 n.3, 171 n.60
   language, function of 19
   ontological vs. human drama 52–3
   theories of xi
tragic drama
   as social phenomenon 113
   see also drama
tragic
   engine of being 13
   "festival" 124
   "hero" 134
   idealism 115, 120, 125, 142
   life cycle 101
   philosophy 122
   unending cycle of 49
The Tragic (Emerson) 153 n.6
transcendentalism 55
transcendentalists 24

thinker 72
The True Chronicle History of King Leir and His Three Daughters (Anonymous) 98, 110
truth 1, 6, 66, 129
Twombly, Cy 51

Übermensch 35–6
Unitarianism 74
"unnatural" 131
Urbas, Joseph 165 n.90

van Gogh 51
victims of tragedy viii, 114, 123
Virgil 7
virtue 61, 63, 97, 99, 115, 127, 132, 135

Wales 3
Weil, Simone 1
   reading Homer 51
will-to-theoretical consistency 75
The Winter's Tale (Shakespeare) 11, 33
wisdom 1, 19, 95, 104, 108, 127
Wordsworth, William 22
world 1, 9, 58, 67, 129, 131, 135
   dramatic 33, 132
   of force 10, 42, 75, 90, 101
   ideal 126
   love in 15–16
   material 78, 126
   natural 57, 66
   of power 10
   social 35, 88
   tragic 14, 32, 43, 49, 83, 93, 111
   unchangeable 37
The World of Odysseus (Finley) 166 n.121

www.ingramcontent.com/pod-product-compliance
Lightning Source LLC
Chambersburg PA
CBHW052113300426
44116CB00010B/1646